TOMORROW'S MANAGERS TODAY

The identification and development of management potential

Andrew Stewart
Valerie Stewart

Institute of Personnel Management

First published in 1977 by IPM as Tomorrow's Men Today.
Second edition published 1981

© Andrew and Valerie Stewart 1976, 1981

Printed and bound in Great Britain at
The Camelot Press Ltd, Southampton

British Library Cataloguing in Publication Data

Stewart, Andrew
    Tomorrow's managers today. — 2nd ed.
    1. Executive ability — Testing
    I. Title   II.   Stewart, Valerie
    658.4'07'125   HF5500.2

ISBN 0-85292-300-7

TOMORROW'S MANAGERS TODAY

Andrew and Valerie Stewart are a husband and wife team of industrial psychologists who have worked on the identification and development of management potential in many British and European companies, as well as in the United States.

Andrew Stewart graduated from Aberdeen University and taught at the University of Surrey before joining IBM (UK) as a personnel officer. As a management development officer with IBM he helped to introduce their assessment programme. From IBM he moved to the Institute of Manpower Studies to work on the validation of management assessment programmes and related topics. He has now joined his wife in Macmillan Stewart & Partners, where they work on improving human performance in industry.

Valerie Stewart is a graduate of Sheffield University and taught at the University of Denver, Colorado, before joining IBM (UK) as a management development officer in the Customer Engineering Division. Since leaving IBM she has worked with her husband in management assessment and is a consultant psychologist in Macmillan Stewart & Partners.

Both authors give seminars on a wide range of applications of behavioural science to industry and have written many articles for personnel and training journals. They have published books on performance appraisal, management development, and Repertory Grid and have others in press on managing the poor performer, stress in industry, assessing management potential and managing professional staff.

Contents

Acknowledgements

The authors and publishers gratefully acknowledge permission to use the following copyright material. The extract from *Pepys* by Richard Ollard by permission of Hodder & Stoughton Ltd. The table from 'Predicting Organizational Effectiveness with a four-factor theory of Readership' by D G Bowers and S E Seashore, Vol 11, 1966, by permission of the *Administrative Science Quarterly*. Tables from *The Journal of Applied Psychology*: D W Bray and R J Campbell, 'Selection of Salesmen by means of an Assessment Center', 1968, 52; H B Wollowick and W J McNamara, 'Relationship of the components of an assessment center to management success', 1969, 53; A I Kraut and G J Scott, 'Validity of an operational management assessment program', 1972, 56; and J L Moses and V R Boehm, 'The relationship of an assessment center performance to management progress of women', 1975, 60, are reproduced by permission of the American Psychological Association. The tables from J M Bender, 'What is typical of assessment centers?', *Personnel*, July–August, 1973, by permission of AMACON, a division of American Management Associations. The example of the bad appraisal form from *Executive Self-Development* by Hawdon Hague, 1974, by permission of Macmillan, London and Basingstoke. The tables from E Anstey, 'The Civil Service Administrative Class: a follow up of post war entrants', *Occupational Psychology*, Vol 45, 1971, by permission of Cambridge University Press. The figures from 'Assessment Centres; an aid in management selection' by R J Campbell and D W Bray, *Personnel Administration*, March–April 1967, by permission of the International Personnel Management Association, 1313 E 60th St, Chicago, Illinois. The figures from 'Who really are the promotables?' by J W Walker, F Luthars and R M Hodgetts, *Personnel Journal*, February 1970, and 'An integrated program for career development', *Personnel Journal*, June 1972, by permission of *Personnel Journal*. The tables from *Industrial Society*, ed Denis Pym, 1968, by permission of Penguin Books Ltd. The tables from *Managerial Behaviour, Performance and Effectiveness* by Campbell *et al*, 1970, by permission of the McGraw Hill Book Company. The extract from J R Huck, 'Assessment centres: a review of the external and internal validities', Vol 26, 1973, by permission of *Personnel Psychology*.

Introduction

Organizations must constantly review and renew their strength if they are to survive beyond their first spurt of growth. To do this, they have to identify and develop the people who in years to come will be the organization's managers – not just the up and coming board members and the high flyers, but the backbone middle managers and the first-line managers whose position at the interface between management and non-management we believe to be one of the most difficult management jobs of all.

In this book we aim to help those with responsibility for the identification of management potential: people concerned with personnel work, management development, training and organization development fall easily into this category. However, we try to cast our net wider than that by taking some of the mythology out of assessment methodology, and parts of this book are also intended for general managers, managers in planning functions, finance managers and managers in production, sales and industrial relations. If you have to make long-term decisions about people, you are one of the readers we had in mind when writing this book.

There is a market for general prescriptions about management effectiveness; there is a large and sometimes gullible market for packaged programmes advertised as selecting, training, or developing managers. It is frighteningly easy to design such a package: a little jargon, one or two memorable visual aids, a flashy speaker or two, all put into a week-long course where natural group dynamics are enhanced to make people feel miserable in the middle of the week and correspondingly more euphoric by the end, and at a high price. Because people usually cannot bear to see something for which they have suffered devalued, they come off their misery making and expensive programmes swearing that the experience has taught them a great deal. The crunch questions 'What are you doing differently as a result of the programme?' or 'How much has the management performance improved as a result of the programme?' are rarely asked. We have made ourselves unpopular in a number of places by asking it. The engineer tests and tests again when he designs a bridge; shouldn't we try for the same precision and set ourselves similar, operational standards of success when we are placing people in jobs?

General prescriptions of what makes for management effectiveness are usually couched in terms which render the task of deriving operational statements from them impossible. Look at some of the terms which are used: *aggressiveness, decision-making, ambition, leadership*, and so on. Get some people to define what these terms mean; their definitions will probably cover a wide range and may conflict. Get them to define what people would have to *do* to demonstrate these qualities and conflict can almost be guaranteed. Go outside your own company, or your own country and further confusion results. The reasons are simple and fundamental to our approach in writing this book:

(i) Management effectiveness has to be defined in terms of what managers *do*. Not their attitudes, personalities, expressed concerns, histories or their ambitions; it's their *behaviour* which differentiates the effective from the ineffective. Any prescription for management effectiveness should be in behavioural terms.

(ii) Management effectiveness varies from firm to firm, from level to level, from country to country and between different functions. A broad prescription that tries to be right for everyone is likely to be exactly right for no-one and the degree of inexactitude may be large.

Though we began our work on the validation of assessment procedures with these views, we were conscious that they were only hypotheses. As we have worked with more and more companies obtaining definitions of effective management in specific positions, we have had our hypotheses confirmed. Management effectiveness does vary enormously between different management jobs and can be defined in practical, behavioural terms. Furthermore, when the definitions are used for management selection, assessment and development, the evidence so far is that these tasks are done better, with fewer mistakes and at less cost in terms of money and people.

In this book we take you through the methods we use to diagnose what makes for effective management in a given type of job. The coverage varies from strategic considerations to practical administration. In the first chapter we examine some of the symptoms which could be presented by an organization where management potential is not properly identified and developed and go on to put these concerns into the context of manpower planning. The second chapter is a brief review of some of the literature about management effectiveness; we have tried to cover some of the more unusual approaches to defining and discovering it, at the expense of the more well-known theories. In the third chapter we cover the history of the management assessment programme, or assessment centre, as a way of identifying potential managers.

The next three chapters are a 'hands-on' guide to doing the research which will lead to definitions of effective managerial behaviour in your own organization; to designing an assessment programme, and to running it. The following chapter discusses how assessment data should be handled both as statistics and as guides for personal development. In the next two chapters we move from the 'hands-on' guide to the validation and costing of assessment programmes. Chapter 8 is a review of the existing literature on validation, which will show what has been attempted by other workers and finishes with a practical guide to setting up your own validation procedures. In chapter 9 we discuss a way of estimating the costs and benefits that can result from an improvement in the identification of management potential. Chapter 10 contains some of the most common questions people ask about managerial potential, and about asessment programmes in particular, and the final chapter is a check-list: what to do next if you wish to follow up the ideas we present.

The practical centre of the book is thus preceded by considerations of strategy and general management concern and followed by guidance on how to make sure that your practical solution is working and giving value for money. There are two points about the practical guide:

(i) The diagnostic procedure we offer is a way of finding out what makes for management effectiveness, irrespective of the method one later uses to discover people who show these characteristics. We concentrate later on the design and running of assessment programmes, but we cannot stress enough that assessment programmes are not your only way of discovering potential. The diagnostic procedure is useful for training needs assessment, the performance appraisal system, management appointments committees, or any other method you may have in mind. Only after the diagnosis are you in a position to decide whether the characteristics revealed by the diagnosis should be sought in an assessment programme, or by performance appraisal, or by some other method. We go into detail about assessment programmes at the expense of these other methods because assessment programmes can have unique advantages and because their design – linked to the diagnosis – has not been discussed elsewhere.

(ii) The validation procedures may look difficult, but we urge the reader not to ignore them. If you go to the trouble of research and development into ways of assessing potential, and do not follow this by some form of validation, you will never know how worthwhile your efforts have been. And if this consideration is not enough, bear in mind that legislative pressures are making the consequences of a wrong appointment increasingly more expensive. If you are not certain that your firm could give valid reasons *in writing* for its selection and promotion decisions, then you need the diagnosis and the validation chapter.

We ourselves are still learning, even as we write this book and gain insights into more and more firms. We are conscious of debts to many people, most of whom we cannot acknowledge here. Special mention must go to Tom Campbell, of BP, for seminal ideas in the chapter on cost-benefit analysis, and to Jeffery Farr, John Bishop, Gordon Lamplough and Derek White of ICI Wilton, for statistical innovations in the analysis of the diagnostic data. Manab Thakur at IPM gave early and vital encouragement to the writing of this book. Sue Beadle-Hill and Helen Piercey at The Institute of Manpower Studies (IMS) typed the manuscript and their good humour and hard work has sustained us through much of the foregoing research. Our thanks also go to our colleagues at the IMS and the people with whom we have collaborated in other organizations. Working in a new area, we have often borrowed research techniques and experience from other people, and we thank them for patient explanations, useful insights, and instructive examples. Responsibility for errors and omissions rests, of course, with us.

Preface to the second edition

In the five years since we wrote *Tomorrow's Men Today* we have worked with many more organizations and in many different countries. We have tried to distil some of that experience in this volume, which has led to substantial re-writing of some chapters. Particularly readers will find a simpler and more robust method of administering the Repertory Grid interview together with some guidance on its administration in groups. The analysis of the performance questionnaire results has been simplified; new examples of performance questionnaires have been provided; and a fresh collection of the assessment factors resulting from such a diagnosis is presented. Six new exercises are described and a re-shaped version of Leaderless Group Discussion is offered, containing a new twist and, incidentally, an implicit recognition of the increasing frequency with which women are encountered on assessment programmes.

The chapter on Observer Training has been substantially re-written to take account of more effective training techniques that are now to hand. More detailed attention is given to the post-programme counselling interview. New validation data are presented, together with information from the UK about the reactions of participants to the programmes. More work has been done on demonstrating the cost-effectiveness of the programmes. More information is offered on the proper role and use of psychological tests.

We would like to thank all those with whom we have worked over the past five years – happily now far too many to mention. They have made this second edition both possible and necessary.

Finally, we would like to suggest that assessment programmes in one form or another have been in use in the UK and elsewhere for some considerable time now. They are no longer new or frighteningly different. The costs of errors in selection, promotion and development of employees have mounted with very considerable speed. Whereas the first edition had possibly something of a missionary purpose, the second no longer needs to perform that function and can concentrate on being a guide to putting some well-tried and satisfactory techniques into practice to help solve a pressing problem.

Andrew Stewart
Valerie Stewart

Note

For the sake of convenience and style, we have used the convention whereby he also means she whenever the context is appropriate.

Chapter 1

Recognizing the problem

This book is about the identification and development of management potential. The reader will discover how various organizations have tackled the job of identifying potential, both in the UK and in other countries; and how we, and other researchers, have tried to answer the question of whether the solutions work and if they give value for money. In particular this book covers the design and evaluation of assessment programmes (or assessment centres, as they are sometimes called) and we offer the reader who wishes to try our ideas on design and evaluation every assistance in the noble art of plagiarism.

There is a stage before any of these concerns may matter to the reader. Why should the reader – a busy manager, an overworked specialist, a man trying to meet tomorrow's problems with today's equipment and yesterday's budget – why should he be interested in the identification of management potential? Is it a problem in his organization? Could better identification of potential lead to the reduction of some of his existing problems? Perhaps he has always thought that identification of potential was a problem, but that it was one of those perennial people-problems which were either incurable or only curable at great cost.

Every doctor and everyone concerned with curing ills (into which category we as industrial psychologists sometimes fall) knows that it is useful to distinguish between the malfunction and the *presenting symptoms*. The complaint the patient makes may be only indirectly related to the trouble he has. When we discuss with managers the problems, experiences and unrecorded triumphs they have had in managing their firms, we keep an ear alert for some of the comments which, in our experience, may indicate that there is a problem in the identification and development of management potential. If we review some of these presenting symptoms, putting them into the words of a fictional manager, maybe we shall assist the reader in discovering the uses he may have for this book.

1 *Too many of our managers are failures*

How the organization defines 'failure' is, of course, very variable. We have known a sales organization in a competitive market prepared to admit that up to 50 per cent of the promotion decisions they made were poor decisions, as measured by the movement of that manager to somewhere else (*not* upwards) within six months of the promotion. On the other hand, there are firms who stoutly maintain to the outsider that everything is running as well as possible, only for that outsider to be button-holed later by people prepared to admit, under their breaths, that such and such a decision didn't turn out too well. Being cynical, one might draw the conclusion that the first firm differed from the second only in its record-keeping and its honesty!

2 *We're not satisfied with our overall management quality*

This feeling sometimes manifests itself as speeches and exhortations by senior management to junior staff; sometimes as requests for better training in every topic from communications to financial management; sometimes as a feeling of unease that opportunities are being missed; sometimes as the sickening realization that opportunities have been missed, when the competition walks off with the account or a strike suddenly erupts.

3 *All our bright chaps seem to leave*

Not everybody regards this as a problem. We know at least one firm which takes a pride in the number of management recruits it loses to its rivals, preferring to feel that having worked for them is a passport to success anywhere in the industry. Most firms do feel uneasy when they see their high calibre people leaving; often in our experience this is the first step towards some simple form of manpower planning. Even more galling is to see people who were not greatly esteemed in one's own firm go into another organization and there make a success. And of course the curious pattern of our economy of late has distorted people's decisions to stay or leave; in periods of wage restraint or high inflation, for example, firms often find that their brighter employees have greater impetus to leave if this is the only way their salaries can advance as fast as they would like.

4 *We always finish up recruiting senior managers from outside*

Surely, people think, there must be plenty within the firm who can do this job, without our having to endure a long gap while the newcomer becomes familiar with our background and the way we do things? But, come the actual decision, the outsider wins nearly every time. Perhaps it is because the outsider talks about his successes, whereas the internal candidate's record of inevitable problems and failings is fully available. Perhaps after the firm has gained a history of recruiting from outside, the internal candidates will feel at a disadvantage anyway. People feel this is an uneconomic way of doing things but are less clear about the possible remedies.

5 *We are never quite sure of the calibre of candidates offered from cross divisional transfer*
Another way this difficulty is sometimes expressed is 'sales division keep passing us their dead wood, with good (but dishonest) recommendations. I won't trust their transfers.' There are a number of possible reasons for this problem. One is the problem of assessing the relevance of the man's previous job experience to the new job in a new division. Will he be planning to the same scale, managing the same calibre of people, expected to respond much faster, or slower? There is a multitude of such questions which should be asked, but it can be difficult to know what the questions are, let alone how to find the answers. Another reason why cross divisional candidates may be difficult to assess is that people recognize that dead wood in one division may flourish in another, but they are not sure how to detect this. The poor sales manager may be being transferred because his technical competence and interest is so great that he would do a better job for everyone in research and development. Or he could be transferred because he is so insensitive that customers refuse to deal with him, which makes him a good candidate (if we may be cynical) for somewhere with no customer contact like building services. In one case the transfer may be valid and honest; in the other case less so, and the problem is how to distinguish between the two.

6 *Why are there no engineers (or personnel specialists or management information specialists etc) on the board, when they are x per cent of the company's employees?*
This feeling can be fed with a variety of fuels; a vague pressure for equity of representation, perhaps, or the sight of a rival firm in trouble because 'the board is nothing but production people' or 'the men at the top are all salesmen and can't manage production' or 'it's managed by accountants and they need some entrepreneurs'. There is a substantial mythology about unrepresentative, self-perpetuating boards of directors, and sometimes this mythology is substantiated by reports issued on companies that have failed or asked for government assistance. This can be damaging to the ambitions of people in the unrepresented areas, if they feel that the very top is closed to them unless they belong to one of the favoured occupations or divisions. In less meritocratic firms, of course, larger numbers of people may have their ambitions similarly pollarded should they feel that ultimate promotion depends upon family or educational connections. The burgeoning of new management sciences, and the changes in approach required in the more traditional areas, may mean that different kinds of talent and experience should be represented on the board of directors.

Recognizing this, and deciding what action to take, is a delicate problem.

7 Two-thirds of our middle managers are coming up for retirement

Where no statistics are kept on such simple matters as numbers of managers and their ages (and there are large firms that do not keep such data) the realization that in five to 10 years' time the company's backbone of middle managers will have retired comes as a great shock. This, in our experience, often happens in firms that grew rapidly from a small start some years ago, with perhaps the original founder still in the background and all the middle managers of long years' service. They have got used to each other and grown old together. In addition they probably have evolved a pattern of communication between themselves and a way of managing which, because it is well established, will leave the organization even more bereft at its sudden loss than would have happened if the pattern had grown gradually. When we are told about this kind of problem, we are on the alert for a possible need to replace not only the numbers of managers but also their skills and abilities.

8 We never seem to be prepared when a management vacancy occurs

It is not comfortable to be managing an operation when one has no idea of the strength of one's reserves. To have to scurry round for a replacement when a management vacancy occurs is wasteful and worrying. It is easy at such times to promise oneself some long term planning to remove the need for further panics. The long term planning may or may not be done and with different degrees of success; sometimes it only leads to the next complaint.

9 The man at the top of the promotion list has been there three years

We once had a lengthy relationship with a firm whose management succession planning was supposed to be computerized. Managers with vacancies reached for the list, on which were recorded the names of candidates for different management posts, arranged in order of their potential judged by managers doing their yearly appraisals. In one part of the firm, the man at the head of the list (therefore the man with the highest listed management potential) remained there for three years while people were promoted from under him. Eventually, of course, people stopped referrring to the list, but the personnel department was immune to any criticism of its methods of assessing and recording management potential; the department had a system, the system was on the computer, the computer never gave any trouble . . . therefore the system was perfect. This attitude – we've got a system, so we're OK – is firmly entrenched in certain organizations and it requires a major catastrophe before they will examine whether the objectives which the system is so efficiently satisfying are, in fact, the objectives which do the organization the best possible service.

10 *We haven't promoted anyone for a long time, so we're all right*

People with this atttiude are forgetting that though their firm may not be growing in size, the people working there are likely to want to grow themselves. They will still be learning, still be changing. If the firm has no use for its employees' management potential, this is no reason to suppose that the employees will be equally uninterested in their own growth.

11 *These things have always been decided by George and he'll be retiring soon*

George may have had an infallible instinct for picking people with potential and for prescribing their development; we have met one or two people who can do this, though they are very, very rare. More often we have met firms where George has promoted only people who conform to a particular pattern, or has promoted only miniature Georges. In one management promotion committee which we observed, a senior manager gave as his reason for refusing a job to a candidate the fact he had made a relatively serious indiscretion some time previously. Only the perspicacity of one of the other managers elicited the fact that this incident was over 20 years old! If the decision-maker has been one man, the decisions may be capricious and will almost certainly not have been followed up to see if they were correct. If the decision-maker has traditionally been a committee, then it is often the case that the candidates appointed for promotion are 'safe' rather than imaginative, and particular decisions may be more influenced by the politics of the committee than by the intrinsic qualities of the candidates.

12 *I'm retiring in four years and I want to know who my successor will be and who will succeed all those people who leave when they find out they are not going to be my successor*

We include this statement, not as an example of a presenting symptom but to provide a contrast to the list above! This was the problem posed to us by the managing director of a small but successful firm who was thinking ahead, realistically.

He was methodically planning the handover of responsibilities, knowing what damage a last minute rush would do. He knew it was inevitable that some people would leave when the successor was nominated. He knew there was not much he could do about that and so he was not asking us to do the impossible. The people who remained were to be strong people fitted for their jobs. Except for a building, an employee is probably among the most expensive long-term investments which a firm makes; employees must therefore be planned for on the same scale, and audited with the same attention to detail as other major expenditures and when they are misused the firm should be concerned to remedy the situation speedily — perhaps more speedily in the case of misused people because people have memories and buildings do not.

We have listed some of the symptoms, complaints, worries and concerns which our experience leads us to believe may sometimes be indicative of the misuse of employee potential. Of course, each of these problems could have other causes; nothing in business, or in the behavioural sciences, is ever simple enough to have one unique cause. But if any of those statements strikes an echo in the reader's mind, and if the reader is not certain that his firm has an efficient, well-validated method of assessing and developing its employees' potential, then he should read on.

Our list of presenting symptoms is taken from the viewpoint of an outsider talking to a senior manager. However, the attentive manager who listens to the kinds of comments coming from the employees in his own firm could also compile his own list of presenting symptoms, taken from the complaints and concerns which people voice when they are asked to air their views. Such employee comments might include the following:

1 *I don't know what a manager does, so how do I know if I want to be one?*
To someone who has spent years in management, it may come as a surprise that there are people who literally do not know what a manager does. We can assure him that such people exist; for example, the specialist we interviewed who, referring to his manager, said 'He's a good manager . . . of course, he doesn't do any *work*, but he's a good manager.' It is not really surprising if a non-managerial employee has only a slight idea of what the job involves, for some good reasons; first, a skilled performance always looks easy, so the person being managed by a good manager may not get a chance to observe the difficult management skills in action; secondly, much management consists of co-ordinating and if you are one of those co-ordinated you get a different perspective on the job. Management is more of an unknown territory to the non-manager than the experienced manager may remember. However, some people may feel that the only way to progress is through management (and in many firms they are, unfortunately, correct) so they are faced with the need to be ambitious for a state which they do not know much about and which may prove profoundly unrewarding to them when they have attained it.

2 *I don't know what help there is to turn me into a manager*
The extent of pre- and post-managerial training varies greatly from firm to firm. So does its effectiveness and the publicity which it is given inside the firm. Some people's anxieties about promotion would be greatly reduced if they knew that their first week as manager would be spent learning about the company's policies, procedures, paperwork and similar parts of the management hardware. On the other hand, we know firms where post-promotion training is offered anything up to two years after one's first promotion; firms where there is no

post- or pre-promotion training; and firms where such training as there is is held in low regard and not taken seriously.

3 I don't want to be a manager

There is increasing concern with the number of professionals and specialists who do not want to become managers, Stewart and Stewart (1974 a).* If specialists and professionals decide that they do not want to leave their specialism behind to become managers, that is their privilege, and it is probably a sign of good communications in the firm that people feel free to voice these opinions. It does imply, though, that serious thinking must be given to the whole issue of employees' potential, career paths, career planning and so on. In this book we write about the assessment of managerial potential but all aspects of individual growth in the job are grist to our mill, and many firms we work with find that they are paying attention to the development of people who have no wish to become managers in the foreseeable future.

4 How do I know what I'm capable of? Nobody asks me

Paradoxically, this is most likely to happen in those firms who complain that they always have to go outside to fill their vacancies. Many firms do not have any fixed system for talking to their people about their capabilities and ambitions. Some firms have an annual appraisal of performance, at the end of which the appraising manager fills in a section on future development, but the employee may contribute little towards this section or may be ignorant of its contents. We often meet people who are better known outside their firms than they are inside, or who feel better appreciated by their customers than they do by their managers. There are some occupations where a built-in performance review is almost essential: sales, for example. But other occupations permit people to grind on for year after year without anyone challenging them about their ambitions, until they reach perhaps middle-age and then go through a difficult, and possibly damaging, crisis. As Dr Peter puts it: 'If you don't know where you're going you'll probably end up somewhere else', Peter and Hull (1969). Guidance and advice on what people are capable of, with actions and plans following, could channel and enhance the capabilities of many people who are not aware how much they are drifting. It is not just the high flyer who needs guidance: the person who has reached his ceiling will often welcome being told this honestly and in plenty of time, so he can plan to get the best out of the 16 hours a day he does not give his employer.

5 I don't feel I've ever been stretched

This feeling, akin to the previous one, is fairly common in middle managers

* All references are given in full in the bibliography on page 255.

who have not had a university education, who perhaps remember the challenge and excitement of active military service in their youth and have never had seriously to pit their wits against a difficult problem since. Part of the appeal of the outdoor challenge courses for middle managers is surely the chance it gives them to find out what they are capable of. Just being given the chance to set oneself high standards and meet them can be satisfying in itself, and it can lead to new self-reliance and to resolutions to do better. If the high standards offered are part of a management assessment programme, simulating a more challenging job, then the man's need to be stretched can be met in a way which will benefit everyone concerned.

6 I don't feel I get a fair chance of promotion

In many organizations, the means by which promotions are made are the subject of involved fantasies. Some of these fantasies have their roots in real issues. If it is true that personnel people never get into line management and that only accountants are considered for promotion to the board, then people cannot be blamed for forming fantastic ideas. The memory of arbitrary promotions lingers long after those who feel they should have been given a chance should have turned their attention elsewhere. Secrecy about how promotions are made leads to industrial relations trouble, and perhaps in extreme cases to white-collar unions insisting that all promotions be made on the basis of seniority or some other criterion which has the sole benefit of being openly acknowledged.

7 I don't know anything about the rest of the company

If people do not know about the rest of their firm, they cannot form a realistic view of the range of jobs they could do. This is a particularly difficult problem because after they have been employed a while people do not like to admit ignorance about such elementary things as what happens in the Manchester factory, and so they may not have the courage to ask. Even knowing the product or the activity cannot completely fill the knowledge gap; one has also to know the kinds of skills needed, the kind of people who work there and so on.

8 I don't know my own market value

This is often said by persons who have got into a rut and is indicative of a possible need to test that market value by applying for other jobs. People who get little feedback on their performance, and who are working in relatively isolated conditions, can lose touch with the salaries and conditions offered to similar employees in other firms. This is likely to happen in firms outside London and the big cities and also in small departments where the employee is the only one of his kind: the manager of the legal department, for example, or the company medical officer. Often the only easy way these people can find out how valuable a commodity they are is by applying for another job. They could well be indicating that they have problems in assessing their own potential.

9 I am underemployed and therefore unpromotable

This is one of the more distressing grumbles for an employee to have and more often heard at exit interviews than in career counselling. In the worst of all possible worlds, it works like this: the firm recruits a graduate to do the job of someone who needs only to be 'A' level standard; in the confines of this restricting job, the man performs badly, not from bloody-mindedness but because it is difficult to do a clerical job well when you are really chafing to do research or go out and meet the customers.

Because he is performing badly, he is ignored when promotion decisions are to be made; it is assumed that as he is not up to his present job, giving him a larger one would be foolish. Perhaps there is a company rule that forbids the passing on of poor performers. The employee may stay and become a troublemaker; he may 'moonlight', getting his job satisfaction elsewhere; he may leave, in which case the firm will never know what it has lost. Formal assessment programmes, in which the management job is simulated and participants are given the chance to try their capabilities at something more challenging, can be the only way for some firms to discover whether they have people working for them in jobs that are presently too small.

If these complaints, and others like them, come filtering up through the management grapevine to the people responsible for manpower planning, it is possible that the assessment and development of managerial potential is not being done as well as it possibly could be. Again, the reader who has heard such complaints in his organization (or who wishes to forestall them) may find this book helpful.

Before we go on to talk about further ways of defining the problem, and to discuss possible solutions, let us offer another argument. Here we anticipate the discussion in a later chapter on validity, but we are sure that some readers will be asking themselves whether these problems we mention are not, in fact, intractable problems which any senior manager has to learn to live with. We offer one example of what can be done.

A company wished to improve its method of assessment of managerial potential. Too many of its present promotion decisions were mistakes; the man had to be moved within six months. This happened with nearly half its promotions. The firm felt sure it could improve on this performance.

We tried, as an exercise, to put some measures on what it cost the client to be making so many errors. What was the lowered performance in the man's position, in the people he managed? Was there lowered performance in the people who could have filled the post but did not get the chance? Had they any notion of the orders lost, customers upset, morale costs to the other managers of knowing that promotion decisions were so capricious, industrial relations costs associated with incompetent managers making mistakes? It was not possible to put money figures on all of these but the feeling was that the money costs themselves were great, even when separated from the human costs. It was worth trying to make some improvement.

We undertook a programme of work in the firm in which we first of all diagnosed the characteristics associated with effectiveness in that firm at the levels of management under consideration. When we had completed the diagnosis and agreed its results with the client, the client asked us to design a programme in which participants' potential could be assessed and development plans formed by putting them through a planned simulation of the management job to be done, during which simulation they would be systematically observed by trained observers looking for the previously-determined characteristics of effectiveness. These observers would be line managers, people who would themselves be involved in the promotion decisions. As a result of the information gained on the assessment programme, and the interviews with participants during which their further development was planned, a full record was available of the participants' managerial potential, objectively recorded and in great detail. This information played a part in any further promotion decisions which the client firm made.

The assessment programme became a regular feature of the client's personnel management strategy and the client tells us that since starting to use the information from the programme, hardly any wrong promotion decisions have been made. Such an improvement, so well-sustained, makes us believe that the costs of the original diagnosis and design, plus the running costs of the programme, have been covered many times over by the tangible and intangible benefits which the programme has produced.

In other words, it is our experience that improvements in the assessment of employees' potential are possible for most firms, whether large or small, and whether the level of management is first-line supervisory or senior director level. This book discusses ways that potential can be assessed and recorded. We discuss how these methods can be validated and costed and (for our own methods at any rate) we try to give the reader as much help as possible in setting up assessment procedures in his own firm.

We hope that this introduction has alerted the reader to the range of presenting symptoms which could indicate that employee potential is not being properly identified and used, and that it has given an indication that considerable improvements might be possible for comparatively small effort and cost.

Having set the assessment of potential into its human context, we should next address the organizational climate and conditions in which potential is to be sought. This will involve us in briefly reviewing the major issues of manpower planning, succession planning and existing employee appraisal systems. We shall not go into great detail about these problems as they are well treated elsewhere, but the reader should understand that it is no good knowing what potential the people employed have unless one also knows how many promotions and transfers one is likely to make within a given time, nor is it any use knowing how many management vacancies one is likely to have unless one has some systematic plans for filling them effectively. We shall therefore describe, in dramatic rather than in quantitative terms, some of the chief concerns of the manpower planning expert.

Manpower planning activities are both subject to, and material for, decisions at policy level. It is perhaps a truism to point out that planning activities refer to the future, but it is important to distinguish between the collection of records for the personnel information system on the one hand, and the extrapolation from these records and other information to clarify future strategy on the other. Manpower planning depends upon personnel records, but up to date personnel records do not constitute manpower planning.

Some people balk at the very idea of manpower planning, maintaining that there have been so many changes in Government policy, the business cycle and world commodity prices that any attempt to plan one's manpower requirements is futile. While we would agree that today's planners probably have a far more difficult task in front of them than at any previous time, we would reiterate that the hiring of a manager or a professional man is almost the longest-lasting investment any company is likely to make; and that planning of capital requirements, while made indescribably more difficult by the switchback economy of today, does not stop because people find the changes difficult to anticipate. In addition, we know of many cases where we could, with perfect justice, have said 'We told you so' to firms to whom we gave advice on their most appropriate manpower strategy some years ago and who, disbelieving that such precision was possible, ignored our advice only to find themselves seriously over- or under-manned.

Properly done manpower planning, based on up to date records, can help with many day to day questions such as: how far is it possible to promote from within, versus recruiting externally? Can we achieve a reduced manning level in time by steady run-down through natural wastage and non-replacement, or should we opt for some immediate redundancies? Can we sensibly offer all our young professionals a long-term career path, or should we be thinking of fixed-term contracts for some people? How many graduates should we hope to recruit this year in order to have a stock of a given size and competency at the end of x years and so on? We can systematize these different areas as follows:

Manpower forecasting

Legislation has been passed which makes it even more difficult than before for a firm to admit that in hiring an employee it has made a mistake. Security of employment is greater. Certain categories of employee have the right to make formal complaint if they feel they are being unfairly discriminated against. The costs of employing women, versus the costs of employing men, have been altered by the Equal Pay Act, by the provision of more expensive pensions for women and by legislation on maternity leave. In addition, the climate of opinion seems to be shifting towards a greater acceptance of the concept of constructive dismissal, so that an employer who removes an employee from a congenial job into one the employee finds less acceptable may find that he is held to have constructively dismissed that employee. In addition to these considerations, which make it important to get placement decisions right, there are the usual ever-changing factors which the manpower planner must take into account. These are:

the introduction of new products
one's expectations of future output
plans for expansion and contraction
changes in technology
possible changes in the structure of the organization (by centralization, decentralization, relocation, reorganization and so on)
financial ceilings or other forms of top limit to one's activity – or, in some cases, bottom limits
existing agreements with the unions and the firm's own personnel policies
environmental and other constraints in the labour supply
current trends in wage rates and other forms of compensation
trends in other forms of costs
demographic considerations about the characteristics of the local labour force.

Faced with such a daunting list of factors to take into account, the manpower planner will have to experiment with a variety of different models before he finds the right one. Then he will have to keep checking it to make sure it is still appropriate. Usually he will try to form projections based upon *time series* in the hope that steady trends will become apparent and that these trends will continue. Most time series exhibit one or more of the following characteristics:

a trend; a gradual, regularly increasing or decreasing series
cyclical movements, undulating in a repeat pattern resembling a wave-form
seasonal fluctuations, as for example the sudden rise in employment in farming at harvest time or the drop in building activity during the winter

a step function, a change in the series from one constant level to another, at
   which it stays
random fluctuations which do not seem to follow any pattern.

Armed with a battery of techniques which can extract patterns from seemingly
haphazard data, the manpower forecaster attempts to form his predictions of
where the organization will find itself within a given period of time, taking
account of all possible factors.

Manpower dynamics

Whereas manpower forecasting operates mostly at the policy level, manpower
dynamics is concerned with the structure and organization of jobs within the
firm in order to achieve the company's objectives. Manpower dynamics, to put
it another way, reflects the concerns usually expressed by people in organization
development or management development, but with a definite emphasis on
measurement, planning and control. An example of manpower dynamics might
be: the investigation of turnover in a factory, the calculation of the cost of the
particular turnover rate for each category of employee, the decision on
whereabouts action should be taken to have the most effect, and the redesign of
the job or the hiring procedure or the training in order to reduce the turnover
rate. Manpower dynamics tends to be a more pragmatic study area than
manpower forecasting, being closer to the operational level and therefore more
subject to day to day constraints and considerations.

Succession and replacement planning

Every organization has a flow of people through its various grades and occupations. The flow will be due to a number of factors, thus:

   voluntary wastage, or resignation
   involuntary wastage, or dismissal
   promotion
   expansion or contraction of manpower requirements
   recruitment
   the age distribution, leading to sickness and retirement
   sideways movements or maybe demotions.

Manpower planning activities in this area will be concerned with the collection
of the appropriate data: the number of people moving through each grade, the
reasons for their movements and the compiling of succession listings and other
data. Typically, voluntary wastage is found to depend upon the type or level of
skill, the length of service, the age and geographical position of employees,
coupled with economic factors and the activities of the competition; involun-

tary wastage depends upon most of the above factors, plus considerations of industrial relations, early retirement, redundancy payments and the current state of industrial law; promotion rates depend upon the sizes and structures of grades available (is the hierarchy steep or shallow sided?) the relative wastage between grades, expected expansion or contraction between grades, age distributions in the various grades, the availability of people suitable for promotion and their wishes for their own career paths. Expansion or contraction of manpower requirements depends upon the current and the predicted success of the organization, allowing for changes in the product mix and for economic trends. Recruitment is the most easily controlled factor, depending upon the external availability of possible recruits, their age, qualifications and experience. And the age mix of an organization is one of the prime determining factors in an organization's succession and replacement planning, involving considerations of normal retirement, early retirement, deferred retirement and increased separation due to sickness. Many firms in this country find that they built up their strength rapidly after the end of the Hitler war and then ceased to expand very much or to think of the potential problem (now becoming real) of suddenly losing a high proportion of skilled and experienced people as they all reach retirement date at about the same time.

Manpower audits or inventories

Generally speaking a manpower audit means listing employees in accordance with certain categories or standards. The 'management inventory' is a common example of the manpower audit. A good inventory will include all the information available on a number of dimensions, such as personal history, skills, interests, appraisal records, career aspirations and present position. Some of the information will be quantitative and some narrative; not all will therefore be amenable to storage on the computer. A review of this information can be helpful when management is examining labour wastage (turnover); the effectiveness and sensitivity of salary administration; the use of development time and money; the rate of advancement of capable people and the balance of exchange across departments. Indeed, some companies have taken management inventories to the point where they feel able to list the successors for any post in rank order of preference, so that the succession is effectively automated. Some firms recoil with horror at what they see as de-humanizing overmechanization. However, what we can say with certainty is that the success of the system, however it is applied, depends upon the appropriateness of the parameters on which information is recorded. To take a silly example: if management success is dependent upon having brown eyes and a certain surname, it is no good collecting data about career aspirations and present performance.

Development planning

This is clearly linked with succession and replacement planning, but concentrates on such issues as the amount and time of development activities that should be planned for individual people and the way these activities are, or are not, directly linked to the firm's prediction about its manpower requirements in the future. This will involve decisions about counselling, supervision, career planning, job rotation, special assignments, advanced management courses, management seminars, educational leaves of absence, sabbatical leaves and correspondence courses. The financial implications of all manpower planning activities are considerable, but development activities are probably the most vulnerable to short-term trimming in the event of a miscalculation or sudden crisis. It is therefore critically important to cost one's development plans thoroughly in order to make sure that the financial and other implications of such short-term pruning can be appreciated.

Manpower modelling

With suitable measures it is not too difficult to obtain a static picture of the appearance of a manpower system. However, it is also important to be able to understand the interactions within the system (its physiology as well as its anatomy, so to speak) and to use this understanding to predict how the system may behave in the future. The purpose of a manpower model is to enable armchair experiments to be conducted: to see what the effect would be of changes in circumstances or different managerial decisions. To do this modelling, the manpower planner needs to understand something about the relationships within a manpower system. The basic relationships can be illustrated quite simply, and table 1 (on page 28) gives a diagrammatic notion of the relationship between the stock of manpower in each grade and the numerical flows acting on it over a period of time. The reader may be surprised to learn that this amount of information is sufficient for quite sophisticated modelling to take place, although certain features of this very simple model might need more detail for real-life simulation to be thoroughly adequate. Table 2 on page 29 shows part of a manpower system, including data about grades and occupations as well as some possible career paths. Table 3 on page 30 takes a single grade and shows some of the influences which can act upon it, and table 4 on page 31 gives a detailed breakdown of the stocks and flows in a single grade by age.

At the moment there are five main kinds of manpower model in existence or under development:

Stationary population models

These are very simple and are often used for gaining initial insights into the

27

Table 1
Basic relationships in a manpower system

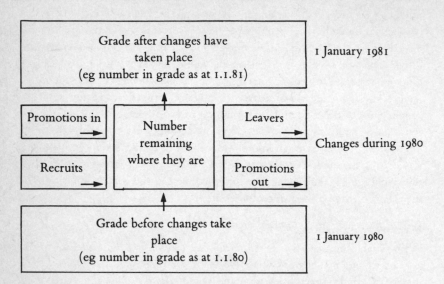

This is a diagrammatic representation of an equation which underlies most manpower models.

Number in grade in 1981 = number in that grade in 1980
  − wastage
  − transfers and promotions out
  + transfers and promotions in
  + recruitment

manpower system. They show the eventual size of a grade assuming the same annual intake and unchanging wastage and promotion rates. It is rather like the hackneyed school problem of the bath filling from a tap at one rate and emptying at another. They are not realistic assumptions but they enable us to say where we would finish if we carried on as at present. There are more sophisticated versions of this type of model available which overcome some of the limitations and can be used to derive, for example, the ideal age structure for each grade and the age at which promotion must occur in order to remain within such constraints as the current age distribution, projected grade sizes and the maintenance of equity between employees.

Programming models

These are rather more complicated and involve the use of linear programming techniques to meet one overriding set of needs while causing the minimum dis-

Table 2
A representation of part of a manpower system

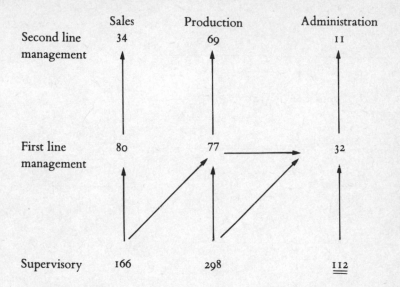

	Sales	Production	Administration
Second line management	34	69	11
First line management	80	77	32
Supervisory	166	298	112

This diagram shows the total number (stock) of employees at one time, classified into broad occupational groups and, within each group, grade level. The numbers show the stocks in each grade at, say, 1.1.80. The arrows suggest typical career paths within the system (ie excluding recruitment and wastage flows)

turbance to the other important factors in the employment situation. For example, it might be necessary to meet reduced demand for one product while minimizing redundancy, where cost is the overriding factor; or it might be necessary to plan the recruitment and distribution of service engineers at an economical rate while maintaining a minimum basic level of service to all customers as an overriding constraint. These models in particular are discussed in detail by Bartholomew and Forbes (1978).

Monte Carlo models

These are used to simulate the movement of individuals in the manpower system, determining individual behaviour by the random application of values from a probability distribution. For example, we might wish to know what is the likely movement amongst people who have been with the organization more than one year but less than two; from the wastage figures we might find that, in the past, 30 per cent of those who have been with the company one year will leave before the completion of two years' service. An individual can now

Table 3
Processes and influences acting upon a single
grade in a manpower system

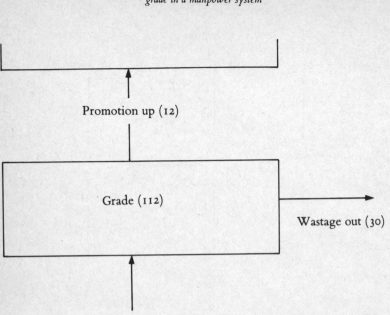

Promotion up (12)

Grade (112)

Wastage out (30)

Recruitment in (42)

This diagram shows typical flows into and out of a single grade: the supervisory, administrative grade in table 4

be predicted as leaving or not leaving within a 12 month period according to whether a number generated at random, to represent that individual's decision, falls between 1 and 30 or 31 and 100. Put at its simplest (and it is a great simplification) Monte Carlo modelling attempts to put the uncertainties of the employment situation into a form which enables us to make useful predictions from probabalistic data.

Renewal models
These begin by taking a record of the number of people in each grade, subtracting the wastage which previous experience leads us to expect and making allowances for expected expansion or contraction. Then different patterns of replacement are tried out in accordance with pre-determined policies incorporated into the model. Renewal models are particularly useful for testing such things as the effect on career prospects and recruitment, of meeting expressed manpower requirements.

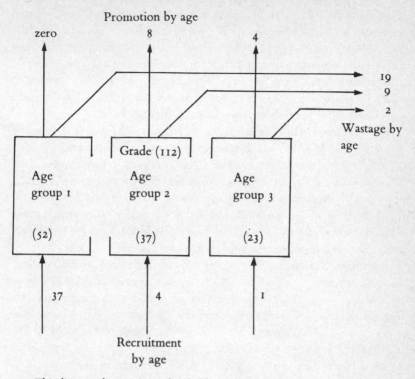

Table 4
Breakdown of stocks and flows according to age in a single grade

This diagram shows a more detailed breakdown of the contents of table 3

Markov models

The logical counterpart of renewal models, they permit the determination of the effect on grade size of satisfying particular career expectations, by expressing all the flows as a proportion of the numbers in the grade and observing the resulting grade sizes.

In this section we have outlined, rather superficially, the possible uses of manpower planning within a firm, thus putting the assessment of managerial potential into its strategical context. Manpower planning is a job for an expert and we have only sketched the areas of expertise and the kinds of results which the expert could obtain. The reader who wishes to pursue the topic further is recommended to some of the books cited in the reference list and to talk to some of the experts in the field. We hope in our lightning sketch to have indicated some of the areas where it would be either useful or essential to have data on the potential for development of one's employees. These areas are manifold.

This first chapter attempts to help the reader discover whether the book could be of some use to him, by indicating the many ways in which poor use of potential could surface as human problems, or as problems of politics. It has indicated the long-term strategic consequences of assessment and potential and some of the ways in which manpower planning techniques can help highlight these consequences and suggest measures for their control. The sceptical reader, though, might have another question. He might formulate this question thus: 'I accept all you say about the importance of correct assessment of potential, but you can't teach me anything; we've been doing it our way for years.'

When someone says this our first impulse is to ask how he does it. If indeed he is doing it well and is satisfied, then we have learned something valuable. This book is full of wisdom we have acquired from other people. But we must admit that we have not often come across firms where the assessment of potential is done to a high standard of reliability and validity and to criteria tailored to the firm's individual, unique needs. This view is borne out by other experts in the field, and so we would ask the sceptic to bear with us until the end of the chapter while we relate some of our experiences and other people's research.

For example, Campbell *et al* (1970, pp 109–11) quote some work by Miner which showed how promotional decisions in one company varied greatly from department to department in their reliance on previous job performance. He compared the extent to which the manufacturing department relied upon past performance with the extent to which the accounting department did so. The reader seeking to protect himself from complacency should guess at this point what he thinks that pattern would have been, before reading on.

In the manufacturing department, promotion decisions were positively related to job performance as follows:

Table 5
Relation between job performance and promotion in the
manufacturing department

	Job performance	
	Judged above average	Judged below average
Promoted	24	5
Not promoted	11	20

Note: the figures indicate the number of persons in each cell of the table.
Source: from Campbell, Dunnette, Lawler and Weick, 1970

and the accounting department showed the following pattern:

Table 6

Relation between job performance and promotion in the accounting department

	Job performance	
	Judged above average	Judged below average
Promoted	8	19
Not Promoted	28	29

Note: the figures indicate the number of persons in each cell of the table.
Source: from Campbell, Dunnette, Lawler and Weick, 1970

Clearly, in this firm the odds were heavily in favour of promotion for manufacturing people with good track records and for accountancy people with poor track records — not something that is easy to predict from an informal knowledge of the requirements of each kind of job. These career patterns were, in fact, probably most influenced by luck, whether they were in manufacturing or accounting departments. It is well worth while, if you think that your own system works well across the whole firm, doing some simple calculations with the aid of the personnel record system to see whether any such inequities have crept in. Company-wide indices of succession do not usually show this information in detail.

Turning from this appealing statistical demonstration to a more anecdotal account (an anecdote that will be repeated, with amplification, later in this book) we were once concerned with developing a list of the characteristics of effective managers in a certain firm. We used a questionnaire technique designed to reduce the emphasis on the 'ideal' effective manager in favour of the real-life effective manager; and several people, highly-qualified psychologists and people from the firm, brainstormed the items for the questionnaire from a combined total of over 30 years' experience. Though the questionnaire was reasonably successful a further simple modification increased the yield of the questionnaire *five-fold*. This modification was designed to remove the bias of the observers (no matter how experienced they thought they were) in favour of the perceptions of the people actually doing the job.

Another time we did some research on a firm's appraisal system; we devised a questionnaire designed to identify which sorts of appraisals were causing managers trouble and took the precaution of (i) predicting the outcome ourselves, and (ii) getting some members of the personnel department to predict the outcomes. Both parties were wrong in a number of significant instances. We have ample evidence to back up the assertion of Campbell *et al* (*op cit*) that armchair theorizing about what effective management should look like, and how to find it, can be at best weak and at worst seriously misleading. We regret to add that sometimes the armchair from which this imperceptive theorizing is done sometimes belongs to the managing director. This weakness is nothing to be ashamed of: human beings are complex creatures and psychologists have been struggling for years to describe human personality in useful ways; an amateur whose expertise lies in other directions should not be ashamed if he cannot achieve the kind of perspicacity about the components of effectiveness which is described in this book.

We have, as a corollary to the above accounts, some experience in talking to firms which use a package assessment programme, bought off the shelf from a consultant or in some cases passed across the Atlantic from the parent firm. The package approach is one that worries us, because it seems to depend upon armchair theorizing and there is usually little attempt to tailor the package to fit the needs of different firms or different managerial levels. We shall present evidence later in this book to show that firms differ so much in their requirements for managerial effectiveness that what would be absolutely right for one firm would be diametrically wrong in another. Of course, most packages compromise and do not go into detail or controversial areas where they might expect such clashes to occur; this leads us to wonder whether it is economic to buy a general prescription, designed to be right for everybody, when it is equally possible to design something exactly right for one's own firm. However, the gravest concern we have about packages has to do with their validity. How much better is the organization performing, according to a strict set of criteria, as a result of the procedure for assessing potential? How reliable are the predictions? How many promotions are successful which would otherwise have been expected to fail? These are the kinds of questions we want to ask about package programmes and we have to say that the manufacturers of package assessment programmes have not been very willing to answer them. In chapter 8 we treat the problem of validation of assessment programmes in great detail, because we are concerned that *all* systems for assessing managerial potential, be they off the shelf packages, or tailored designs such as we describe in the body of this book, or any other methods that could be used, should be validated against proper criteria so that the firm concerned can see if it is getting its money's worth. We ask the sceptic who is satisfied with his present system of assessing potential to look at the chapters on validation, to see whether his present system could be tested and perhaps improved.

For other readers, we shall assume that our argument has been made. It is important, for all sorts of reasons, to assess what the organization's workforce is capable of in the future. It is important to get a picture of one's future manpower needs, qualitatively as well as quantitatively, and to marry these two assessments. On the specific topic of potential to become a manager in a particular firm, it is worth distrusting armchair theorists and package deals and pursuing instead the solution that best fits one's own particular firm and its unique requirements. It is possible, and highly desirable, to conduct this pursuit scientifically, with an eye to measurement and objectivity, for what cannot be measured cannot be controlled. This book records some of our experiences in the assessment of potential, in the hope that we can put the ability to ask and answer these important questions into the reader's hands.

Chapter 2

Managerial effectiveness
and how to spot it

In this chapter we have two purposes: first, to review some of the existing literature on managerial effectiveness, recording the views and the evidence on which these views were formed; and secondly to discuss the different methods by which, it is advocated, potential managers of various kinds can be spotted in advance. Though we shall occasionally take a critical view of existing methods, the reader who wishes to see existing methods thoroughly examined should bear in mind that in the chapter on validation we treat the existing methods in a more rigorous fashion than we do here.

We must begin by lamenting the dearth of existing empirical work on what makes for managerial effectiveness. Campbell *et al* (*op cit*) say that 'the business literature is full of commentary, speculation and expressions of opinion about possible answers', and go on to point out that speculation far outweighs the evidence. We cannot but agree with them. One of our purposes in writing this book is to help the reader detach himself from speculation and conduct his own empirical research into what makes for effective managerial behaviour in his own firm.

Turning to the first of our purposes, ie the existing views of managerial effectiveness, we began by reviewing some delightfully empirical work on what managers actually do. Rosemary Stewart's *Managers and Their Jobs* (1967) analyses the results of 'diaries' kept by a sample of managers in a wide variety of jobs in different industries, in terms of the time spent on different activities, the nature of those activities, the direction of face to face contacts, the nature of the communications media and so on. She was able, as a result of factor analysis, to differentiate five different kinds of managerial job:

1 *The emissaries*, people whose work brings them into close touch with the outside world and who might be away from their desks for days at a time. Typical emissaries are sales managers, general managers who have a large

responsibility for representing the company to the outside world and civil engineers who have to oversee contractors. The emissary spends more of his life on company business than do other managers and a greater proportion of this time is spent unprofitably in travelling.

2 *The writers*, managers who spend markedly more time in reading, writing, dictating and figure work. They are solitary only in comparison with other managers, spending half their time with other people as compared with an average of two-thirds spent thus by the other managers in the study. This group includes specialists and head office advisers, as well as managers whose primary function for their own department was a paperwork function, for example a payroll manager. Dr Stewart also points out that this group includes, somewhat surprisingly, several production and works managers.

3 *The discussers*, managers who spend the most time with other people and with their colleagues, especially in one to one contact and in contact with their peers. This type of manager is the least easy to typify in terms of a likely job or position, as managers with widely differing responsibilities fall into this categorization.

4 *The trouble shooters*, managers whose diaries show large numbers of fleeting contacts, reflecting the extent to which their job consists of coping with crises. A works manager is likely to be a 'trouble shooter', spending a larger than average proportion of his time with his subordinates and a larger than average proportion on inspection; rarely leaving his own factory, rarely going to committees and having little opportunity for uninterrupted work.

5 *The committee men*, who have a wide range of internal contacts and spend a large amount of time in group discussions. The typical committee man works for a large company, spends a large amount of time on personnel work, has few external contacts and more opportunity to work uninterrupted. The chief determinant of whether a manager will be a committee man is a combination of the type of production, the size of the firm and the policies of the company.

Rosemary Stewart does not attempt in her book to prescribe what makes for managerial effectiveness; she confines herself to describing what managers actually do. In so doing she contributes to our understanding of managerial effectiveness in at least two ways. First, she is commenting on the work of British managers and this book is written from the UK point of view. There is good evidence that what makes for managerial effectiveness in the UK can be unproductive in the USA and for this reason we have to take transatlantic work through a mental 'translator' before applying it in the UK. Secondly, Rosemary Stewart is one of the few people who actually attempt to distinguish between the different requirements of different jobs in different firms. This is an axiom to

37

which many writers pay lip-service but most of the work on the different requirements of different jobs consists of comparing and contrasting two jobs only, eg manager of a sales office versus manager of research and development. Many other factors should be taken into account when assessing the unique requirements of different jobs in different firms and comprehensive evidence is thin; Rosemary Stewart reviews a wider range than the great majority of writers.

Citing similar work in the USA, Mintzberg (1973) contributes another non-prescriptive analysis of what managers actually do. He distinguishes 10 managerial roles which managers are called upon to perform, to different degrees, depending upon their job and position:

figurehead, in which the manager has to perform certain routine duties, usually of a social or legal nature, just because he is a manager
leader, in which he is responsible for motivating and activating his subordinates and selecting, training and counselling them
liaison, in which he must develop and maintain a network of outside contacts who provide information, favours etc
monitor, in which he seeks special information so as to improve his understanding of the organization and its environment
disseminator, in which he transmits information received from outside and inside sources to other members of the organization
spokesman, in which he transmits company sanctioned information to outsiders or serves as an expert on the particular organization's industry
entrepreneur, in which he searches inside and outside the organization for opportunities for improvement and initiates and follows through any such projects
disturbance handler, in which he is responsible for the necessary corrective action when the organization faces important, unexpected disturbances
resource handler, in which he is responsible for the allocation of resources; in other words, making decisions
negotiator, in which he represents the organization at major negotiations.

Mintzberg, like Rosemary Stewart, refrains from making prescriptions about managerial effectiveness as a result of these different roles. He also presents some discussion of the relative salience of these roles for different jobs and different firms. We quote him for two purposes: first because in our own work on managerial effectiveness in different firms, it has often proved useful to compare our actual results with Mintzberg's more widely-known descriptions to aid understanding. Secondly because Mintzberg takes issue with the many writers on management who have ignored or diminished the 'figurehead' role. We have to report that in many of our investigations, even at fairly junior levels in the hierarchy, 'figurehead' type behaviour appears as a distinguishing characteristic of the effective manager.

Turning now from the work on what managers actually do to the larger body of work on what a good manager actually is, we are faced with a more difficult analytical task. Perhaps we can illustrate the difficulty by quoting Lewis and Stewart (1961) who tell of the questionnaire sent by *Fortune*, the American business journal, to 75 top executives who were asked to indicate the importance of the following qualities: initiative, integrity, drive, foresight, energy, human relations skill, decisiveness, dependability, emotional stability, fairness, ambition, dedication, objectivity and cooperation. Nearly a third of the executives thought that all the qualities were indispensable. The sting is in the tail: these 75 executives, asked to describe what they understood by the various trait-names, managed to describe the word 'dependability' in 147 different ways.

Jurgenson (1966) asked personnel men and executives to sort 120 adjectives to describe 'the type of person most likely to succeed as a key executive in top management'. He took out the 12 adjectives rated as most descriptive and least descriptive:

Table 7

Most descriptive of key executive	Least descriptive of key executive
decisive	amiable
aggressive	conforming
self-starting	neat
productive	reserved
well informed	agreeable
determined	conservative
energetic	kindly
creative	mannerly
intelligent	cheerful
responsible	formal
enterprising	courteous
clear-thinking	modest

Source: Jurgenson (1967), by permission of the author

This work is perhaps one of the more scientific collections of opinions, but it should be apparent to the reader that some of the findings are of questionable utility, on grounds both of definition and of accuracy. For example, what does 'productive' mean? Lots of work, or small amounts of high quality work, or working to time? How many times has the reader seen genuinely bright, creative, intelligent and aggressive young managers have their fire quenched by senior managers who, though they might *say* they value these qualities, actually promote yes men who have never done anything noteworthy for good or ill? In one or two of our own studies, qualities listed by Jurgenson as characteristics *least* descriptive of executive high-flight have been shown to characterize the *effective* manager in a certain firm. Furthermore, it often seems that these descriptions reflect the Samuel Smiles, 19th century capitalist view of the manager as go-getting entrepreneur in a market of perfect competition; whereas, as Stafford Beer points out in his unusual book *Platform for Change* (1975), it is likely that for most firms and most managers the key issue has changed from being one of *profit* to being one of *survival*. As the *Economist* has pointed out at various times recently, it is virtually impossible for anyone to start a firm nowadays and hope to run it as a profit-making venture; ever-changing legislation of ever-increasing complexity makes the weighing of risks difficult and company taxation makes them unlikely to succeed; in this light, one asks oneself, should one so automatically state that the key executive in top management will be a determined, aggressive entrepreneur? The point is worth pondering the next time the reader encounters a glib prescription for managerial effectiveness.

Campbell *et al* (1970) depart from the notion of the trait list to give us a list of opinions, collated from many sources, of what managers have to do in order to be effective. Though sceptical about the value of collecting opinions, they say that opinions about activities are more useful than opinions about traits, a view with which we would agree. Successful managers are said to show most of the following job behaviours:

they manage work instead of people
they plan and organize effectively
they set goals realistically
they derive decisions by group consensus but accept responsibility for them
they delegate frequently and effectively
they rely on others for help in solving problems
they communicate effectively
they are a stimulus to action
they co-ordinate effectively
they co-operate with others
they show consistent and dependable behaviour
they win gracefully
they express hostility tactfully.

One of us once had the misfortune to take part in an interminable discussion with people employed at the public expense, the object of which was to agree a set of objectives for a research project. In despair at the meeting's lack of purpose, which expressed itself in quibbling over whether we should begin by settling the aims or the objectives or the roles or the goals or the purposes, your author delivered the opinion that 'the important thing is to get it about right'. Sad to relate, this contribution was taken seriously instead of being realized for what it was; and the same objection can be levelled at so many of the 'behaviour statements' which we quote from Campbell et al. So many of those statements contain the adverbs 'realistically' or 'effectively' without going on to answer the important question of what, exactly, constitutes effectiveness in these circumstances. The answer cannot be assumed, as we shall show clearly in the later chapters.

For brief and salty comment, whether on managerial effectiveness or on any other aspect of running a business, one cannot do better than consult Robert Townsend's Up The Organization (1970). For Townsend, the best manager is first into the office and last out; the best manager does not mind how low a job he does if it helps one of his people to reach his objective; he protects his people from the intrusions of outsiders including senior managers; he preserves the long-term view of the business strategy so that he, and his people, do not over react to swings in the business cycle. On the subject of spotting a true leader, Townsend says that though they come in all sorts of shapes and sizes there is one clue: the true leader can be recognized because somehow or other his people consistently turn in superior performances.

Our own findings are that there seem to be one or two behaviours characteristic of effective management almost irrespective of the firm and the job and the job level; and Townsend has pinned down most of these common factors in his comments.

In most of the firms we have looked at, for instance, the effective manager has a habit of giving his people the credit for good work, protecting them in public and delegating to them the challenging rather than the donkey work; he will have one or more of his subordinates ready to take his place and, particularly at senior and middle levels, he will be able to exercise the 'helicopter effect' so viewing his information, and his decisions, from the point of view of their effect on the company and its range of business and its long-term plans.

More brief comment on the kind of man to get to the top is contained in Lewis and Stewart (op cit) where the authors mix solid demographic data with a spicing of humour and Machiavellianism to provide a guide to how and why people have reached the top. For instance, they point out that it is no good doing good work unless it is noticed by one's superiors; in support of this argument they cite the case of the two naval officers who, on leaving Dartmouth as midshipmen, made a brotherly pact that, throughout their service careers whenever either of them heard the other's name mentioned in conversation, he would chip in with the remark, 'Did I hear you say old So-and-So? He's a marvellous chap, simply marvellous.' Both of them ended as admirals.

Writing in 1961, Lewis and Stewart point out that a public school education was a decided advantage in getting to the top in British business; between one-third and one-half of top managers came from public schools and the major public schools were over represented in this proportion. Family connections were also an advantage, especially to people joining small or medium sized firms. Being technically trained, as opposed to having an arts or legal or accounting background, was a distinct disadvantage; and (a thought-provoking finding) those who had been successful in business had rarely changed companies. We should bear in mind the age of this study, but it does make clear the nonbehavioural characteristics on which success has, historically, depended to some extent. Needless to say, the authors did not think it necessary to point out how few of the successful managers were female. They also made the point that most of the trait names associated with off the cuff estimates of business effectiveness can be found in the biographies of a number of successful businessmen, eg Ivar Kruger, Horatio Bottomley, Clarence Hatry, who finished their careers in jail. Since they wrote we could add the names of Bloom, Cornfeld and Savundra and many others, all of whom were well-equipped with ability, optimism, ambition, winning ideas, ability to grasp opportunities, self-confidence, application and determination – all except integrity and the ability not to be found out.

More recently, Kellner and Crowther-Hunt (1980) investigate quite thoroughly the 'Oxbridge' bias in Civil Service recruitment into its higher grades concluding that, despite the protestations of the Civil Service Commission, such bias can still be demonstrated. It should be noted, however, that the picture is not quite so clear as is often made out and that it is perhaps only the bias towards candidates from the private sector in education which remains truly mysterious. Campbell (1980) is even more direct:

> First, the dominance of just two Universities, Oxford and Cambridge, in providing recruits for the senior ranks (of the Civil Service) has no parallel elsewhere. Second, in no other Western bureaucracy has the generalist administrator managed to retain his primacy over professionally qualified specialists. In Canada and the United States such people end up selling insurance. Whitehall takes essentially facile, glib individuals and runs them through a selection process geared to assessing the extent to which people have these qualities.

It is as if Fulton had never existed. We shall return to this issue in the chapter on validation.

A fairly down to earth treatment of managerial effectiveness is found in Koontz's book *Appraising Managers as Managers* (1971). He suggests a checklist against which to assess managerial effectiveness:

- setting his unit short-term and long-term goals in verifiable terms, that are related positively to the goals of the superior and the firm
- making sure the goals are understood by the people reporting to him
- assisting his people to set their own verifiable and realistic goals for themselves
- following the accepted company policies and practices when planning for the future
- understanding the company policies himself and making sure that his people also understand them
- solving his subordinates' problems by helping them find their own solutions rather than issuing rules or doing it himself
- helping his subordinates get information they need
- seeking for a range of possible answers before making a decision
- recognizing the critical requirements and the limiting factors in coming to a decision
- recognizing the size of the commitments his decisions involve
- checking and following through the plans he makes
- making decisions that allow for flexibility of time if necessary
- considering the long-term and the short-term implications of his decisions
- putting up proposed solutions whenever he has to put up a problem to his superiors
- organizing the management structure underneath him so as to reflect the major result areas
- delegating sufficient authority to match the responsibility he has delegated
- making his delegation clearly
- formalizing in writing his subordinates' goals, job descriptions, and extent of authority delegated to them
- clarifying responsibility for the contributions he expects from his subordinates
- maintaining adequate control when delegating his authority
- delegating responsibility as well as authority
- making sure that once he has delegated authority to a subordinate he does not 'claw back' the decisions for himself
- making sure that his subordinates properly delegate their authority when necessary
- maintaining unity of command
- using staff advice when necessary, recognizing that it is only advice
- teaching his subordinates the difference between line and staff relationships
- making clear the scope of delegation of functional authority

using service departments only when necessary to control or efficiency or service

not creating excessive levels of organization

not using committees for decisions that should be taken by individuals

making sure that committees have proper agendas and that they are served in time with appropriate information

distinguishing between lines of authority and lines of information

developing people to meet known future requirements

taking full responsibility for staffing his department, even when he uses assistance from the personnel department

making it clear that promotion is based solely on merit

making sure his subordinates have adequate training

making sure he coaches subordinates himself

not keeping subordinates whose ability is questionable

hiring people who are adequately skilled (in other words, not hiring dull people against whom he will shine by comparison)

appraising his subordinates regularly against appropriate goals

recommending people for promotion on the basis of accurate judgement of their potential

taking such steps as he can to make sure his subordinates are well motivated

guiding his subordinates to get their acceptance of company goals and policies

using effective and efficient communication downwards

engaging in appropriate amounts of face to face contact

creating an environment where people are encouraged to suggest innovations

being receptive to innovative ideas, no matter where they originate

expecting and welcoming suggestions and objections to policies his subordinates regard as wrong

being readily available to his subordinates for discussions

helping his subordinates understand company policies and objectives

balancing correctly the demands for participative leadership on the one hand and authoritative direction on the other

being effective as a leader

tailoring his control techniques to his plans

using control techniques to spot deviations from plan well in advance

developing reliable and effective information systems

developing controls that point out exceptions and critical points

developing control techniques that are understood by the people who must take action

taking prompt action when deviations occur

helping subordinates to take action when deviations from their plans occur

operating effectively to budget

44

using devices of control other than budgetary devices

understanding the need for network analysis of his control systems

utilizing newer techniques of planning and control

helping his subordinates use effective control techniques and develop new ones where appropriate

keeping his superiors informed of significant problems and errors in his operation, together with reporting his actions to correct them.

This is a long checklist. Any attempt to move from woolly ill-defined phrases to more precise, objective, behavioural language will involve rather a lot of detail. We do not see this as an objection to Koontz's checklist; a car wiring diagram, for instance, is much more complicated. Not all of Koontz's managerial virtues pass the tautology test but in fairness we must add that in his checklist, which takes up a fair amount of his book, he does elaborate on what he means by 'effective' or 'appropriate' so as to reduce the degree of uncertainty. Koontz's list, however, does fall victim to the objection that as it is a general list, meant for managers everywhere, there will be areas where it does not fit a particular firm; this misfit could be quite important. For example, Koontz's manager is supposed to take full responsibility for staffing his department, whether or not he has help from the personnel department. There is one large British firm, commonly held to public view as a paragon of efficient and humane management, where the manager has very little control over the appointment of subordinates and must usually accept whomsoever the personnel department recommends. There are some areas of managerial responsibility which Koontz does not mention: the figurehead role suggested by Mintzberg, for example, is not addressed, and Koontz's manager is strangely free of customers and suppliers. In addition, he does not offer any way of putting these criteria into priority order. Many other management counsellors do not attempt this either, but we cannot refrain from mentioning that the diagnostic method which we recommend later in this book will provide the reader with criteria of effective management in his own firm in detail and objectivity similar to that suggested by Koontz and with priority order attached.

Let us not criticize Koontz too harshly. His detailed thinking is an object lesson to managers who refuse to believe that qualities of 'leadership' or 'delegation' can be, and should be, analysed in detail before they can be used in the assessment and development of managerial ability.

P J Sadler, in Dennis Pym's *Industrial Society* (1968) quotes a questionnaire administered by the Research Department of Ashridge Management College, reported in 1966: 1,500 employees in two companies were questioned to determine what type of leader they thought they would most enjoy working under. Though these labels were not used in the questionnaire, the four styles were *autocratic, persuasive, consultative* and *democratic*. The preferences they showed were as follows:

Table 8
Leadership styles: stated preferences of different groups of employees

	Auto-cratic	Persua-sive	Consult-ative	Demo-cratic	No reply
Managers (n = 126)	8	16	71	2	2
Professional and technical (n = 660)	7	23	67	2	1
Salesmen (n = 196)	7	30	61	—	2
Supervisors (n = 61)	18	31	46	2	3
Clerical and secretarial (n = 354)	14	25	39	16	6
Blue-collar (n = 113)	15	19	47	17	2

Note: the figures in the cells of the table represent the percentage of each group of employees.
Source: Sadler (1968) by permission

showing a clear preference for the consultative style, though more higher grades of employee prefer it to lower grades. The participants were also asked to indicate the styles they thought their own managers actually employed, with the result shown in table 9 on page 47.

In this table it is obvious that many people who say they would prefer the consultative style of leadership do not come under the influence of this style from their own managers. Of course, there could be all sorts of reasons for this preference, one of them being the 'grass is greener' syndrome and another the popular wisdom of the time, which esteemed consultative management highly. However, the Ashridge workers go on to report the views of the subordinates about their managers' effectiveness along certain dimensions, ie their own job satisfaction, their own satisfaction with the company, their confidence in their managers and their rating of their immediate managers' efficiency. The results may be seen in table 10 opposite.

This in summary indicates that it is better to have a distinctive leadership style, whatever it is, than to have an indeterminate style.

Sadler's report is interesting because it looks at a neglected area in the study of

Table 9
Leadership styles attributed to the managers of the employees quoted in Table 8

	Auto-cratic	Persua-sive	Consult-ative	Demo-cratic	None of these	No reply
Managers (n=126)	15	30	36	6	12	2
Professional and technical (n=660)	15	25	25	5	28	3
Salesmen (n=196)	22	23	27	1	21	4
Supervisors (n=61)	34	20	15	8	20	3
Clerical and sec-retarial (n=354)	26	19	18	6	20	10
Blue-collar (n=113)	23	16	16	5	36	4

Note: the figures in the cells of the table represent the percentage of each group of employees.

Source: Sadler (1968) by permission

Table 10
Relationship between leadership styles and subordinates' attitudes

	Auto-cratic (n=320)	Persua-sive (n=352)	Consult-ative (n=367)	Demo-cratic (n=379)	None of these (n=381)
High job satisfaction	72	81	84	81	66
High satisfaction with organization	86	90	93	87	82
High confidence in management	76	87	89	70	50
High rating of manager's efficiency	38	30	35	27	12

Note: the figures in the cells of the table represent the percentage of employees claiming particular styles for their managers who reported satisfaction with the different aspects of their jobs.

Source: Sadler (1968) by permission

managerial effectiveness, namely, what the subordinates think of their manager. We suspect that there are, in fact, many studies of subordinates' perceptions of their managers locked away in the files of personnel departments and research departments, but there is little incentive for them to be published and quite a sizeable argument against publication. And there is no visible market for books on how to appraise your manager but a large one on how to appraise your subordinates. Perhaps we might make a plea for more publication?

One common prescription for managerial effectiveness is to be found in the managerial grid, as discussed by Blake and Mouton (1969). The grid philosophy is tied firmly to a commercially available training programme; we have been unable to find validation data for a grid exercise that is not open to serious questioning on a number of grounds, chiefly the lack of control groups and the absence of precautions against Hawthorne effect from going on a training course and cognitive dissonance reduction on returning from a stressful training course. Blake and Mouton take the view that managerial attitudes can be classified on two simple dimensions: *concern for people* and *concern for production*. The ideal manager exhibits maximum concern for people and for production, which on a nine point scale describes him as a 9.9 manager. Less effective managers show favouritism to one or other of these dimensions, so that it is possible to be a 9.1 man resolving all conflicts in favour of getting the production targets met; a 1.9 man sacrificing the production targets in favour of keeping people happy; and of course all kinds of combinations of scales are possible.

It seems that there are a number of objections to Blake and Mouton's characterization of managerial effectiveness along these two dimensions. One objection is that *concern* expressed in a questionnaire or a group discussion is quite different from actual *action*, and it is the manager's actions which influence the work. (As an example, Neil Rackham told us of a training course he once ran in which participative management was offered as a subject for group discussion. One manager was enthused by the notion and discoursed at great length on what a splendid idea participation was. During this discussion she was observed to interrupt, talk over or otherwise shut out other people's contributions no less than 81 times, while she invited comment from other group members, surely the sign of a really participative manager, just once.)

Another objection is that there are other things in management besides concern for production and concern for people. There is the ability to plan to the appropriate timescale; the ability to manage oneself; and the ability to negotiate internally and externally, to name but three factors which our diagnoses have found to be important but which do not appear in the people-production grid. There are also many managers who do not have much control over production: the payroll manager, for example, or the manager of the legal department, whose notional 'production' should be a nil return if he is doing his

48

job! (Most service departments have the problem that if they are doing well, nobody notices they are there.)

More psychologists and management theorists have looked at the notion of *leadership* than at managerial ability. We shall conclude this section reviewing the work on managerial effectiveness by turning to three classic papers on the personal qualities of leaders, but we must caution the reader to beware: 'leadership' is not the same as 'management' in our view. The manager has to lead, but he has to do many other things well which are not commonly identified with the functions of leaders. And *leadership* is often written about as if the only places it manifested itself were in armies in wartime, ignoring the fact that most of our young workforce has had no military experience and would not recognize army style leadership, even if the situation demanded it. (Imagine, if you will, Field-Marshal Montgomery in charge of the keypunch operators or Nelson as marketing director). With these warnings, let us examine first Stogdill's (1948) review of the personal factors associated with leadership. He surveyed well over 100 studies of leadership in all sorts of situations and we have condensed his already tightly condensed review into table 11 below.

Though now somewhat elderly, Stogdill's study is valuable for drawing to our attention some of the obvious facts about leadership which people have traditionally preferred to ignore; facts such as the leader's physical characteristics and even physical attractiveness, his socio-economic status and his social skills. There is a feeling in some quarters that the current trend towards egalitarianism, eschewing any form of élitism, should make us unwilling to recognize that factors over which a person has no control can nonetheless play a part in his achievements. This feeling would make it unfashionable, or even illegal, to mention that a person's colour, sex, physical attractiveness or height could have a bearing on his likely effectiveness as a leader. As scientists we take the view that to ignore the effect of, say, sex on perceived promotability is as shortsighted as to ignore the effect on promotability with International Business Machines (IBM) of having the surname Watson.

Table 11
Stogdill's survey of personal factors associated with leadership

1 *Chronological age:* most studies found leaders older but some found them younger
2 *Height:* most studies found leaders taller
3 *Weight:* most studies found leaders heavier
4 *Physique, energy, health:* most studies found leaders had greater physical prowess and athletic ability, energy and health; some studies found these unimportant
5 *Appearance:* nearly all studies found leaders presented a better appearance

49

Table 11 continued

6 *Fluency of speech:* leaders almost always more fluent and confident

7 *Intelligence:* most studies found leaders brighter; some studies found that great differences between leaders and followers militated against leadership

8 *Scholarship:* almost all studies show leaders' scholastic records superior

9 *Knowledge:* specialized knowledge *and* ability to apply it both important

10 *Judgement and decision:* leaders are more likely to make sound judgements and not go back on them, and to make quick, accurate decisions

11 *Insight:* leaders show alertness, the ability to evaluate situations, social insight, self-insight, and sympathetic understanding

12 *Originality:* highly correlated with leadership

13 *Adaptability:* leaders are more likely to recognize changes and to take action in anticipation of these changes

14 *Introversion-extraversion:* some studies found leaders more extraverted, fewer studies show leaders more introverted

15 *Dominance:* most studies found leaders more dominant and ascendant; some studies showed bossy, domineering persons rejected as leaders

16 *Initiative, persistence, ambition:* leaders more likely to show initiative and willingness to assume responsibility; more likely to persist in the face of obstacles; more likely to show ambition; more likely to apply themselves

17 *Responsibility:* leaders more dependable, trustworthy and reliable

18 *Integrity and conviction:* associated with leadership sometimes to extremes, eg one study where leaders characterized by unwillingness to change their minds

19 *Self-confidence:* many studies report leaders more likely to show self-assurance and absence of modesty

20 *Mood control, mood optimism:* some studies report leaders more controlled in mood, many studies report leaders as more cheerful and optimistic

21 *Emotional control:* most studies found leaders more stable and emotionally controlled; some studies showed leaders less well controlled

22 *Social and economic status:* most studies show leaders coming from higher socio-economic background, a few studies show it makes no difference

23 *Bio-social activity:* leaders usually judged as lively, active, restless, daring and adventurous

24 *Social activity and mobility:* leaders participate in more group activities and show a higher range of social mobility

25 *Social skills:* leaders are more likely to be sociable and to show tact and diplomacy

26 *Popularity and prestige:* leaders are more popular and more admired

27 *Co-operation:* leaders are more likely to be co-operative themselves, to be able to enlist other people's co-operation and to work for the group.

In addition Stogdill reports the large numbers of studies in which leadership traits differ markedly with the situation.

NB In producing the table, we have omitted the phrase 'than their followers' in all comparative statements: thus 'most studies found leaders older than their followers' and so on.

In a later review of the literature, R D Mann studied the personality variables which had been shown to relate to leadership and to popularity (1959). He reports that most studies find a high degree of correlation between intelligence, adjustment and extraversion on the one hand and leadership on the other. Leadership was less strongly, though still significantly, related to dominance, masculinity and interpersonal sensitivity. Authoritarianism (the necessity to see things in black and white, to have rules, to punish offenders etc) was negatively related to leadership.

Popularity with one's followers, however, was correlated with fewer of these personality variables; extraversion, intelligence, adjustment, and conservatism were all found to be positively related to popularity, but Mann could find no convincing evidence relating the factors of dominance, masculinity and interpersonal sensitivity to popularity.

The third of our classic papers on leadership was written by Bowers and Seashore (1966). They begin by providing a review of many American studies of leadership, based on factor-analytic methods. The factors of leadership according to Hemphill and Coons, for example, are:

> maintenance of membership character
> behaviour likely to lead to attaining the objective
> behaviour likely to facilitate group interaction.

According to Halpin and Winer (1957), the factors of leadership are:

> consideration, friendship, trust, warmth
> initiating structure, organizing roles, patterns, systems
> production emphasis, getting the job done
> sensitivity, social awareness.

A study by Katz and Kahn (1951) presented four dimensions of leadership:

> differentiation of supervisory role
> closeness of supervision
> employee orientation
> group relationships.

Kahn (1958) presents four supervisory functions:

> providing direct need satisfaction
> structuring the path to group attainment
> enabling goal achievement
> modifying employee goal.

Bowers and Seashore go on to present the work of Cartwright and Zander (which shows leadership in terms of two functions, group maintenance and goal achievement); Mann's differentiation of skills into human relations skill, technical skill and administrative skill; Likert's prescription that effective supervisory behaviour depends upon supportive relations, group methods of supervision, high performance goals, strong technical knowledge and the ability to coordinate, schedule and plan.

Bowers and Seashore then describe their own work, in which they issued questionnaires to employees in a life insurance firm in order to discover what leadership traits influenced effectiveness as indicated by the many measures of effectiveness which the firm was able to supply. The firm's own measures of effectiveness could be classified into seven types, thus:

(a) high staff and clientele maturity
(b) business growth
(c) business costs
(d) advanced underwriting
(e) business volume
(f) manpower turnover
(g) regional manager's personal performance.

These were then correlated with various leadership measures, ascertained from questionnaires given to the managers' fellow managers and superiors. The correlations they found are simplified in table 12 on page 53 in which asterisks indicate the variables which were significantly inter-correlated.

Bowers and Seashore go on to discuss the implications of these findings for the firm, making clear incidentally that 'leadership' alone is not sufficient to predict effectiveness as a manager. We quote Bowers and Seashore because theirs is one of the most accessible summaries we know of previous American work on leadership; partly because it is instructive to see the detail they go into, making clear that managerial effectiveness is not a simply described matter; and thirdly because it illustrates a point which we have tried to bring out during this discussion, namely that managerial effectiveness varies enormously from industry to industry. Though theirs is not a comparative study, it does go into one industry in such detail as to convince the reader that some of the measures of effectiveness will be largely determined by the nature of the work.

The reader who has borne with us through this review of other people's work on managerial effectiveness will probably be feeling a little overwhelmed by all this information, some of it contradictory and some of it perhaps unclear. Let us spare the reader any additional worries he may have about theories of effectiveness; we promise that we are not going to advocate any theories of our own. Instead we shall advance some propositions to be borne in mind by anyone seeking to investigate managerial effectiveness, thus:

behaviour which is effective in one country cannot be assumed to be effective
in another, even in the same firm

the requirements for effective management may differ greatly between
different levels of management, even in the same firm

the requirements for effective management in one firm may be vastly different
from the requirements for effective management in another firm. Some of
this difference may be due to differences in product or service; some may be
due to size; some to geographical dispersion; and some to the history and
internal politics of the firm

what people *say* constitutes effective management may be different from their
behaviour when actually judging and promoting people, and what people
say about their own management style may be different from the way they
behave

empirical studies of what, at present, is regarded as effective managerial
behaviour may yield information which is surprising or unwelcome. This
information is ignored at one's peril.

Table 12
Relationship between leadership traits and job effectiveness

Leadership measure	Performance factor						
	(a)	(b)	(c)	(d)	(e)	(f)	(g)
Peer:							
support	—	—	—	—	—	—	—
goal emphasis	*	—	*	—	—	—	—
work facilitation	*	—	*	*	—	—	—
interaction facilitation	*	—	*	—	—	—	—
Manager:							
support	—	—	—	—	—	—	—
goal emphasis	*	—	—	—	*	—	—
work facilitation	*	—	*	*	—	—	—
interaction facilitation	*	—	—	—	—	—	—

Source: Bowers and Seashore, 1966, by permission

We believe that general prescriptions of effectiveness are most unlikely to be a
perfect, or even a good fit, for the manager who wonders how over the next
two years he is going to fill the expected six new vacancies for junior managers;
nor will it be much help to the retiring managing director who wants to have his

succession planned to take care of the two rapid shuffles he predicts will occur within six months of his retirement. We believe it is much more important to be able to diagnose what the characteristics are of effective management in a given firm at a given level and the evidence we have suggests that we are right. The time for presenting the reader with general theories is not yet ripe: not until we can help the harassed line manager to go from the general to the particular without losing his grip.

A second consequence of our propositions, especially the proposition advocating the difference between managerial requirements in different levels of job, is that there will be many cases where the employee's track record will not help much in predicting his performance in a higher job. This was particularly the case in a grocery wholesale organization with whom we worked. People were recruited to work on the floor of the depot and supervisors and depot sales managers were drawn largely from this initial intake. When it came to appointing people to the next level up, Regional Sales Manager, the requirements were so different that it was nearly impossible to grow top management from within, given the initial recruitment strategy. It could be said that the Regional Sales Manager position was, in fact, the first true management position. Track record was of little value. It was perfectly possible to be an excellent Depot Sales Manager and yet to be clearly and quickly a disaster as a Regional Sales Manager.

Blind adherence to the track record is, of course, one of the organizational predispositions for becoming victim to the Peter Principle, where every employee is promoted to his level of incompetence. The difficulty in relying on track record for prediction becomes particularly acute at two stages in the typical organization; first, at the transition from non managerial job to managerial job and secondly at the transfer from divisional responsibilities to general responsibilities. There may be other equally important schisms in particular firms, but no firm we have encountered has been free from these two. This belief that track record may not give all the information necessary underlies our concentration on the assessment programme as a way of assessing managerial potential. We do not advocate assessment programmes exclusively; judgements of certain levels of potential can be more economically arrived at by other methods. The decision depends upon the diagnosis of effective performance which we describe in chapter 4. We conclude this chapter, therefore, with a brief discussion of some of the methods other than assessment centres which have been used to predict managerial potential; although the most common method is some variant on the performance appraisal procedure, there are other methods which we shall look at first.

First then, we should admit that one way of assessing potential is to assume tranquilly that the good men will rise to the top of their own accord, like the skin on boiling milk. There are not many books and manuals written on this method. When we were researching for this chapter we found a number of books on general management and personnel management whose sections on promotion or succession planning gave the reader no hints on how to decide whom to promote, confining their advice to the need to keep neat records. In the extreme case, the system of record keeping will be confused with the system of potential spotting, so that the intrepid personnel manager can confront discontented employees from the strength of his box of records. Not many firms admit to having this system but it is quite common.

Secondly, methods of self-assessment are sometimes marketed, with varying degrees of plausibility and scientific reliability. One of the more interesting of such contributions is a book by Gunter Klinke, *Test: Have You Got What it Takes to Reach the Top?* (1972). The book looks workmanlike, covering everything from an analysis of newspaper advertisements to many self-administered tests of managerial requirements. Unfortunately, the author does not see fit to present us with evidence on whether the tests actually separate effective from ineffective managers in real life, and one has some doubts about its effectiveness when one comes across items such as:

Are you regarded as a man of vision?
Do you get genuine respect from your colleagues?
Do you notice when some object has been moved from its usual place?
Can you digest adverse criticism from your boss?

and so on.

Some of these questions are logically impossible to answer from some points of view; if you don't notice when an object is out of place, you don't have the information on which to answer no. And some of the other questions make impossible demands upon the average reader's honesty and are likely to give a perfect example of what people say being different from what they do.

We cite this example because it encapsulates some of the difficulties involved in self-rating. W H Whyte's *Organization Man* (1956) contains enlightening advice on how to fiddle a test or interview to present a desirable picture. All of which should by no means rule out self-ratings as a means of assessing potential; one merely has to exercise great care to make the ratings sensible, intelligent and unsusceptible to conscious or unconscious manipulation. From time to time we have experimented with personality tests on assessment programmes, though our conclusions are based on too small a sample for us to state them with any certainty. Many people have used vocational guidance forms as part of their career counselling procedure, or attitude tests such as the Edwards Personal Preference Inventory, or the Allport-Vernon-Lindzey Study of Values Test.

And many firms provide a Preparation For Counselling form for their employees to fill in as part of the performance appraisal and career counselling procedure. The consensus here seems to be that self-ratings can be useful for helping the potential promotee to clarify his thoughts on possible careers, and therefore help the manager to make a better promotion decision; but a paper and pencil self-administered test of managerial potential is unlikely.

Thirdly, as an interesting method of assessing potential, Pamela Ramsden (1973) maintains that the observation of body movements will give strong clues to managerial ability. She claims that managerial abilities can be classified ninefold into: investigation/exploration, confrontation, determination, decision, anticipation (used not in its dictionary meaning, but connoting planning), presentation, dynamism, adaptability and identification. Each of these abilities, she maintains, can be detected by observing body movements, which are charted by trained observers on a special scale. Unfortunately she gives us no clues as to how these scales are derived and how the observed behaviour maps on to each scale; she does not tell us how the observers are trained, though she tells us they are reliable; she does not give us evidence to relate known measures of managerial abilities to the body movements she proposes, so that we have nothing but her word that certain types of gesture are related to certain types of personality. In addition, she gives no satisfactory evidence of validation (it is not enough to say that the client liked it and is still making profits) and some of her statistical manipulations are impermissible. All of which is a matter for regret, because there can be no doubt that non-verbal communication plays a large part in business activity and that some of that communication would stand up to a statistical analysis. (For example, a salesman told us that in his business if the customer took notes during the discussion the salesman could be sure he would not close the deal on the first visit.) We would very much welcome a more rigorous treatment of the theoretical basis on which Miss Ramsden's prescriptions are founded, because she is drawing attention to an important and neglected area of business performance. Lamb and Watson (1979) provide a more accessible account of the work Ramsden discusses, but there is still no demonstration of the validity of the approach.

Fourthly, the most traditional method of assessing potential and probably the most widely used: the appraisal interview with an additional part, the appraisal form with a box for the manager to record his opinion of the employee's potential. Sometimes this works well as an assessment device; at other times less well.

One key difference between appraisal practices in different firms is the number who appraise on personality traits versus the number who appraise on performance measures. Campbell *et al* report that about one-third of American companies were appraising on the basis of personality traits at the beginning of the present decade; and Hawdon Hague (1974) cites a splendid example of a bad appraisal form, an example noted for its restraint, for we have seen far worse.

By 'worse', of course, we mean appraisal forms which are difficult to administer, unreliable in use and productive of employee discontent. At least one

An Example of a 'Bad Appraisal Form'

Department ....   Name ....

Section ....   Age ....

Position ....   Length of employment ....

1 General assessment
  (Tick as appropriate, any important qualifications can be given in general remarks)
                                        Exceptional Good Adequate Moderate Poor

    accuracy
    attendance record
    energy and willingness shown
    initiative shown
    intelligence
    interest in his job
    knowledge of his job
    output
    performance in his job
    personal appearance
    punctuality
    quality as a leader
    relations with fellow employees

2 How long has he been working for you?   ....years ....months

3 Do you consider that he/she is fully and
  properly employed in the work he/she
  is doing?   ....
  If not, give reasons and state either:
  (a) whether you wish to retain him/her
      on your staff?
  OR
  (b) whether you recommend that
      he/she
      (i) be retained in the company's
      employ in another capacity   ....
      or
      (ii) should be encouraged to find a
      job elsewhere?   ....

Source: Hawdon Hague (1974) by permission of Macmillan Ltd

UK firm has been forced to change from trait appraisal to performance appraisal by the pressure of employee opinion. Both Campbell *et al* (*op cit*) and Williams (1972) make it clear that trait based appraisal forms are likely to be carelessly and unwillingly used by managers who are reluctant to state an ill opinion of anyone, especially if they are likely to have to back it up with facts; this can lead, as it did in one firm, to 98 per cent of the employees being rated above average.

Williams, in a workmanlike book, presents evidence from attitude surveys in which employees gave their opinion on their appraisal practices. Over a variety of companies he found that in general two-thirds of employees were satisfied that their superiors knew about their current performance; only 31 per cent felt that they knew how their superiors regarded their potential and future prospects. This broad finding accords well with our own research in companies, research not connected with the assessment of potential, but merely investigations into the appraisal programmes, where typically we found that employees were not satisfied with the discussion of their potential and that managers did not feel themselves equipped, either with knowledge about career paths or with counselling skills, to enter into discussions on potential.

Stewart and Stewart (1977) point out six different reasons why a conventional performance appraisal system may fall short when prediction of potential is asked of it in addition to its legitimate function. The reasons are that most of the measures used are too simple; that managers tend to lack confidence in assessments of potential made by performance appraisal; that the manager is being asked to assess potential for a position about which he may not know very much himself; that discontinuities between specialist and management functions (or between management in one area and another) are too great for track record to be a reliable guide; that the reason for poor performance may be that the man is in the wrong job and not that he has little potential; that the appraisee is given no opportunity to discover for himself anything about the post for which he is being considered.

In our experience, firms who use the performance appraisal system for the assessment of potential, and who achieve some success in doing so, follow most or all of these guidelines:

they appraise on performance, not on personality (except insofar as that affects performance, eg appearance or social skills)

the performance traits they appraise on have been empirically related to success in the job(s) for which potential is being assessed, and are clearly and operationally defined for the appraising manager

the appraising managers are effectively trained in interviewing and counselling, and have good back-up information on career paths, succession plans etc the appraising managers never, never use the appraisal interview to promise the man a job

the employee has, by means of a Preparation for Counselling form or similar device, plenty of opportunity to structure his own thoughts before the interview, and has a clear idea of what is involved in the possible jobs to which he may be promoted

there is cross checking of potential ratings, by a committee or by the appraising manager's manager or by the personnel department

the firm employs 'generalists' rather than specialists, so that transfer of training between one job and the next is increased

the firm is in a 'buyer's market' for senior staff, which is possible whether the firm is expanding or contracting

the firm has a good reputation, amongst its own staff, for fair assessment of employees' potential.

If it is possible to follow these guidelines, then in some circumstances it is possible adequately to assess managerial potential by means of the appraisal interview, though we are basically sceptical that this system will suffice to overcome the two great divides we mentioned earlier. However, the diagnostic methods we give in chapter 4 should enable the reader to discover what the criteria of effective management are in his firm; if it transpires that these criteria can be efficiently sought by means of the appraisal interview, perhaps with some restructuring of this interview, then this is a satisfactory solution. We continue to think it likely that other methods of assessing potential would prove more valid and fruitful in the long run, and it is with this method in mind that we devote our next chapter to a review of the uses of the assessment centre or management assessment programme.

Chapter 3

The assessment programme: a brief history and general description

From the previous chapter it will be apparent that serious objections can be levelled at a number of traditional ways of assessing managerial potential, based on the well-founded hypothesis that a man's track record may not tell you how he will perform when translated to a different, more demanding job. A good pragmatic solution to this difficulty would be to put the man into a simulated version of the new job and watch how he performs, judging him according to the criteria of effectiveness which are thought to be appropriate to that job. There have been many attempts to conduct this planned simulation of the new job and, contrary to popular belief that everything innovative comes from the USA, in both the UK and Germany during the Hitler war work was done on the assessment of officer potential which antedated the American work in the field.

We are pleased to report, for the sake of historical accuracy, that the British were first on the scene some centuries before. Samuel Pepys (quoted in Ollard, 1974), when Secretary to the Navy, proposed many times that more systematic assessment of abilities be undertaken by the board. He leaves us full notes on the way he proposed to assess the candidates for the chaplaincy at Bridewell, having the applicants preaching sample sermons while he assessed them under the following headings:

Prayer (set or extempore)
Text
Appositeness
Action, voice, tone and style: 'Presbyterian,' 'ordinary,' 'stiff and schoolboylike'
Age

60

Countenance: 'Tolerable,' 'Grave,' 'Very Good'
Length: 'Convenient,' 'Five Quarters,' 'An Hour'
Within-book (ie well read)
Learning: 'Little,' 'Much Latin,' 'None'
Orthodoxness.

We wonder whether the criteria of episcopal potential would differ greatly today. Pepys also encourages us by recording that it took two years of lobbying and committee mongering before he obtained agreement on his proposals for more accurate assessment of Naval officers; a time-span not much different from that required to move many of today's bureaucracies.

As with so many innovations, this one lay fallow for many years. Then during the second world war, the major combatants were faced with the need to select (from a wide variety of sources) soldiers with potential to become officers. In the UK this led to the development of the War Office Selection Boards (WOSBs) devised by psychologists, psychiatrists (and existing officers). In the WOSBs, participants were given a variety of tasks in which they had to get things done, usually in a group, by exerting officer potential to overcome great odds – material difficulties, shortages, lack of information, unco-operative personnel and so on. The participants were watched by trained observers (with a strong emphasis on the presence of psychiatrists) and their potential assessed. Whether or not the ultimate validation consists in having won the war, there is other work, published by Reeve (1971) on the validity of WOSBs as a selection device for officer potential.

In the UK, emphasis shifted after the war from WOSBs to CSSBs, as the Civil Service Selection Boards were rapidly christened. The CSSB is the main instrument for selection of civil servants who are likely to rise to higher posts in the Civil Service; typically, the undergraduate or graduate who enters the Civil Service as Assistant Principal and will rise within 15 to 20 years to the level of Assistant Secretary or Head of Division. Anstey (1971a), who has been closely concerned with the CSSBs since their inception, describes the typical content of a CSSB thus:

a leaderless group task, in which a group of candidates with no appointed leader is given a discussion topic by the three assessors, who observe during the discussion each participant's participation and helpfulness, dominance, acceptability and the content of his contributions

committee meetings, in which each candidate in turn takes the chair for a group discussion. This discussion is based on some individual work the candidates have completed the day previously, in which they have had to study the dossier on a problem and reach some conclusions. During the committee meetings, each candidate's ability as chairman is assessed according to his grasp of the relevant points for discussion, his control of the group, the success with which he keeps order and the degree of integration he achieves between different points of view

extended interview boards, in which candidates in groups of five to seven are seen by a group of three interviewers for a series of tests and exercises which can include: scrutiny of application forms; written examination; cognitive tests (intelligence, general information and statistical inference); other psychological tests; written tests (especially those designed to assess the ability to write tactfully and diplomatically); personal interviews; and ranking by candidates of other candidates.

Candidates are not given feedback on their performance in the tests; either they get an offer of a job or they do not. The psychologists and others in charge of the CSSB are aware of the need to keep their assessments as consistent and reliable as possible and research is continually being undertaken to ensure that standards are maintained and improved. In the chapter on validation we discuss some of the findings of CSSB validity which have been published.

The reader will see that the tasks set at the CSSB (particularly the group tasks) mimic the civil servant's job and allow for the assessment of characteristics that could not be reliably sought for in interviews or paper and pencil tests.

The War Office and the Civil Service have their own unique requirements: what steps have been taken to discover the managerial requirements of industry?

In the USA, many organizations saw the advantages of the military procedure and adapted it for themselves. Byham (1971) cites the following organizations in which this method is used: The Huyck Corporation; American Telephone and Telegraph; General Electric; J C Penney; The Ford Motor Company; Cummins Engine; Sears Roebuck; Shell Oil (USA); International Business Machines; Standard Oil (Ohio); Owens-Illinois Corporation; Steinbergs Ltd; Merrill Lynch; Pierce, Fenner and Smith; and in addition Edgar's Ltd in South Africa; Northern Electric Co in Canada and Caterpillar Tractor. Some of these firms, notably AT and T, Standard Oil (Ohio) and IBM, have published research data on the programmes they employ. Others refuse to let outsiders have the slightest inkling of the procedures they use. In addition, some consultants and similar organizations, for example, the American Management Association, have produced assessment centre programmes which they make commercially available.

A semantic point is raised here. The Americans talk about assessment centres; the British talk about assessment programmes. What is the difference? Simply that in the earliest programmes in the States, the procedures happened in a separate building, which was known as the assessment centre; by a transfer of epithets, the name became attached to the actual programme of events, so that irrespective of whether it took place in a specially dedicated building the programme was known as an assessment centre. We prefer to talk of assessment programmes, first because this is likely to be more accurate even for a one day programme and secondly because an assessment programme for certain types of job could if necessary last 18 months (using planned assignments, for instance) and the phrase then becomes ridiculous.

What does a typical American programme look like? We shall describe one of the longer in-company programmes, operated by an American multi-national in the States (the programme is slightly different overseas).

A typical programme consists of two days of assessment followed by three days of developmental work based in part on the results of the first two days' assessment. There are normally 12 participants, with four observers and a programme manager who has secretarial assistance. The participants are people who have been rated by their managers as promotable within the next 18 months and they are usually not yet managers. The observers are line managers, preferably two levels senior to the participants but not in a direct reporting relationship to them. Line managers are used because it would probably be politically unacceptable and bad management practice to have a staff of professional assessors from the personnel department as observers; the reason they are not in direct line of reporting with the participants is to minimize the influence of their previous knowledge of the participants and to ensure that they concentrate on their observations made during the programme.

The programme manager is a capable administrator who is thoroughly trained and familiar with the method. He may well be a professional psychologist, but if he is not and psychological tests are to be used on the programme, a psychologist will be on hand.

Before the programme has begun, the observers will have been given a two day course on the elements of observation. During this course they will have been lectured on common faults made during observing; they will have had much practice in observing live group discussions and video-tapes of previous assessment programmes; each observer's recordings will be checked against everyone else's and any deviations or problems will be examined and rectified. Nobody is allowed to be an observer until he has had this training and shown himself a reliable and consistent observer. Also, during their training programme, observers thoroughly discuss with each other and with the trainer the criteria against which the participants are to be assessed, thus evolving a common standard and a common understanding.

The assessment part of the programme begins on the Sunday evening as participants and observers assemble for an informal get together over dinner, followed by a meeting in which the programme manager or other senior person welcomes them to the programme and attempts to set at rest some of the fears and concerns which people will naturally bring to a programme which they know will have some bearing on their future. Besides administrative matters, the programme manager will probably have to answer questions on whether or not there are hidden microphones, whether they will have to stay up until four o'clock every morning and whether the participants are competing against each other. It should go without saying that every attempt is made to reduce artificial stress and uncertainty – there is no secret microphone or camera!

Beginning the next day participants take part in three group tasks and three individual tasks:

Group exercise – leaderless in which each participant has a brief on a promotion; he has to absorb the information on his candidate and then with the others, discuss the candidates until they are agreed on one candidate for promotion and the rest are put in rank order. No leader is appointed for the group. They have a time limit (it is, in fact, quite rare for the group to finish on time) and they are told that each participant has an aim to get his own man promoted but that the group as a whole will have failed if no one is promoted.

Group exercise – task force in which a particular business situation (usually the sudden news that an account has been lost) is outlined and the task of the group is to arrive at agreement about which of three courses of action is to be taken. Each man is given a brief containing his position briefing and his proposed solution. There is an opportunity to form alliances and pressure groups (among six participants with only three courses of action such alliances are inevitable) but it is up to the group members to make them and take advantage of them. As before, each man is concerned to have his alternative adopted but the group as a whole will be held to have failed if no solution is forthcoming.

Group exercise – manufacturing game in which groups of six participants have to manufacture products, buying their raw materials and selling the finished objects, their aim being to make a profit. Various complicating factors are introduced to create additional pressure, and the purpose is to observe how well individuals combine the need to get things done quickly with the need to obtain co-operation from a group.

Individual exercise – writing sample in which the participant writes about his present job, an unstructured task giving data from which the observers will make inferences about his self-insight, breadth of understanding etc.

Individual exercise – in-basket in which the participant is given one and a half hours to go through the in-tray associated with the new job into which he has

64

supposedly been promoted, with no opportunity to ask for help or get further information. Here a number of characteristics are being examined: his ability to work under pressure, to delegate effectively, to use all the information he has, to adhere to common sense and to company policies and procedures. Later on in the programme there will be an interview with the observer responsible for marking the in-basket exercise, concentrating solely on his performance in this task.

Individual exercise – presentation in which the participant has to put together a presentation on the basis of an ill-assorted collection of information about the management development needs of a mythical organization.

In addition, some programmes have included psychological tests of both personality and ability.

For all the activities, both group and individual, the task of the observer is made as easy as possible by the provision of prepared record forms and guidance specific to each exercise: guidance covering what to look for, clues on how to recognize it (which clues reinforce the learning that took place during the observer training) and guidance on how to present one's report of the exercise. In this way, as far as possible, the observers are watching the same behaviours in the same way at the same time and are thereby producing more comparable results. During the third day of the programme, the observers and the programme manager come together and agree a summary statement about each participant, which will form the basis of the feedback interviews which are considered to be an essential part of the programme.

In the second part of the programme the emphasis shifts from assessment of the participants to development of their skills and knowledge in areas where they appear weak. It is difficult to generalize about what the last half of the programme includes, as it varies with the needs of individual participants and with the resources that the training department can lay on at short notice. However, most participants at the level where the programme usually operates require training in communications skills, effective group behaviour, self-development planning and work organization. To assist in this training there may be videotape playback of the assessment exercises, personal interviews, films, seminars and visiting speakers; the training department has to stand by alertly whenever an assessment programme is running.

On the programme which we are describing here, two sorts of feedback to the participants are used. *Developmental* feedback is given directly to the participants in two phases: the interview based on the in-basket exercise, which concentrates on work organization and the relative weights given to task problems and people problems under the wide range of circumstances portrayed. The second developmental interview usually takes place at the end of two days' assessment, before moving on to the development phase. Normally this interview takes place between the participant and one observer, though other observers may be asked to contribute. Here the participant's strengths are listed and up to three areas of improvement are identified, together with some suggestions about what the participant can do about these areas. At the end of a successful interview the participant will have a general idea of how well he performed in comparison with the rest of his group, and will have the beginnings of a personal development plan. He is not told his precise ratings and rankings, nor is he given the results of his psychological tests except in the most general terms. In any case, these tests serve only as back-up information and do not carry the weight of the other parts of the assessment programme until and unless they are shown to make a unique, reliable and valid contribution to the overall programme.

Development feedback will only reach the participant's manager through the participant himself. The immediate manager receives no feedback directly from the programme at all. However participants are strongly recommended to involve their immediate manager in drawing up and implementing specific development plans.

Assessive feedback, combined with the developmental feedback outlined above, is stored by the programme manager or by some other individual whose job it is to keep this information under conditions of strict security. The assessive feedback is released to higher management as and when a particular participant is being considered for a specific promotion. The data are not released except to the manager or managers who are to make the final decision, and it is preferable that the data are only released when one of the promoting managers has himself been an observer on an assessment programme (not necessarily the one on which the participant was assessed) so that he knows what sort of information the assessment data are founded on.

A comparison of this brief description of an American programme with the CSSB approach shows some interesting differences, not so much in the content of the exercises as in the use which is made of them.

For instance, the American programme uses line managers who are taken from their jobs for a two days' training programme and three days' work on the assessment programme, while the CSSB uses a permanent staff of observers. Secondly, the American programme places great weight on giving feedback to the participant, whereas the CSSB gives no feedback at all; thirdly, the American programme contains at least as much emphasis on development as it does on assessment. Fourthly, though the CSSB and the American company both use a leaderless group discussion exercise (in fact, most assessment programmes do; it is nearly always a useful device) the purposes for which they use it are quite different as a reading of the group discussion contained in Anstey *et al* *(op cit)* will show. In the CSSB the observers are looking mostly at personal relationships and social skills, whereas in the American example the observers are looking for specifically task-related skills as well, for example, memory for detail.

The reasons for and the consequences of these differences are interesting. Having line managers as observers removes the objection, often heard otherwise, that 'no outsider and nobody from the personnel department is going to tell me who I can and cannot promote'. Giving feedback to participants is considered wise because it provides a great learning opportunity for the participants and it seems wasteful not to give them the chance to take it; also, most American participants would ask for it vociferously and spread unpleasant rumours about the assessment programme were it to be withheld. The emphasis on developmental activities as part of the programme is unusual. Most firms we know of give some developmental counselling but do not go as far as providing developmental activities as part of the assessment programme itself. And the notion that one exercise can serve a number of assessive purposes is a notion both fruitful and dangerous, for it indicates the care which must be taken in priming the observers on what to look for.

The programme we have selected, lasting a week, is one of the longer ones. Some programmes can be as short as one day, albeit a very hard-working day, and one that leaves some tidying-up to be done at the end, with the observers needing to take extra time to complete their ratings and probably with final feedback interviews postponed until the following day or up to a fortnight later. One commercially available package covers an in-basket exercise, a presentation exercise, a leaderless group discussion, a group production task and paper and pencil tests, in one day's work. Interestingly, we saw this package demonstrated to a group of UK managers who watched a film about the procedure. The film was American, and professionally presented, with equal opportunity clearly indicated. However, the sympathy of the British audience was almost totally lost when it became apparent that the observers were still assessing the participants during the time they ate their box lunches together, each observer carefully buttonholing a participant and observing his social skills while they ate! An interesting and delicate question.

Many assessment programmes are broadly similar to the American example we gave above. Under the gaze of trained observers, participants go through a series of tasks, group-based and individual, which are intended to simulate the managerial job for which potential is being assessed; if they are not a direct simulation, then they are designed to bring out the managerial qualities in some other way. Observers record their observations according to fixed criteria for each exercise and then pool their assessments so as to arrive at assessive and

67

possibly developmental conclusions, which may or may not be fed back to the participants.

The appeal of this procedure is enormous. Bernard Ungerson (1974) lamented that the face validity of an assessment programme is frighteningly high. Having described what one programme looks like, perhaps we can persuade the reader to consider some of the factors in this programme which, from the point of view of overall effectiveness, are of crucial importance if one is to avoid a programme of high face validity which is doing the wrong job. We can identify a number of such factors crucial to the success of an assessment programme:

Attitude of participants

It is useless to try to assess participants who are rigid with fear or competitiveness, unless of course your organization runs by having its managers frightened out of their wits 24 hours a day. We once visited a firm where, at the mention of the word 'assessment', people shrank away and indicated that there were dark secrets; within a few days we were told that 18 months previously, on the declaration of a vacancy at second-line management, an untrained management development manager had gathered together 12 first-line managers on an assessment course which was highly competitive, involved deliberate overwork, gave no feedback on performance and had no clear criteria of success. It is going to be difficult for even the most scientific and rigorously designed programme to be introduced into that firm. Participants should ideally come to the programme wanting to find out more about their own capabilities and how to develop them; propaganda, rumours or actions which contradict this belief should be discouraged.

Attitudes of observers

Observers need to realize that they are there to observe to a protocol, a protocol which is standardized between observers and between programmes because of the need to have all participants 'measured' against the yardstick. There is no place on an assessment programme for the individual observer's fads, quirks and private beliefs about human behaviour, though after the observers have proved themselves able to work to a protocol it can be useful to allow individual skills to re-emerge. There are several good reasons for this requirement that the observers be mutually consistent. If a participant discovers that observer A is rating his contributions as (say) helpful proposals, while observer B judges the same behaviour to be distractions, he is rapidly going to lose faith in the programme and rightly. Another reason is that great emphasis is usually placed on having the observers record their observations and it is quite likely that, in a feedback interview given by one observer to one participant, that observer will be relying on his co-observers' ratings. He has to know what these ratings mean.

And since in the programme we have described, the observers are often line managers who will later on receive data from assessment programmes about people they are considering for promotion, it helps if they understand these data in the form they were recorded.

To anticipate a subject we shall treat in detail in chapter 6, it is not difficult to train observers to a high standard of reliability, given that the criterion behaviours they observe are relatively few in number and well-defined. When we undertake observer training we aim to achieve a 90 per cent standard of inter-observer consistency with nearly all observers. Oddly enough, the single class of people with whom we can guarantee difficulty in achieving this standard is the class which includes psychologists, personnel people, group trainers etc because they have their own frameworks of how people 'should' behave and in many cases find them difficult to discard.

The moulding of observers' attitudes is one of the most difficult potential problems, especially if they are line managers of some seniority. All the programme manager's tact and resources may be needed to deal with the manager who says he does not need training in observing, or whose observations differ from the rest of the observers'. Unless the observers do work in harmony, the assessment programme runs a high risk of appearing useful while in reality being riddled with failings.

Clarity of purpose

Decisions must be made, and constantly kept in mind, about the purpose of the programme. Is everyone eligible to be assessed? Or just the people already spotted as high flyers? Is the programme to be a pass/fail instrument? Are people to be encouraged to think of promotion as automatically following the programme? Are people free to nominate themselves or must they be nominated by their manager? Will there be resentment from the people not selected and how will it be dealt with? If participation is to be voluntary, what steps will be taken to find out whether people who would rather not be considered feel that they have to take part? How long will the assessment results be kept? How many steps ahead are to be considered, just one promotion or several jumps? All these questions and more need to be considered when deciding the purpose of the assessment programme and they need to be reviewed from time to time. Some ideas about the uses various organizations make of their assessment programmes are found in table 13 on page 70 from Bender's article, *What is 'typical' of assessment centres?*

It is not easy to prescribe which course of action will be right for a particular firm but we shall try to indicate some of the consequences of these various options at the appropriate points of this book.

	Yes	No	Not checked
Assessees are provided immediate feedback on their performance	21	12	1
Feedback is given orally to the assessee	33	0	1
Feedback is given in writing to the assessee	10	22	2
Feedback is given through the line organization	16	15	3
Feedback is given only by assessment centre personnel	21	12	1
Assessee's evaluation is made available to top management	24	8	2
Evaluation results are used to prepare a formal plan of development for the assessee	23	9	2
Follow up of an assessee's continued development after assessment results are reported is a routine function of the assessment centre	14	17	3

Source: adapted from Bender, 1973

Administration

A well designed assessment programme can fail for lack of smooth administration. Indeed, we give a whole chapter to the back up services needed to conduct an assessment programme, but we cannot stress too hard the need for exact time tabling, adequate equipment in the right place and the other facilities necessary for trouble free activities. The reader who is contemplating the introduction of assessment programmes must realize from the beginning that there is less 'play' in the system than there would be on, say, an ordinary training course, and that there is proportionately more house work to do and more need for continuity of administrative services etc.

Selection of criteria and design of exercises

We have left the most important of these crucial issues until last. How does one know what behaviour to look for in the participants? How does one structure the assessment programme so as to provide maximum opportunity for distinguishing people in terms of the criterion behaviours? These are complex questions, deserving large chapters (4 and 5) to themselves. We should indicate the salience of these questions here, because it was to the question of derivation of criteria that we first addressed ourselves when we were examining assessment programmes for the first time.

In chapter 2 we reviewed many theories of managerial effectiveness and lamented the lack of specificity which many of them showed. This lack of specificity becomes a handicap when one tries to design an assessment programme to bring out these nebulous characteristics and one usually finds that assessment programmes use tighter definitions of behaviour than (for example) appraisal forms. Bender's review articles lists the evaluation parameters most frequently used in the assessment parameters he surveyed, with the results shown in table 14 below.

Table 14
Evaluation parameters most frequently used in assessment centres

Parameter	Response frequency
Oral communication skills	30
Leadership	29
Organizing and planning	27
Decision making skills	25
Resistance to stress	24
Problem analysis	24
Written communication skills	23
Energy	21
Use of delegation	21
Oral presentation skills	21
Behavioural flexibility	21
Forcefulness	19
Impact	18
Creativity	17
Perception	16
Salesmanship	16
Risk taking	16
Management control	16
Independence	14
Range of interests	12
Listening skill	12
Attitude towards peers	12
Attitude towards superiors	11
Self-evaluation	11
Inner work standards	10
Attitude towards subordinates	8

Source: adapted from Bender, 1973

One needs to ask at least two questions of any set of criteria used on an assessment programme. First, are the criterion behaviours defined sufficiently rigorously: for example, is guidance provided on how to distinguish 'leadership' from bullying, or from talking a lot; and is the leadership to be participative or authoritarian, is it to be consensus-seeking and so on? Secondly, are the criteria the right criteria for that firm? A good middle manager in an oil company might be an abject failure as managing director of a woollen mill; a good line manager in ICI might not make a good staff group manager in the same company. Do the criteria chosen for assessment reflect what we all know, that individual firms are widely different from each other and that each one is in some way unique?

We have evidence that in many firms the selection of the initial criteria is not done as objectively as possible; indeed, we know of several firms where the criteria were arrived at in committee meetings with no pretence to scientific research in the field. In addition, there are studies showing that after analysis the criteria used may collapse into far fewer factors than the total number of criteria suggests. If we examine some of these studies, we shall gain insight into the differences between firms and the problems of establishing criteria; thus:

American Telephone and Telegraph use 26 rating variables, from which the following eight factors emerge after factor analysis:

1 General effectiveness
2 Administrative skills
3 Interpersonal skills
4 Control of feelings
5 Intellectual ability
6 Work oriented motivation
7 Passivity
8 Dependency.

Contrast this list with the factor analysis of the rating variables of Sohio, who use 13 rating variables which reduce to five factors:

1 Group task effectiveness
2 Need for structure
3 Interpersonal effectiveness
4 Quality of independent thinking
5 Work oriented motivation.

Sohio's effective manager is thought to possess independent thinking; would this get him very far in AT & T, where they assess on the basis of passivity and dependency? Or compare these two with the IBM assessment programme, where the 12 rating variables reduce to three factors in total:

1 Overall activity and general effectiveness
2 Administrative skills
3 Resistance to stress.

In IBM, it would appear, overall activity and general effectiveness are impossible to tell apart; though people use different words and think they are using different rating variables, the man who is active is more likely to be judged as effective irrespective of the quality of his work. Perhaps the company motto should be amended from THINK to THINK ON YOUR FEET.

The IBM factor analysis also shows that resistance to stress is a quality esteemed in their managers. Anticipating our own results, we have found in many companies where we have undertaken diagnostic exercises that the effective manager is more likely to improve his performance under short-term stress. Sometimes we worry about this, because those who improve under short-term stress are often the same people who go to pieces when they have to work with no immediate pressure on them, and senior managers in particular should be kept free of short-term pressures so as to concentrate on the long-term.

Another company for which factor analytical data are available is Sears, Roebuck, who use no less than 40 variables from which nine factors emerge:

1 Overall executive orientation
2 Independent administration and control
3 Organization and planning
4 Decisive action orientation
5 Courtesy and understanding
6 Information acquisition and transmission
7 Profit and cost orientation
8 Human relations orientation
9 Casual informality.

This list presents an interesting contrast to the first three. It is the only one that mentions finance and the only list that mentions information handling. Independence rather than dependence is the keynote and the man is expected to get on with the job.

It is easy to see that designing a programme to assess the characteristics in any one of these lists would require special tailoring of that programme. Certain exercises would be more useful than others and the same exercise would be used to bring out different behaviours in different countries. Quoting yet again from Bender's article, we can see in table 15 on page 75 the distribution of different exercises and tests across different companies and each can be used for a multitude of purposes, depending upon its content, the time pressures involved, the amount of disagreement to be resolved and so on.

The examples we have cited should have indicated to the reader that quite a lot of preliminary diagnosis is necessary before an assessment programme can be got under way. The characteristics of effective management differ from firm to firm. The degree of insight into these characteristics varies from person to person in the firm and needs checking. Exercises cannot be designed until one knows what the characteristics of effective management are in one's own firm and until one has decided whether these characteristics are to be perpetuated or in some way changed. Indeed, it may be that after one has diagnosed the characteristics of effective management it becomes obvious that there is no need for an assessment programme; this has happened to us on more than one occasion, with perfectly satisfactory results. It should follow, therefore, that to buy an assessment programme off the peg, or to accept a programme designed for a different part of your organization unquestioningly, is to run the risk of getting something that does not fit, that wastes time and opportunities and at the same time gets people highly committed to it. Much of this book is devoted to showing the reader how he can avoid these pitfalls by proper diagnosis and design.

To summarize, therefore, in these three introductory chapters we have tried to show that the assessment of managerial potential is an important area for the stability and growth of a business and that in many firms the means for accurate assessment do not exist or do not work well. We have tried to show that managerial effectiveness varies widely from firm to firm and job to job, and that it needs to be carefully and objectively defined. We reviewed some of the ways currently being used for the assessment of managerial potential, nearly all relying on a reading of the man's track record – and we indicated that there were many circumstances where the track record would not make a good predictor of future performance in a different job. We then moved on to the assessment programme as a way of simulating the new job under controlled circumstances, with careful ratings by trained observers who would look for the criteria of effectiveness in the participants' behaviour; this appealing and fast growing procedure has many advantages, but in its advantages lie some hidden dangers unless the criteria of effectiveness are the right ones for the unique needs of the firm and the particular managerial job in question.

The next four chapters are a distillation of our own experience in designing assessment programmes, starting with the methods by which the criteria of effectiveness can be extracted, moving on to programme design, observer training, administration and the feedback and developmental activity that follow an assessment programme. Our aim in writing these four chapters is to

Table 15
Primary evaluation devices used by companies operating assessment centres

	Yes	No	Not checked
In-tray exercise used	31	3	
Business game exercise used	30	4	
Assigned roles	19	11	4
Not assigned roles	20	12	2
Leaderless group discussion exercises used	31	0	3
Assigned roles	23	9	2
Not assigned roles	23	9	2
Films used	5	29	
Video tapes used	15	19	
Psychological tests used	20	13	1
For the most part, assessment devices are locally produced	23	10	1
For the most part, assessment devices are purchased externally	9	24	1
An in-depth background interview is given to assessees	22	12	

Source. Bender, 1973

give the reader an alternative to an off the peg solution, so that he can design and run his own assessment centre. Even if the reader does not wish to proceed all the way to assessment programmes, he may find that the methods for deriving the criteria of effectiveness are useful should he wish to conduct a training needs analysis, or to re-examine the performance appraisal programme or to review the selection procedure. Similarly the chapter on programme design may contain exercises useful outside the context of assessment of potential.

Chapter 4

Devising the criteria of effectiveness

Some management assessment programmes sold as commerciai · available packages depend upon general prescriptions of the characteristics of effective management. We admit to a degree of scepticism about any such general prescription, partly because they are often not written in operational terms (what *is* good personality, leadership, decision-making ability? What should the man do in order to demonstrate that he has good personality?) and partly because we suspect that what is generally right for management overall is unlikely to be exactly right for a specific level of management in one particular firm. Perhaps we may relate two case studies to illustrate this point:

We were introduced to the internal assessment programme of a certain firm, were shown the glossy manuals and the careful costings, saw the videotapes of previous participants and heard the glowing accolades of the firm's managers. We asked to see the criteria on which assessments were made. There was a list of 10 factors, not very specific. We queried what some of them meant; what, for example, was *decision-making ability*? Did it mean making quick decisions or taking hard decisions or deciding not to act when it is not necessary or taking black and white decisions or taking decisions so loudly that everyone could hear? We went on with this line of questioning until it became apparent that the people running the programme had not thought out the assessment factors in depth. So we asked how they had been arrived at and were finally told that a committee had been set up to decide what the factors should be and these were the results of their deliberations! We have run into this problem on training courses (giving the group a discussion task of deciding what makes a good manager) and we have seen the way criteria are arrived at; partly by a search for the broadest sounding words, partly wishful thinking and partly because every member should contribute at least one item. The usefulness of such a list is dubious, to say the least; there should be a way of getting closer to the real culture of the firm than by appointing a committee of its own employees.

Another of our experiences concerns some work we had been doing with a firm with a strong engineering background whose middle and senior managers were nearly all ex-military men. The management fashion at the time was for participative management and a request came down to the training department that managers should be trained to improve their participativeness. The inference was that effective managers in this firm were already participative and that training should make up the deficiencies. It seemed likely to us that the real culture of this firm was strongly against participation and that training in participativeness, while perfectly possible, would be against rather than with the current practice. We therefore devised a questionnaire containing a number of opposing statements about what a manager does and asked some managers in the firm to fill it in twice, once with their most effective subordinate manager in mind and once with their least effective manager in mind – the constraint being that they should describe *real* people, 'warts and all'. Some examples of the kind of item used in this questionnaire are given below.

He asks for his people's ideas before making a decision	☐ ☑ ☐ ☐ ☐	He takes decisions without consulting his people
He asks for help when he needs it	☑ ☐ ☐ ☐ ☐	He refuses assistance
He does not let other people know what he is busy with	☐ ☐ ☐ ☑ ☐	He lets other people know what he is busy with

and so on, about 80 items in all

From the answers to this questionnaire it was possible to calculate which items significantly distinguished between managers who were perceived as effective and managers who were perceived as ineffective. It transpired that in this firm the effective manager was not at all participative as perceived by senior managers; he kept himself to himself and neither consulted his people before taking decisions nor let them in on his problems; kept other people out of his operation and did not communicate freely with his colleagues.

We were then able to make the point that training in participativeness, while perfectly possible, would have greater repercussions around the organization than had been foreseen when the original request came in. This experience convinced us that it is always worthwhile trying to determine something of the prevailing culture of a firm before buying a blanket prescription and that simple questionnaire techniques could assist in making this diagnosis.

Whenever we have worked on assessment programmes or in related areas we have begun by diagnosing what, in the present perceptions of the client organization, constitute the characteristics of the effective manager at a given level in a given type of job. Our earlier suspicions have proved well founded; while there are some factors common to effectiveness everywhere we have investigated so far, there are differences so profound between firms that it is obvious no off the shelf prescription could meet all their needs. In addition, our experience in developing diagnostic techniques has led us to the point where we are usually able to derive a list of 60 to 80 objective, observable ways in which effective managers differ from ineffective managers, which is a great advance on the list of 10 or 20 broad general characteristics which would result from a committee meeting or a perusal of many authors' advice. We would go further and claim that as far as possible the techniques we use for this diagnosis are almost free from the bias introduced by the observer, be he an internal employee or an outside consultant.

This lack of bias is inherent in the special interview procedure, where the interviewer extracts information from the interviewed without imposing any of his own preconceptions. The diagnostic procedure we use takes one of two forms, depending upon the size of the firm. Above a certain size it is possible to use techniques of statistical analysis which would be inappropriate in a small firm; in a smaller firm we would use a technique of interviewing in depth which we shall describe later. The two approaches have something in common, though, which is the basic form of the interviewing technique used.

The objectives of the diagnostic stage are:

to obtain, in objective behavioural terms, a statement of those characteristics which differentiate the manager who is perceived as effective at a given level (and perhaps in a given function) from the manager who is perceived as ineffective at the same level and function in the firm concerned

to obtain, in objective behavioural terms, a statement of those characteristics which are associated strongly with perceived effectiveness at a given level in that firm

to obtain, in objective behavioural terms, a statement of those characteristics which are associated strongly with perceived ineffectiveness in that firm at a given level.

These objectives are to be obtained with the minimum of bias from the people performing the diagnosis, using statistical techniques that are both reliable and easy to understand. Let us first look at the diagnostic procedure in a fairly large firm (the size will become apparent as we discuss the statistical requirements). It is easier to begin discussion at a point some way through the diagnostic stage and then work back to the beginning later; our instrument of diagnosis is the performance questionnaire which we described in embryonic form earlier, on page 77.

Suppose we want to discover the characteristics perceived as belonging to effective and ineffective *first line managers*: we draw up a questionnaire consisting of a series of opposing statements about the behaviour of first line managers. The constraint is that all these statements have to be about objective, observable characteristics. Thus:

He is a good leader ☐ ☐ ☐ ☐ ☐ He is a poor leader

would not be an acceptable item because it does not tell the reader what the man *does*, it merely expresses an opinion about his leadership; but

He gives his people
credit for their ☐ ☐ ☐ ☐ ☐
successes

He takes the credit
for his people's
successes

is a better item, because it deals with observable behaviour about which outsiders would find it easy to agree.

We draw up a questionnaire containing between 80 to 120 such items, trying to cover all appropriate areas. Then we issue this questionnaire to *second line managers* (managers of the position in question) and ask them to think of their most effective subordinate first line manager and to fill in the questionnaire with this manager in mind, using the five point scale to indicate degrees of strength or frequency of the behaviour. If at all possible they are to try not to use the middle box. We ask them to fill it in 'warts and all' about the manager but we do not want to know his name.

After about three weeks, when all these first questionnaires have been returned, we send out a second batch, identical with the first, except that this time we ask them to bear in mind the most ineffective first line manager subordinate they have and describe him.

At the end of this chapter the reader will find excerpts from some of the performance questionnaires we have designed, for different firms and different levels of management, and an example of the introductory instructions we use. For the statistical tests we use to be reliable, we need a minimum of 50 managers to respond to the questionnaire and it is better to have more – hence the restriction of this technique to large organizations.

We believe that the calculations should be easily understood by the layman, and easily performed by the inexperienced non-statistician. On a purely political point, these results will have to be explained and defended to a variety of managers within the firm and some of these managers may not be easy to persuade. If the persuasion has to depend upon complex statistics whose implications are not immediately obvious, then the persuasion may fail.

The statistical operations are quite simple, as will be seen from the following instructions which we quote from a typical report to a client:

Statistics performed on performance questionnaire data

As each questionnaire is received, the check marks for each item are transferred to a master questionnaire; there is one master questionnaire for the effective (A) group and one for the ineffective (B) group. When all the questionnaires have been returned, the tally marks on the master questionnaire are transformed into figures. Taking item 3, for example, the A master read:

He works best when he alone is accountable	16 / 14 / 5 / 12 / 5	He works best when the accountability is shared

and the B master read:

He works best when he alone is accountable	7 / 11 / 3 / 17 / 15	He works best when the accountability is shared

These raw scores are next given a weighting, so as to reflect the greater statistical importance of the extreme scores. So the two outside columns are multiplied by 3, the next two inside columns are multiplied by 2, and the centre column remains unchanged. Following through item 3, the weighted A score read:

He works best when he alone is accountable	48 / 28 / 5 / 24 / 15	He works best when the accountability is shared

and the weighted B scores read:

He works best when he alone is accountable	21 / 22 / 3 / 34 / 45	He works best when the accountability is shared

Note: this weighting procedure also renders unimportant the occasional items where one or two people have been unable to make up their minds or have had no experience from which to answer; though 53 people returned questionnaires, the raw A scores add up to only 52. One or two discrepancies such as this do not matter greatly, though if a large number of people found they could not answer then the item would have been dropped.

Three operations are now performed on their weighted scores. The first operation is designed to extract the items which maximally differentiate between the effective and ineffective manager, and which strongly differentiate; which differentiate adequately, and which ones do not differentiate at all. The second is designed to give a picture of the effective manager, listing those characteristics which apply to him strongly or adequately. The third operation gives a picture of the ineffective manager according to the characteristics which apply to him.

For the first operation (finding which items differentiate the effective from the ineffective manager) the weighted scores are examined to find out where the highest scores occur. In item 3, for the ineffective manager the extreme right hand column contains the highest score, 45; and the effective manager has the highest score, 48 in the extreme left hand column. We conclude therefore that there is the maximum possible separation between the two managers on this item and that it therefore differentiates maximally between the effective and the ineffective manager. All the items which differentiate maximally are listed using this procedure; then those items where the separation is one column less – these items are considered to differentiate strongly; then those where the separation is less by one column again – these items differentiate adequately. There are then left those items where the maximum scores occur in columns next to each other or in the same column. These items are considered not to differentiate at all.

The second operation (getting a picture of the effective manager) uses the weighted scores from the A questionnaires only. The purpose of this is to see how strongly the characteristics are associated with effectiveness. Taking item 3 again, the procedure is to add the extreme right hand column to the inside right hand column ($24 + 15 = 39$) and then add the extreme left hand column to the inside left hand column ($48 + 28 = 76$) and to subtract the smaller sum from the larger ($76 - 39 = 37$). This score of 37 is the *separation score* for this item. Clearly, the more unequivocally people judge the effective manager to have the characteristic referred to, the larger will be the separation score. So if this procedure is repeated for all the items, they can be ranked in their order of 'unequivocalness' so as to give a picture of the effective manager. The separation scores here range from 140 as a maximum to 0. This range is split into three parts – 0 to 47, 48 to 93, and 93 to 140 – and those items with separation scores in the highest range are considered to be strongly characteristic of the effective manager; those in the middle range to be characteristic of the effective manager, and those in the bottom third to characterize not too adequately the effective manager.

The third operation is exactly the same as the second, but this time the data are taken from the weighted B questionnaire. For item 3, the arithmetic is $(34 + 45) - (21 + 22) = 36$; the range of scores is from 1 to 117, so that the range is split 0 to 39, 40 to 78, and 79 to 117.

The three operations serve different purposes. The first provides information on which to distinguish the effective from the ineffective; the second provides information for specifying developmental objectives; and the third gives a picture of what to avoid.

Item 3 is a very good one for distinguishing between the effective and the ineffective manager, but is less useful when one tries to paint the picture of the effective manager. This apparent contradiction arises because, though the majority of the weighted scores come at the extreme ends of the scale, thus giving rise to the good distinguishing qualities of the item, there is still a wide spread of the remaining weighted scores so that the item has a relatively small separation score. For assessment and developmental purposes, then, both the list of distinguishing items and the picture of the effective manager need to be considered.

As the questionnaires are returned, they are logged in and the results from each individual questionnaire transferred to a master copy containing all the results for the effective manager or the ineffective manager, as appropriate. This is a simple clerical task and a skilled person working in undisturbed conditions can process about 100 questionnaires a day. The subsequent arithmetical operations are best performed with a pocket calculator; there is no need to use a computer. Though the tasks here could be delegated to clerical staff, we must admit to a preference for doing it ourselves. One needs to be thoroughly acquainted with the data so that later discussions can be as wide ranging as possible and this part of the research is often very exciting as the results take shape under one's eyes. Personnel departments do not often get presented with the opportunity to make new discoveries and analysing a performance questionnaire may provide a real job enrichment.

At the end of the statistical operations quoted above, the researchers will have three lists of characteristics. One list is of those items which differentiate, at different degrees of strength of differentiation, between the perceptions of the effective manager and the ineffective manager. Then there will be a list of items strongly or less strongly associated with effectiveness, and a similar list of items strongly or less strongly associated with ineffectivness.

Readers will probably be wondering about the possibility of putting the results through a cluster analysis or similar exercise, to determine which items are correlated with each other and with what strengths. The answer is that when we are working with a single firm we do not usually have the resources, or the large number of questionnaires necessary, to make full use of a cluster analysis programme. In our research, however, assembling data from many different firms, we do use cluster analysis and other higher order statistics. When working in a single firm at one managerial level, it is not usually convenient to perform a cluster analysis and we also have to recognize that such sophisticated techniques might render the results inaccessible to managers who would be able to understand a simpler presentation.

Under pressure from managers who requested a simple presentation of the performance questionnaire data we have often turned the listing of effective manager separation scores into a narrative account of the effective manager, stressing that this is a picture of the paragon, not the typical, effective performer. In producing the narrative, one has to perform a mental cluster analysis, labelling the clusters into which the data appear to fall. We give two contrasting examples of the kind of narrative we have sometimes produced below:

Summary of assessment factors in Company X

1 *Self-assessment* Accurate assessment of own performance. Not made over-confident by success; recovers quickly from failure.
2 *Coping with stress* Works best at own pace; can still work when others set the pace. Performance improves under greater-than-normal pressure. Can work when there is no pressure. Finds his way around quickly, and adapts to the unexpected. Stays calm when attacked. If one job is delayed, gets on with something else. Does not avoid doing unpleasant tasks.
3 *Concern for improvement* Is aware of his mistakes; learns from them; does not repeat them. Asks how he can improve his results; is ambitious and an optimist.
4 *Decision-making* Assigns priorities. Leaves decisions alone once made. Can distinguish what he can and cannot control; and between fact and opinion.
5 *Preference for quality* Prefers quality work to volume, though would sacrifice technical excellence to marketability. Would pay premium to ensure high quality.
6 *Scale of operations* Prefers big picture to details. Plans several steps ahead; deals with strategy not tactics. Better when planning for future than when dealing with day to day problems.

7 *Absence of self regard* Admits when he doesn't know answer. Asks for help and does not refuse assistance. Can tolerate compromise. Listens to people even when he does not like what they say.

8 *Technical competence* Good safety and security records. Understands finance easily. Assesses capital requirements accurately. Absorbs technical information rapidly and retains it well. Meets his objectives; assesses time to meet objectives correctly.

9 *Delegation and consequence* Delegates when he should, clearly. Does not assume that people know what is expected. Checks progress frequently. Makes heavy demands on people. Protects his staff in public and can work from a brief which someone else has prepared for him. Gives his people credit.

10 *Training staff* Tells them when they have made mistakes; helps them find their own way out of difficulties. Recommends them for training; brings them up to date about customers. Forms correct opinions on people's potential; their performance improves over time; one or more could step into his place.

11 *Personal relationships* Tries for co-operation, not conflict, in his team. Works best when people like him; would rather be respected than liked. Seen at all times, not just at crises; will discuss his people's personal problems.

12 *Social skill* Appears relaxed, at ease, skilled with people. Deals with people better than with paperwork or technical problems.

13 *Communications and paperwork* Communications timely, in all directions, and clear. Clear on the telephone. Documentation well organized.

14 *Working in groups* Works better in groups than alone. Invites only those who need to attend. Most effective as chairman. Does not insist on rank/seniority prevailing. States his position openly; would rather co-operate than compete.

15 *Company policy and public relations* Anxious for good public picture of the firm. Decisions in accord with company policy. Good realtions with unions. Adapted to multinational working. Up to date on current affairs.

Summary of assessment factors in Company Y

1 *Analytical ability* He analyses situations at speed, both qualitatively and quantitatively. He makes systematic analyses. He is not bothered by the lack of a formal system for doing things. He is better at the 'big picture' than the details. He is better at prevention than cure. His administration is neat and tidy.

2 *Relations with the engineers* He would rather spend time helping the engineer learn how to fix machines than fix them himself. He checks engineers' performance frequently, but not necessarily through direct accompaniment. He would rather have all his team perform to a moderate standard than to have some very good and some bad. He will not correct the engineer in front of the customer.

3 *Relations with customers* He tries to calm angry customers down before turning to the machine. He does not use technical language to the customer. When his customers have problems he tries to deal with them from the office rather than going straight out to see them.

4 *Relations with boss* He is selective in what he tells his boss and can plan his own actions without constant checking back. He keeps his boss informed of important matters but is prepared to act independently.

5 *Relations with sales force* He tries to co-operate with the sales force and keep in touch about mutual problems. He will not blame the sales force in front of the customer.

6 *Speed of action* He spots problems early and follows changes on time. He can analyse

situations quickly but he does not always respond at top speed if the situation would subside of its own accord. He would sacrifice some present gains for greater gains in the future.

7 *Handling a budget* He can read a budget statement. He uses his budget as a tool for monitoring progress. When he draws up a budget it contains realistic contingency plans.

8 *Cost effectiveness* He does not always go for the perfect solution when a cheaper or quicker one would do the job. He encourages his engineers to think likewise. He is prepared to accept that some customers and some standards of service to customers, are unprofitable.

9 *Facing up to difficulties* He gets on with unpleasant tasks. If delays and frustrations occur he can turn to something else. He admits his mistakes. He can reproduce accurately the points of view of people who disagree with him. When things are going wrong he admits it and when things are going well he wants to understand why. When his morale is low he keeps quiet about it to the engineers.

10 *Running meetings and giving presentations* He plans for meetings and presentations. He gives clear presentations whether formal or informal. He can persuade other people to change their minds.

However, we should emphasize most strongly that the actual sentences and phrases used in the narratives are taken directly from the performance questionnaire and suffer no interpretation from us. In addition, we stress that the labels placed on the factors should not be a temptation to further expansion or addition (or contraction); they are there for convenience only. We admit that we resisted the pressure to provide narrative accounts until it became obvious that if we did not do it, people might go ahead and produce their own narrative without perhaps using strict standards of objectivity. In discussions on the interpretation of the data, we try to steer the conversation away from the narrative and back towards the individual items. This is particularly important to bear in mind when designing and conducting the training of observers on assessment programmes.

Where do the questions on the performance questionnaire come from?

We have introduced the reader to the design of diagnostic procedures by starting him in the middle of the actual process. We apologize for now having to take him back to the beginning, but it is easier to understand the early stages if one has in mind the end product to which they are directed, namely (in large firms) the production of a performance questionnaire.

We are able to record in this section one of the few instances where behavioural scientists have been able to produce a 'many times over' improvement in the yield of their instruments. This improvement happened after we had been using performance questionnaires for some time. One of the authors had been involved in the production of three performance questionnaires using the now superseded method of getting together a group of people from the personnel department, outside experts, behavioural scientists, interested line

84

managers and so on, and asking them to brainstorm items for the questionnaire until exhaustion set in. The author had used a similar technique in a study he conducted within IBM; we also knew other researchers also using performance questionnaires who designed it using the same approach. In every case the results were similar, a questionnaire of about 100 items, from which between 10 to 20 items would significantly differentiate the effective from the ineffective performer.

For the first exercise in assessment of managerial potential on which the two authors collaborated, we decided to test a hunch that this yield from a performance questionnaire was not good enough. In addition, we have a continuing concern that any outside observer may prejudice the results he discovers just because of his own history, experience and point of view; we are constantly on the look out for ways of removing the observer bias from our investigations.

This led us to examine the utility of a technique which has been known to clinical psychologists for many years, ever since it was published by George Kelly (1955) and adopted with expertise and enthusiasm in the UK by Bannister and Fransella, among others (1971). Kelly had been led to the invention of the technique by a number of concerns; there was the constant concern of any clinical psychologist, that a patient visiting Freud would turn out to have Freudian problems, whereas one visiting Jung would have Jungian problems and one visiting a behaviourist would be diagnosed as having problems which a behaviourist approach would cure. In other words, he was worried that the nature of the observer biased the nature of the observations. A second concern, best understood in the context of the times, was that psychology was becoming obsessed with statistical observations of masses of people, in order that statistically reliable results be produced. Just as the behaviour of one molecule cannot be predicted, but the behaviour of an aggregation becomes subject to well established physical laws, so the psychologists of the time believed that in order to gain predictable results they had to deal with people in the mass. Kelly, as someone concerned with the individual problems of individual people, found this approach unhelpful and sought a way of describing the thought processes and attitudes of individual people with the minimum intrusion from the investigator.

His technique is known to clinical psychologists as the Repertory Grid, and when used in clinical applications it is a thorough interview or series of interviews probing deeply into the subject's thought processes. For our purposes we adopted only the very first stage of the grid interview, where the interviewer discovers the thoughts which the subject uses in construing the world as it appears to him. The simplest way to illustrate our process of interviewing is to give an example of the dialogue between interviewer and interviewee in a typical interview as we would conduct it.

First the interviewer is introduced, checks that the interviewee knows the broad purposes of the interview and specifically checks that the interviewee does not think that *his* managerial effectiveness will somehow be revealed from his answers. Then the interviewer presents the interviewee with a series of 5″ × 3″ record cards, nine in all. He asks the interviewee to write on the first card an event where he feels that he has performed well. The restriction here is that it should be an *event* or *activity*, not a role or an area of responsibility; thus, *doing an appraisal interview* is an acceptable response but *Personnel* is not. A good rule of thumb is that the statement should have a verb in it. The more concrete and directly observable is the event under discussion the better. It follows that the statement is likely to be specific rather than general: *an* appraisal interview, not appraisal interviews.

On the second card the interviewee is asked to write down an event or activity where he feels that he failed to live up to his own expectations. The third card asks for an event which was important and which he could not see coming and so it was a bit of a surprise. The fourth card is a routine event he enjoys. The fifth is a routine event he dislikes. The sixth is an important event requiring mainly managerial skills. The seventh is an important event requiring mainly technical/professional skills. The eighth is another event where he feels that he performed well. The ninth is any other event which helps round out the picture.

Other series of questions are possible. There is nothing sacrosanct about the list of nine above. Two variations that we have used from time to time are:

Variation one

Card 1   Something you do which is very important
Card 2   Something you do frequently, or which takes a lot of your time
Card 3   Something important and unlikely to appear in your plans
Card 4   Something else you do which is important
Card 5   Something else frequent or time consuming
Card 6   Something else important
Card 7   Something else time consuming
Card 8   Something you do alone
Card 9   Something you do involving other people

Variation two

Card 1   Someone you know who you judge to be successful
Card 2   Someone you know who is not performing well
Card 3   Someone who has been around a long time
Card 4   Someone who is relatively new to the business
Card 5   Someone who is happy in his work

Card 6 Someone who is unhappy in his work
Card 7 Yourself
Card 8 Someone else who is successful
Card 9 Someone else who is not performing well

It will be noted that 'variation two' does not employ events but people. Conventional wisdom amongst Repertory Grid users is that to use people about whom the interviewee is likely to have strong views (significant others, in the jargon) can be dangerous because it may lead the interviewee into deep waters rather fast. While we would agree where such significant others as 'father', 'mother', 'sister', 'brother', etc, are being used, our experience in industry leads us to conclude that, provided the people concerned are *people at work* there is little or no difficulty. Many interviewees find it perfectly possible to give good responses to this set of trigger questions when the activity series has proved a problem for them.

There are as many different sets of trigger questions as there are purposes for conducting a grid interview. A fuller account of methods of starting a grid interview will be found in Stewart and Stewart (1981). Whichever schedule is used, the interviewer refrains from suggesting the kinds of answers which he is expecting, confining his input to ensuring that the events, activities or people mentioned are really specific or operational.

The interviewer then takes the cards, three at a time, according to a pre-arranged sequence and the interview carries on as follows:

Interviewer I am going to hand you three cards and I would like you to tell me one way in which any two of these events or activities resemble each other that makes them different from the third. You can pair them any way you like.

Interviewee Well, Planning and Travelling are both solitary activities, but Selection intervewing involves other people.

(The Interviewer records *Solitary – Done with others*)

Interviewer Thank you. Now three different cards about which I am going to ask the same question: in what way do any two resemble each other that makes them different from the third?

Interviewee Taking telephone messages and Attending management meetings, they're both run of the mill, nothing's going to be disastrous immediately if you fail, but independent arbitration in disputes, that's important, you could have the whole edifice crashing round you if you make a mistake. One's got a serious immediate outcome, the other two less so.

(The Interviewer records *Serious Outcome – Less Serious Outcome*)

Interviewer Thank you. Now a further three cards, with the same question . . .

Interviewee Meeting with my group, I have to be here in the office for that,

87

whereas the other two can be done anywhere. There's another difference too, in the staff meeting I'm usually responding to their requests, questions and so on, whereas the other two are much more concerned with my initiating things myself.

(The Interviewer records *Done in office – Done anywhere,* and
I respond – I initiate)

The interview carries on like this until all the prepared triads on the interviewer's record sheet have been used up, or the interviewee appears to have exhausted his store of replies. At one time we had a carefully prepared sequence of triads to use in determining which set of three cards would be presented next. We soon realized, however, that the process could be greatly simplified by increasing the number of cards from eight to nine! In fact, because the precise content of the cards must be unknown to the interviewer until the interviewee has filled them in, the precise order of presentation cannot matter in terms of substance. In order to avoid over working some cards and missing others, or repeating some cards too quickly and in order to eliminate the possibility of using the same combination of three more than once, the little diagram illustrated below is very helpful:

Triad control

1	2	3
4	5	6
7	8	9

It is now possible to navigate one's way around this diagram with the greatest ease. For example, one would present cards 1 2 3; 4 5 6; 7 8 9; 1 4 7; 2 5 8; 3 6 9; 4 1 2; 6 9 8; 7 5 3 and so on.

A little study of the procedure (or an experiment in the reader's own office) will show that the interviewer has suggested virtually nothing of the responses produced in the interview. All the interviewer has done, in fact, is to provide a structure within which the interviewee compares and contrasts aspects of his job and expresses those comparisons in his own words. The interviewer merely records the utterances, technically termed as follows: the nine items on the cards are called *elements,* and the bipolar statements expressing the comparisons are called *constructs,* because that is the way the interviewee *construes* his environment. The bias which would come from the interviewer's classifying the job according to his preconceptions is minimized.

It will also be apparent that the constructs are not dissimilar from the items in the performance questionnaire, a little adjustment is all that is needed to turn the interview results into a questionnaire.

However, there are some more steps remaining in the actual interview. It is unlikely that each triad will produce a fresh construct; some triads will produce several, others merely a repetition of an earlier one. The lowest number of constructs we have recorded is seven and the largest was in the 60s! The novice interviewer who thinks he is not extracting enough constructs has a safety net in the next two procedures. First, the interviewer goes back to the very first construct, and says: 'Now, in your first answer, you said that planning and travelling were both solitary activities, but that selection interviewing involved other people. Could you tell me, in your job which of those two kinds of activity is it important for you to do well? Is it more important for your effectiveness that you do solitary things well, or that you do things involving others well?'

The interviewer records, with plus and minus signs, the judgement that the interviewee makes. Sometimes the judgements are very hard but he should not allow an equivalence judgement unless the interviewee is adamant that he cannot decide.

When this procedure has been exhausted with all the constructs, the interviewer who wants more data can go back to the first construct again and say: 'You said that in your job it was more important for you to do well the things that involve other people. Would you like to tell me some more about that?' Another possible question is 'Why?'

It is usually necessary at this point to be able to write fast; people who have had trouble making the triadic comparisons to begin with may find that this question breaks the log-jam.

Whether or not he elects to ask the interviewee to elaborate on the reasons behind his preferences, the interviewer spends the last part of the interview asking if there is any more information or opinions which the interview has prompted; they have been talking about how the interviewee judges his job and the kinds of skills and activities which are more or less crucial to success; now does the interviewee have anything further to add? In our experience this invitation usually leads to one of two responses: some people say that they have uttered things about their job which they themselves did not know before the interview. Other people find that the interview procedure has opened up a new mass of insights which they are anxious to share. In this case, the interviewer records the comments assiduously.

At the end of this interview, the interviewer has a record of the constructs generated, plus the evaluations given to those constructs and any other information which the interviewee may have volunteered. To design a performance questionnaire, we take a sample of people doing the job for which potential is to be assessed, and interview them in this fashion, producing at the end of the interview phase a list of constructs, with evaluations, composite for all the interviewees. This in itself can be invaluable information, as it gives a picture of the way a section of managers view their jobs, obtained without any of the biases usually associated with such questionnaires. One such eye-opening picture was obtained when a sample of middle managers in a large manufacturing firm was interviewed thus, and none of the 21 interviewed mentioned any constructs with financial or budgetary overtones despite the fact that they were responsible for many millions of pounds' worth of plant.

So far we have only discussed the conduct of Repertory Grid interviews with one individual at a time. It is usually the case that this is much the preferred route, as it enables one to handle individual queries and adaptations as the need arises and with no embarrassment or time constraint imposed by others. However, it can sometimes be the case that a client is unwilling or unable to devote the amount of time needed to conduct the interviews singly. Under these circumstances it is possible to make the best of a bad job by conducting group grid interviews. It should be emphasized that this is not our first preference for discovering the characteristics of effective managers, but if all else fails this remains a possibility.

For a group administration, settle as many as are going to take part in a room where they are unlikely to be disturbed and where they have sufficient room to write without being overlooked or crowded. After a general introduction to the purpose and the method, exactly as for an individual interview, all present are given 10 cards of a light colour and about 50 white cards. On the coloured cards they are to write their elements. Each element elicitation question is given by the interviewer to the whole group and they are each asked to write down their response on one of the coloured cards, remembering to write the question number in the top right hand corner of the card. In this way each interviewee assembles his own element list from a generally administered series of elicitation questions. It is advisable to have someone walk round the group answering questions concerning the procedure and ensuring that all interviewees are indeed writing down observable activities, events, discrete names of people, or whatever has been requested by the interviewer. The tenth card is simply there in case of mistakes. It has no other role.

Once all the interviewees have completed their nine element cards the interviewer can proceed to construct elicitation. We find it best if the little matrix that we introduced earlier:

1	2	3
4	5	6
7	8	9

is written up on a board or flip-chart where all interviewees can see it clearly. The sequence is then introduced and each stage in the sequence, 1 2 3; 4 5 6; 7 8 9; etc, is announced after a suitable interval. It is made clear to the group that if anyone wishes to go faster or slower than the rate at which the sequence is being announced, he is entirely free to do so. The interviewer might say, therefore:

> I want you to start by taking your coloured cards 1, 2 and 3. Now will you please think of a number of ways in which two of the activities (events, people, etc) which you have written down are like each other and different from the third one. Please write each construct down on a separate white card from the pile that has been given to you. You may think of as many constructs as you like, and you may combine and recombine your three elements in as many ways as seems to you to be productive. Try not to repeat any construct too often, but if you genuinely want to use the same construct more than once, then you are entirely free to do so.

The group then proceeds, each individual at his or her own pace, until exhaustion or boredom sets in. The interviewer should prompt movement on to the next combination in the sequence at a frequency dictated by the pace at which most people in the group are working. The interviewer should also walk round the group ensuring that everyone has understood the procedure and that the constructs that are being produced are bipolar. This is important as, unprompted, there is a tendency for people to forget to provide both ends of the construct. At the end of the allotted time, all are asked to bundle up their cards, elements together on top, and to secure them with the elastic band provided and to add on the top of the whole pile a single card on which is written his name and job title. It should be emphasized that this is simply for purposes of classification during the analysis and that the promised anonymity will be preserved.

The advantages of the group method are that it is relatively quick; that as many as 30 or 40 people can be interviewed simultaneously; and that the data are usually fairly simple to analyse. The main disadvantages are that it is difficult to be sure that everyone is following the procedure all the time; that repeated constructs are more likely to occur; and that there is some loss of detail because it is not possible to ask the follow-up questions ('Can you tell me some more about that?' 'Why?') It is possible to ask the preference question: 'Which end of each construct is more representative of the effective manager in your view?', but there is a danger that not everyone will properly understand what is required. When we have asked the preference question in a group interview we have sometimes found value judgements being recorded which simply do not accord with what we have already learnt of the organization and which are very much the opposite of what we would have expected. It is difficult to know whether we are tapping genuinely dissenting value systems or whether it is merely that the procedure has been misapplied. Provided that one accepts that the information will be at a more superficial level, then the group administration of Repertory Grid is quite possible and has yielded valuable data. It remains our second choice, however, if individual interviews are at all feasible. More sophisticated versions of group grid are discussed in Stewart and Stewart (1981).

The results of the interviews must now be transformed into the performance questionnaire. From a sample of 20 or so managers we usually have around 400 raw constructs, some of them duplicated many times over, some of them occurring singly. It is our aim to have a performance questionnaire on which all these constructs are represented as far as is possible. This is not too unrealistic a task as some will differ only slightly. Very few constructs are incapable of being turned into performance questionnaire items.

The designing of a questionnaire is a difficult procedure the first time it is undertaken but it becomes progressively easier as light dawns. It is not possible for us to give a strict procedure which the reader can follow, but we can usefully describe what we have done whenever we have taught someone to design his own questionnaires.

One of us sets aside two or three days for working with the firm's staff. Probably a small group from the personnel department, some of whom may have been involved in the Repertory Grid interviews earlier. With a listing of constructs in front of us, we take the first construct and think of as many possible bipolar items, of performance questionnaire format, which could be made from this construct. We adopt the brainstorming approach, putting up the item on a chart and recording all our guesses; thus, suppose the first construct is *done with people – paperwork*, an imaginative group might produce the following items:

he is better with people	he is better at paperwork
he prefers dealing with people	he prefers dealing with paperwork
he delegates dealing with people	he delegates the paperwork
he judges others on their ability to deal with people	he judges others on their ability to deal with paperwork and so on.

It is important for the group to discover for itself the many different operational prefixes which will turn a construct into a questionnaire item. The brainstorming process, taking each construct to the point of exhaustion, should probably be performed with the first six to 10 items, so that people become skilled in producing and (later) evaluating a wide range of possible items. At that point, probably halfway through the first day and some little time after people have wondered despairingly whether they will ever complete the questionnaire at this rate, they go back and select which of the items already produced should, in fact, go into the questionnaire. This judgement will not usually be difficult;

some items will be less operational than others, some will have a greater scope than others.

When these operations have been performed on the first few constructs, the group can usually go ahead with the design of the questionnaire at greater speed, taking each construct in turn and arriving at one item, perhaps two, or sometimes agreeing that a previous item has covered the issue. Most often the construct will consist of apparent opposites like *people – paperwork*, but sometimes the two ends to the construct will have no apparent connection like *industrial relations – foreign language*, and this type of construct will generate two questionnaire items.

It is our experience that collections of constructs gathered from managers at the same level in the same firm will give between 80 and 120 items in the questionnaire. In addition, of course, the interview data may suggest further questionnaire items. The top limit of numbers of items which people will agreeably complete is probably around 120, although we have gone as high as 180.

It is not necessary to have the questionnaire designed by a group, and an experienced designer can do the job quicker and just as thoroughly single handed. When a group designs the questionnaire, care needs to be taken to see that its members facilitate rather than hinder each others' operations, by using a rubric like the rules of brainstorming. To learn the art of designing the questionnaire, we know of no more reliable way than to force oneself to dwell on each item, producing bipolar operational statements deriving from it, until each item naturally suggests its derivatives. The novice will be helped by a sight of the performace questionnaires from which we quote later in this chapter, though he should also be warned not to plagiarize them unaltered; they come from widely differing firms and from very junior to senior management and their specificity itself will render them less suitable for borrowing. It is almost as easy, and much more exact and exciting, to do one's own diagnosis in one's own firm.

When the items for the performance questionnaire have been assembled, they should be put in random order around the five point scale, with the 'good' and 'bad' sides (insofar as one can predict what these will be) jumbled. We caution the reader against accepting items in the form such as:

He lets me know what
his plans are   □ □ □ □ □   He does not do so

because there is some evidence that the 'he does not do so' statement carries less strength of meaning than a fuller statement of what he does instead. Better to write 'he does not tell me what his plans are' and thus remove any possible bias.

The reason for the five point scale is: we have found that if people are not given a mid point they return more spoiled papers than if they are given a mid point but encouraged not to use it except when pressed. Seven discriminations is too large a number for many people to make meaningfully.

The questionnaire is carefully proof read and examined for any unfortunate conjunctions of items, preferably by a stranger; the designers will be so familiar with the document by now that their ability to spot mistakes or unclear phrases is impaired. Then the instructions are written (a sample set of instruction sheets are given on pages 98–99 and the questionnaire printed and sent out to be analysed as set out above.

The reader will remember that we introduced this section with reference to the Repertory Grid method of interviewing and our concerns to remove interviewer bias from our questionnaire design. We stated earlier in this chapter that our experiencing of designing performance questionnaires by brainstorming the experts had led us to expect a 10 to 20 item yield. The first performance questionnaire we designed using Repertory Grid interviews as the basis gave us a yield of 67 items significantly distinguishing the effective from the ineffective performer!

This huge increase in productivity was totally unexpected and we have not been able to explain it completely to our own satisfaction. However, it is a consistent finding; every questionnaire we have since designed has given us a yield of between 60 and 85 items and we feel that this well justifies the time spent in preliminary interviews.

We also stated that there will be times when a performance questionnaire will not be possible because of limitations of numbers. The higher up the organization, the more likely this will be, though there is no theoretical reason why performance questionnaires could not be devised in respect of board members. When a performance questionnaire is not possible, we use the interview alone but this time we take a much more thorough approach. Our objective in conducting the small series of interviews we have with the people occupying the jobs under consideration is to get from them a full listing of the constructs they use, plus their evaluations and this implies that everyone interviewed is taken through the phase of 'telling us some more about that' when we review with him the evaluations he has made. Whereas an interview for the purposes of questionnaire design might take an hour and should not take more than an hour and a half, the thorough interview is likely to last for three hours and to follow every lead, to press for evaluations and judgements at every point and generally to exhaust the interviewee's knowledge of his subject. It was after one of these interviews that one managing director said that we had got from him things about his job which he himself did not know he knew. At the end of this exercise the constructs themselves, plus the evaluations given, must form the basis on which the next series of judgements (about the assessment of potential) must be made.

It is to this series of judgements that we now turn our attention. Using the diagnostic procedures described in this chapter, we have obtained for the client a set of results showing how managers who are perceived as effective in a given type of job differ from managers who are perceived as ineffective, with variations on the way these data are presented. In order to emphasize how important it is that this stage of the process be thorough and searching we have come to call it *interrogation*. To allay any fears that might be aroused by the use of such a word we do try to make it clear to the managers concerned that it is the results that are being interrogated, not the managers. We as outsiders cannot take part in this set of decisions, though we have learned the need to put two questions to the firm's manager and to wait for him to decide the answer. The first question is: 'Here is today's picture of perceived effectiveness: do you wish to perpetuate it, or are there any changes (ie, in the business, in the market, in your attitudes) which make you wish to change it in any way?'

Few of the firms have seriously wished to change their pattern of future managers in ways that differ greatly from the pattern presented, though some have added small changes of emphasis. It is quite right that this should be so. There is nothing intrinsically right and prescriptive about the picture of effectiveness that emerges from the diagnosis. However, even were a firm to wish to change its management style completely, the diagnosis would still have helped it by providing an appropriate working vocabulary with which to discuss its new preferences. Indeed, the specificity with which people come to observe management style after they have been concerned in a diagnostic exercise is one of the spin-off benefits of this procedure.

For example, a managing director in a large manufacturing company, after looking at the results of a diagnosis, suggested that he wished to add three items: the ability to achieve results through others (which, surprisingly, had not been mentioned by any of the existing senior managers); intelligence (he pronounced himself tired of being surrounded by 'stupid managers'); and abrasiveness ('this organization has gone to sleep on its feet'). As might be imagined, his third requirement generated some discussion. At the end of that discussion it was agreed that, while his first intention, abrasiveness downwards only, was a non-starter, it might be possible to encourage people to be a good deal more frank with each other about disagreements. This was actually implemented, with highly favourable results.

The second question we must ask – or get him to ask himself – is: 'Having got your picture of the characteristics of the manager of the future at this level in this job, what are the most reliable and efficient ways of looking for him?'

Often it is worth going through the results item by item, deciding what sort of evidence would be necessary to make this judgement about an employee, and going on to decide how one discovers this evidence – is it in the man's track record and available in the existing appraisal scheme, could it be obtained by some form of job analysis, by studying his written output, by putting him into an assignment eslewhere and seeing how he behaves? It may be the case – although not always – that some key characteristics can only be found out by putting the man into a situation that simulates the management job under consideration; or that these characteristics could most economically be observed in such a simulation. In this case, we may go on to discuss the design and running of an assessment programme. We regard it as just as satisfactory an outcome if the results of this decision are to have a fresh look at the management appraisal system, or to reorganize the personnel information system, or even – it is possible, though it has not happened yet – to decide to do nothing, if the diagnostic stage has demonstrated that current practice is as efficient as could be hoped.

In the following chapters we discuss the design of assessment programmes; there are, though, some small points remaining from this chapter.

First, the reader may be interested in further applications of the repertory grid technique, with or without a performance questionnaire. It is a fruitful technique and can be adapted to many industrial uses. Market researchers, for instance, frequently use it to get consumers' views. They would use different products as the elements, and record the constructs as before. We ourselves have not used this application, but one of us has used it in selection interviewing (1976) with useful results. In addition, the performance questionnaire can lead to immediate information for the re-design of the selection mechanism system, which enabled one firm to halve the wastage rate among new salesmen, and would prove very useful to a personnel department worried about having to give written reasons for its selection decisions.

Secondly, we should warn the reader that the repertory grid is a powerful technique for probing people's thinking and it should not be used frivolously. It was designed, after all, as a clinical tool for individual diagnosis. The reader will find the recommendations we have made for its use to be perfectly harmless, but we would caution him against trying any other applications without first consulting an expert and perhaps undertaking a course of training. These and other issues are expanded on in Stewart and Stewart (1981).

Thirdly, a small political hint: one of the regular banes of the researcher in the behavioural sciences is the person who, when presented with one's hard won results, says 'Well, I could have told you that in half an hour.' It is our experience that these predictions are rarely true but there is no counter-argument. However, after the design of the performance questionnaire but before its distribution, it can be useful to ask one or two people to predict what the results should be. The researcher, if internal to the firm, should always do this himself to test that his day to day perceptions are reliable; it is not often that one gets a chance to check oneself. Asking a potential troublemaker to make his predictions is excellent insurance against the later objections; if he is right, he can be asked for his secrets; if he is wrong, he should not be crowed over but this is an opportunity to gain his interest and, perhaps, his respect for one's techniques.

Finally, a point that often comes up in discussion: is not the performance questionnaire analysing only perceived effectiveness, not real effectiveness? We admit that we worried about this question until we heard an accountant trying to define profit. Having sat through many different definitions of profit, we were foolish enough to ask for the real definition and were told that these different fomulations represented different viewpoints about what profit really was. We thought that if accountants could live with that degree of non-specificity in their chief area of concern, then we who were better used to living with probabalistic data could also tolerate it. However, we admit that this does not fully satisfy the objection and we have two further points to make. One is that the procedure gets such a full, operational, workable measure of perceived effectiveness that it is likely to be better than most of its competitors. For when we see how the diagnoses differ from firm to firm and are specific to each firm, we are encouraged in that belief. Secondly, we would add that most methods of examining managers' performance depend upon perceptions, as for example appraisal systems or management succession committees, so it makes sense to find out systematically what those perceptions are.

Performance Questionnaire Examples

XYZ Industries

Assessment of management potential

As you will know, Central Personnel Department has been carrying out an exercise to provide a description of the characteristics of an effective plant head, in order to improve the methods whereby we select and develop future plant heads. In order to complete this stage of the work we are asking you to complete two questionnaires. The first is attached.

Will you please call to mind *the least effective plant head you know, or have known*. It is important that he should be a real person, but we do *not* want to know his name. We would like you to complete this questionnaire about him, good points as well as bad.

To remind you how to complete the questionnaire: every item in the questionnaire consists of a pair of statements with a five point scale between them. For each item, will you please decide which statement best describes the person you have in mind and then put a tick in the appropriate space. For example:

Example 1

He arrives for work on time ☐ ☑ ☐ ☐ ☐ He arrives for work late

This would mean that you think he usually turns up for work on time, but not always.

Example 2

He keeps a tidy desk ☐ ☐ ☐ ☐ ☑ He keeps an untidy desk

This would mean that you think his desk is a mess

If you genuinely cannot make up your mind on a particular item, then please tick the centre space. Try to use this space as little as possible.

Later on you will receive a second questionnaire, with a different set of instructions. We shall not be troubling you for further information after that.

Thank you for your co-operation.

When you have completed the questionnaire, will you please return it to:

XYZ Industries

Assessment of management potential

A short while ago you completed the first of two questionnaires to do with obtaining a description of the characteristics of an effective plant head, in order to improve our selection and development procedures. You will find attached the second and final questionnaire.

Will you please call to mind *the most effective plant head you know, or have known*. It is important that he should be a real person, but we do *not* want to know his name. We would like you to complete this questionnaire about him, bad points as well as good.

Every item in the questionnaire consists of a pair of statements, with a five point scale between them. For each item, will you please decide which statement best describes the person you have in mind and then put a tick in the appropriate space. For example:

Example 1

He arrives for work on time ☐ ☑ ☐ ☐ ☐ He arrives for work late

This would mean that you think he usually arrives for work on time, but not always.

Example 2

He keeps a tidy desk ☐ ☐ ☐ ☐ ☑ He keeps an untidy desk

This would mean that you think his desk is a mess.

If you genuinely cannot make up your mind on a particular item, then please tick the centre space. Try to use this space as little as possible.

Thank you for taking the time and trouble to complete both our questionnaires. The problem of selecting and developing future plant heads is becoming increasingly critical. We appreciate the help you are giving us to find better solutions to these problems.

When you have completed the questionnaire, will you please return it to:

PERFORMANCE QUESTIONNAIRE

Example 1 First-line supervisors – Insurance industry

1 He is most at ease when dealing with his subordinates — — — — — He is most at ease when dealing with his superiors

2 He is best at paperwork — — — — — He is best working with people

3 His first priority is his clients — — — — — His first priority is his staff

4 He finds ways to assist his staff with ongoing problems — — — — — He gets involved with his staff's work only to check it

5 He is at his most effective with his superiors — — — — — He is at his most effective with his subordinates

6 He says 'How can we improve on the results we achieve?' — — — — — He says 'Under the circumstances we're doing a grand job?'

7 He does not tell his people when they have made mistakes — — — — — He does tell his people when they have made mistakes

8 He is interested in his staff's personal problems — — — — — He does not want to know about his staff's personal problems

9 He repeats his mistakes — — — — — He learns from his mistakes

10 He is more effective in dealing with people in groups — — — — — He is more effective in dealing with a single person, face-to-face

11 He under-uses his staff — — — — — He makes excessive demands on his staff

PERFORMANCE QUESTIONNAIRE

Example 2 Senior middle managers – Chemical industry

1 He checks if his decision will affect other people — — — — He doesn't check if his decision will affect other people
2 He confers with them by telephone — — — — He seeks people out when he wishes to confer
3 He gets rid of poor performers — — — — He tolerates poor performers
4 He is surprised by the effect of new legislation — — — — He anticipates the effect of new legislation on his operation
5 He prefers to set his own standards for his work — — — — He prefers to have standards set for his work
6 He will take action even though results will not be apparent for a long time — — — — He will only act if the results are likely to be apparent quickly
7 He uses his authority when the situation demands it — — — — He is reluctant to use his authority
8 His visual presentation of data is unclear — — — — His visual presentation of data is clear
9 Safety to him is a people and technical problem — — — — Safety to him is a technical problem
10 He avoids travelling — — — — He will travel anywhere, any time
11 He is concerned to present XYZ to the public in the best possible light — — — — Public relations do not concern him
12 He prefers to work through influence, lobbying and politics — — — — He prefers to work through the formal channels
13 He tells his people what his job involves — — — — He does not tell his people what his job involves
14 He sees unionization as greatly inhibiting his freedom to plan — — — — He sees unionization as another factor to be managed
15 He builds his own reputation — — — — He builds his team's reputation
16 He asks people to précis for him — — — — He reads everything for himself
17 He issues detailed instructions — — — — He issues broad, general instructions
18 He contacts people face to face — — — — He writes messages to people
19 He absorbs the workload created by crises — — — — He gives all his attention when he is in a crisis
20 He can make accurate long-term predictions — — — — He cannot make accurate long-term predictions
21 His assessment of people's potential is correct — — — — His assessment of people's potential is incorrect
22 He imposes systems on his people — — — — He lets his people develop their own systems

PERFORMANCE QUESTIONNAIRE

Example 3 Senior managers – International bank

The real person whom you have in mind. . . .

1	Prefers to work in the field	Prefers to work in the office
2	Is better at relationship skills	Is better as a technician
3	Would rather work through others	Would rather act directly
4	Reacts	Anticipates
5	Is better at handling subordinates	Is better at handling superiors
6	Prefers action	Prefers evaluation
7	Is more concerned with form	Is more concerned with substance
8	Imposes structure	Allows his people to go their own way
9	Prefers psychological problems	Prefers business problems
10	Recognizes what is within his control and what is not	Does not recognize what is within his control and what is not
11	Would rather achieve targets	Would rather deal with organizational matters
12	Controls the time available	Is controlled by the time available
13	Would rather explain a situation	Would rather improve a situation
14	Knows when to cut losses	Does not know when to cut losses
15	Prefers to handle small specific issues	Prefers to handle large diffuse issues
16	Prefers the client to set priorities	Prefers the Bank to set priorities
17	More concerned with short-term (less than 2 years ahead)	More concerned with long-term (2 years or more ahead)

Chapter 5

Programme design

After we have discussed the results of the diagnostic stage, we may have to design an assessment programme. Of course, the assessment programme will not tell the firm everything they need to know about the participants' management potential, but it may be the most convenient way of assessing evidence that is not readily available elsewhere. We have a library of tasks and exercises which we use in designing programmes, but the content of many of the exercises will vary so as to tailor them to the firm's own background. Needless to say, there is no such thing as a standard assessment programme. Each is designed to meet the firm's unique needs and constraints and every programme we have designed so far has included a number of totally new exercises developed specifically for that programme. The shortest programme so far has been a one day event (though a very long, hard working day!) and the longest we have been associated with has been a week long programme combining assessment and developmental work. We know of other firms where programmes of a fortnight long are run, though we are not aware of any attempts at rigorous validation of these events.

In this chapter we discuss some of the exercises and tasks which we have assembled so far, and then go on to the art of combining these into an economical and effective programme. In the next chapter we treat the related matters of observer training, administration, accommodation and secretarial back up required.

In Table 16 on page 105 we reproduce a table prepared for one organization when we were discussing the design of an assessment programme. The left-hand column lists the assessment factors relevant to this firm (the reader should remember that these are abbreviated descriptions of much fuller statements and try not to fall into the trap of substituting the shorthand for the real thing). Across the top are listed the exercises we had to offer them, with a rough indication of the utility of each exercise to each assessment factor. This diagram is used initially to check that adequate coverage is given to all factors and that the factors which are judged to be of greatest importance receive the most frequent attention. It can also be used as a control document in the sequencing of exercises to make sure that the same set of factors is not pursued in two or more exercises in succession. As new ideas about exercises emerge, or as new priorities about the factors are agreed, so the diagram can be used to map these changes and to achieve a quick visual check that the various balances are being maintained.

1 The In-tray Exercise

Here the participants work individually, against time pressure. They are given a brief which tells them that they have just moved into a new job and that this is their first morning in it; it is a Saturday morning and they have come into the office for an hour and a half before leaving to catch a plane to somewhere where they will not be able to carry on their office work. There is no one else in the building and the switchboard is shut down; they have a full in-tray in front of them which they have to cope with as best they can in the time provided, knowing that they will not be back until next Wednesday. They are to attach notes to each item indicating the action they are taking, and *not* in the form 'If I were X I would . . .' but in the form 'I *am* X and I am doing . . .'

The actual managerial position which is mimicked depends upon the level of the assessment programme and the mix of people. Obviously, the position must bear some relation to the level of management ability for which the participants are being assessed; it is no good using director level material when the participants have not yet reached first line manager. Sometimes, when a specific post is under consideration and the programme is designed to look at abilities to fill it and no other, the content of the exercise is taken directly from the experience of the present occupants of such posts. On the other hand, it may be necessary to specify a position for which none of the participants is likely to be directly in line: if they come from a variety of divisions within the organization it would be giving some of them an unfair advantage if the in-tray was drawn from one of those divisions; thus we have asked a mixture of line managers from different operating divisions to imagine themselves as the personnel director, a position for which none of them was being considered. This tactic needs using with care, to make sure that the broad principles underlying the quality of decision-making are the same in the make believe job and the positions for which the people are being assessed; the choice of personnel director may be unfortunate, as we shall indicate later.

What sort of problems and information does the novice manager find in his in-tray? We usually try to provide a selection of the following:

useful information, such as a note from his predecessor, or a day to day planner, an organization chart or policy manuals (if the client firm uses them). The note from the predecessor often contains thumbnail sketches of the people the

Table 16
Example of matrix of assessment factors and suitable exercises in one firm

	Leaderless Group Discussion	In-tray	Manu-facturing	Consult-ancy	Politics	Real Life	Psychological Tests				
							AH6	SDQ	JCQ	W-G CTA	16PF (A)
Management and Leadership	√	√	√√		√	√					√
Generalist	√√	√√	√	√	√√	√√					
Intellect	√	√√	√	√√	√	√√	√√			√√	
Personal	√		√√	√	√	√					√√
Cultural and Political		√			√√	√					
Stability	√	√	√√	√√	√	√		√√			√√
Drive	√√		√√	√√	√√	√			√		√√
Planning and Organization		√√	√√	√							
Command and Impact	√√	√	√	√√	√	√				√	√
Numerate		√	√√	√√			√				

√ √ means that the factor will emerge particularly strongly in that exercise new manager will have working for him, and the use he makes of this information is material for the assessment

information he simply hasn't time to deal with, as for example a draft report from a firm of consultants on an attitude survey just completed, a questionnaire on how many school leavers etc he will want to employ six months hence, or his requirements for new office furniture. Some people will plough doggedly through these weighty documents; others will see that they are not urgent and put them to one side

operational matters on which he has to shape a decision and then delegate it to one of his staff. The actual content of these matters depends on the position but a sensitive participant will use the predecessor's notes, and the organization chart, in delegating and will draft his instructions clearly

operational matters which should not be brought to his attention until the decision has been taken; perhaps the predecessor will have indicated that one of his staff is indecisive and liable to push all decisions upwards unless he is clearly told to use his own judgement

matters which he has to delegate upwards or sideways. A good example would be the presentation of a long service award to Joe Bloggs next Tuesday, brought to his attention by a routine reminder; he has (a) to spot that he will not be there next Tuesday, (b) to realize that this is sufficiently important for his place to be taken by one of equal or greater seniority and (c) to ask for this to be done

matters which are nothing to do with him, for example a letter from a solicitor about one of his staff involved in an accident for which the firm may be liable. Unless the programme is actually simulating the job of managing the legal department, the participant will probably be best advised to take no action on it himself and to hurry it to the legal people

matters where there are possible exposures on areas of current concern; we have often used safety, security and industrial relations items.

The items themselves can take many forms, ie memoranda, notices from bulletin boards, newspaper clippings etc. The date should only be omitted when this is done for a purpose. There should be sufficient items in the in-tray that no one could expect to do them all; the participants are then assessed on whether, and how accurately, they assigned priorities to the items they found.

As we have indicated, the actual content of the items need to be decided in close consultation with the firm, working preferably with a line manager currently occupying the kind of position for which potential is being sought. We usually show him a previous in-tray exercise to give him some idea of it and he gives us some ideas in response; these are then drafted into a provisional in-tray which he then considers, alters and guides us on the correct and incorrect ways that it should be tackled. We rarely specify the 'right' action ourselves and have often been surprised at the totally different ways in which the same item would be treated in different firms, underlining the point that effective managerial practice varies from firm to firm. It is usually a good idea to have the observers go through the in-tray in detail, agreeing preferred and non-preferred responses to each item. In this way both their knowledge of the in-tray and their commitment to the programme are increased.

Because we have to discuss in detail the range of possible ways of tackling the in-tray, getting the firm's views on good and bad practice, we have to rely on the objectivity of the people with whom we discuss this. Here we have the explanation for our possible caution at making the in-tray that of a personnel director: our discussions at this stage are usually with a personnel manager and there can be a whiff of incestuousness if the personnnel department goes within itself to find material.

There are some actions which are common to all good in-tray performances in the firms we have so far worked with; all good managers put their material in priority order, take note of their diaries, arrange to have a report back when they return and appoint a deputy to take their place while they are away.

The in-tray exercise is useful in assessing a number of characteristics:

the ability to work under short term pressure
specific aspects of decision-making as they relate to the firm, for example preference for quality over volume
ability to distinguish between fact and opinion
specific aspects of delegation and control
clarity of communication
knowledge of and adherence to company policies and practices
sensitivity to subtle issues of concern to the firm
and the technical content of the items can usually reveal the participant's technical knowledge and skills

In addition, rich opportunities are provided for feedback and discussion to the participant as there is a great deal of hard information around which to interview. We usually try to design an individual feedback interview on the in-tray exercise alone when we include this task in a programme although in many programmes this interview is a further exploration of the participant's decisions with an observer to ensure that the observer has fully understood the participant's intentions.

2 Listening exercises
Here we are concerned to assess one particular characteristic which has often

been shown to be associated with effective management: the ability to listen to information and opinions which one does not like while staying calm and absorbing the material. In addition these exercises can be adapted to examine clarity of verbal communication.

The usual practice is to arrange participants in small groups of four to six people and to give them a topic to discuss. They may be told that they have a time limit within which to agree a joint statement; the topic should be one on which controversy can reliably be expected. After they have been discussing for 20 minutes or so, each participant is given forms on which to summarize the views of each of the other participants. Each participant is then given all the forms which relate to his views and has to score them on a five-point scale for (a) completeness and (b) accuracy. In addition, the observers will be monitoring each participant's output, certainly for its content and probably also for its clarity, so that when the time comes to assess the participant's performance on this exercise they have information from several sources.

The listening exercises can be adapted to include a wider variety of content, if the topics to be discussed also test technical knowledge, say, or company policy. Our experience suggests that it is quite sufficient to use this exercise to examine listening skills only, because it is such a subtle and difficult to test matter.

Selection of topics can be a problem. Sometimes the firm suggests current areas of controversy which they are certain will arouse passions: who should bear the cost of meeting the quota of disabled employees, or how should out of territory points be shared? We also have some topics ourselves if necessary, for example, the banning of smoking in offices, payment for travel on company business in one's own time. It is sometimes wise to place the listening exercises towards the end of the assessment programme, when one has a better idea of the groups to form and the topics to give them.

3 Presentation exercise with or without preparation

One example of this exercise is the *management development presentation*, which we shall describe in detail. The individual participants are given a sheaf of notes which are supposed to have been prepared by a colleague who was drawing up recommendations for a management development programme in a strange firm. There are many figures on manpower stocks, vacancies, graduate intake, promotion rate, projected trends and previous experience. It is the task of the participant to get this information into some sensible order and (perhaps) prepare a standup presentation lasting 10 minutes which he will later deliver. To prepare the material (against a time deadline) he has to sort the trivial from the important, and also do a fair amount of cross referencing and amalgamating within the information provided. We have drafted possible solutions which show different degrees of skill and alertness; there is not much doubt about the best possible answer but it can be attained with different degrees of completeness.

The participants may be asked to write up their solutions, or they could have to prepare a presentation, in which case they are assessed according to the characteristics of effective presentation within the firm. We cannot be more specific about what these factors are because they vary widely from firm to firm. In the context of this particular exercise one of us received an early lesson in cultural differences: a team of visiting Americans, who had developed an assessment programme within IBM in the United States, was demonstrating the programme's virtues to people from IBM World Trade, mostly European but also Japanese. They showed three films of possible presentations, telling the viewers that one was good, one bad and one mediocre and asked them to rate the presentation. Without collusion the World Trade viewers agreed on a rank order that was the exact reverse of the American one! Presentation styles do differ widely but the observers can be trained and briefed to look for the performance appropriate to their own firm.

The *management development exercise* examines characteristics such as working under pressure, coping with large quantities of strange information, numeracy, ability to take the long view, and ability to present information clearly. Used as we have used it, it does not address specific aspects of technical competence but, given a different 'flavour', technical skills could also be involved.

4 Negotiation exercise

We freely admit that we 'borrowed' this exercise from Rackham (1972). He recommends it for training purposes; with some adaptation we have fitted it to the assessment programme.

Participants are divided into two groups, physically separate but not too far apart. They are given a problem to which they have to negotiate a solution; the problem should be real, one with whose solution they will have to live afterwards. Each participant has a piece of paper and a pencil; observers sit with each group. The programme manager or his assistant selects one group arbitrarily and announces that he will take a message from that group to the other. To decide the message, the following must happen:

 (i) individually, each participant notes down the message he would send
 (ii) as a group, with a time-limit of three minutes, they discuss their individual messages and agree which one shall be sent.

The programme manager leaves to take the message to the other group. In his absence, the group will (one hopes) discuss their strategy, tactics and aims, to which the observers will pay close attention. The programme manager visits the other group, reads out the message and asks participants to prepare their answer using the two stage format above, first the individual replies and then the group-agreed replies. This procedure carries on until the time limit (at least two hours) is reached.

This exercise generates two sorts of information and the brief to the observers reflects this fact. First, because a written record is available of each individual's messages, these messages can be analysed by content according to appropriate criteria. Does he attack? Does he compromise? Does he state his own position? Does he wait for the other fellow to back down? Does he crow over a defeated enemy? The criteria vary; in one firm we worked with it was characteristic of the effective manager that he should play his cards close to his chest in negotiations; in another firm the effective manager stated his position openly. However, we have here a record of the participants' first thoughts on the message presented, a useful guide to their conduct in real negotiations. Secondly, the observers will attend to the discussions that go on while the messenger is out of the room, using such criteria of effective group behaviour as seem appropriate, with special stress on their approach to negotiations – how is agreement reached? how are the bargaining ranges, aims and constraints agreed? whether the group uses any special skills of its members, how it copes with conflict etc.

The choice of problem on which to negotiate is a nice task. The problem must be one that matters: it is no good negotiating about whether we should come out of the Common Market but better to negotiate about a menu for the farewell dinner and better still to settle on a real company problem which is giving current concern, such as the fair allocation of limited car parking space.

This exercise requires strong administration. A time limit of three minutes from delivering the other group's message must be strictly enforced by the pro-gramme manager (or whoever else is going from one group to the other). If he is not careful, he will be trying to take down the message in writing and find that the group members are telling him to erase and alter as he goes along, thus stretching the time they have for discussion; he must be prepared to blow the whistle on them after three minutes and say that if they have no message com-pleted he will go to the other group and tell them that this one cannot think of anything to say. This need to assert authority from time to time makes the job of message carrier unsuitable for an observer, who could be seen to be losing his neutrality; if the job must be done by an observer, he should not try to make any observations during that time.

5 Politics exercise

This exercise is particularly useful for multinational organizations whose managers have to adjust to and deal with cultures far removed from their own. There is no reason, incidentally, why non-British companies should not use something very similar to help their nationals prepare for work in the UK. It is designed to test cultural and political sensitivity and awareness of the public relations dimension that can easily enter multinational companies' awareness rather too late.

A fictitious national operation is outlined, together with bare details about the kind of country in which they are supposedly operating. Some indications are given of local natural resources, the political climate, the availability of skilled and unskilled manpower, particular communication problems and transport infrastructure, the relative size of the company as an employer in that country and, of course, the product range and how it fits in to the national plan. Six problems are then posed containing elements drawn from labour relations, religious conflicts, inappropriate technology, international financing arrangements, bribery, climatic problems, family and social adjustment difficulties, changes in the way in which the host country wishes its commodity market to be handled, escalating shipping costs, unrealistic demands from UK head office, surprise visits from senior managers and so on. If at all credible we usually add something to do with an unfavourable report on the company's activities threatened by a UK television team.

Each participant is asked to write brief notes on how he would settle each of the problems. He is made aware that the purpose of these notes is to crystallize his views and to provide the observers with a record of his starting position. The participants are then brought together and required to agree a view amongst themselves of how they would settle each difficulty.

6 Railway planning exercise

In this exercise the objective is to see whether the participants can handle largely numerical data and make rational decisions based upon these data. An outline map of a railway system is provided, with distances and traffic densities marked on it, together with indications of the population contained in each of the towns or villages which the network serves. The participant also receives information about the number of train sets available and their capacity, average service speeds under varying conditions and staff availability to drive and service them. Aided by historical figures of utilization of the various services during the day the participant's task is to optimize the use of the available plant and people while providing the best customer service possible.

Clearly this is a task which some parts of British Rail would find entirely familiar, but airlines, road transport firms, bus companies, shipping companies, anyone indeed who has to plan to use inadequate resources to do a complicated job will find this exercise of interest.

7 Leaderless group discussion

In this exercise the participants are required to handle a typical clash of objectives. They have individual aims which they are expected to pursue with vigour and they share a group objective which will be at variance with all the individual objectives present except, ultimately, one.

Each participant is given the job description and man specification for a post which has, supposedly, become vacant in the organization. Each participant has, in addition, a description of a fictitious subordinate whose candidacy for the post he is supposed to advocate to the best of his ability. The man and job specifications are drawn, as far as possible, from life in the organization. The fictitious subordinates are so constructed as to be as nearly in balance as possible, with equal numbers of strong and weak points. Before the group discussion takes place each participant has 10 minutes in which to become acquainted with his candidate, during which time he may take notes if he wishes. The original description of his candidate is then taken from him and he has five minutes in which, on the basis of his notes, to prepare a three-minute maximum presentation of his candidate to the rest of the group. The presentations take place one after the other, in random order, and in order to make sure that flights of fancy and concealment of weak points do not reach too fine a pitch, each participant has the description of one other participant's candidate. The participants do not know who in the group has the check description of their candidate, but they do know that someone will be able to tell if they depart too radically from the profile provided.

After the presentations have been given there follows a group discussion, usually of about 45 minutes' duration, in which the participants have to agree (on the basis of what they have heard and their further discussion) which one of the candidates they are prepared to put forward for the vacancy.

The observers are equipped with a specification of what to observe according to the criteria of effective group behaviour which derive from the diagnostic stage. Besides bringing out the general aspects of effective group behaviour (organizing, building on ideas, getting agreement, bringing people in) this task can demonstrate how well participants can take the 'helicopter effect' of seeing the effects of their own decisions on a wider area of the company. They can also see how well they can argue to a brief which someone has prepared for them, a frequently occurring characteristic of effectiveness. The group rarely does all that is asked of it and no sanctions are imposed on participants for 'failing'.

The preparation of descriptions of candidates needs close consultation to make sure that we give appropriate descriptions of realistic sounding people, and that the firm's manager agrees with us about the different faults and advantages in each candidate. Some of the faults we use fairly often are: not being able to delegate, spending too much time on outside activities, having a roving eye for the secretarial staff, being unable to do arithmetic, not being able to stand up to stressful overwork. Where the job has been predominantly male, zest can be added to the discussion by making one or more candidates female.

The leaderless group discussion exercise is a good method of seeing how participants cope with the unpleasant and common managerial predicament of having to balance personal success against the possible success of the group to which one belongs. This is an adjustment which some dedicated specialists find difficult to make and the opportunity to try it on an assessment programme, for their benefit and the firm's, has been of great value to one or two people who have participated in programmes with which we have been associated.

8 White paper exercise

This is an individual task and one more suited to assessment of potential for higher managerial positions. The participants are given a white paper, green paper or an official publication of some kind and asked to write a report on it, detailing its implications for the company as a whole or perhaps for a specified part of the company. The material needs to be chosen with care, something freshly issued on which only a little popular wisdom will already have been generated. The Health and Safety at Work Act, when newly proposed, was useful to us; nationally published accident reports similarly. Obviously the assessment will partly cover the clarity and thoroughness of writing and will also touch on sensitivity to the real implications of the material; again, this means close liaison with the firm in preparing model answers.

9 The book review

We use this exercise for specific purposes relevant to the needs of many firms: the ability to absorb and react rationally to unpalatable information presented in a hostile fashion, and the ability to digest large quantities of technical material in a short time. Our usual practice is to obtain a book written from an anti-business standpoint and get the participants to review it, swallowing their antagonism to the presentation and style in order to get at the meat of the argument. We have frequently used a book called *The Hazards of Work* (Kinnersly, 1973) which has, from our point of view, the great merit of being virulently anti-business while having a number of indisputably valid points to make about the inadequacy of our occupational health and safety practices. The participants' task is to react rationally to the way the book is presented while recognizing the points it makes and summarizing them fairly. This book is good for use with production managers, engineers and some R and D managers; the same firm also publishes a book called *Your Employer's Profits* (Hird, 1975) in which balance sheets are examined from a Marxist viewpoint; this could serve a useful purpose with participants experienced in this area. Assiduous combing of bookshops may be necessary to find material for other participants!

10 The job report

This is again an individual task, in which the participant has to write an essay about his present job. We have experimented with two sets of instructions: in one we ask the participant just to write about his job, its successes and failures, challenges and what he feels about it; in another approach we ask him to write as if he were leaving a brief for his successor. The analysis performed by the observers follows a well-defined set of criteria covering such questions as:

is he honest about failures and successes?
does he give his people credit (if already a manager)?
does he give other departments credit?
does he talk about the job in day to day terms, or in long-range company wide terms?
does he mention his colleagues and in what terms?
does he give evidence of ambition and purposeful self-management?
does he give evidence of having learned?

Because this is a deceptively easy task to assess, the observer's brief needs to be especially clear and self-limiting. Again we should warn the reader not to take this list of questions as fixed; others might need to be added and some of the above might not apply in the reader's own firm.

11 The consultancy exercise

This exercise covers some of the same ground as the presentation exercise, though their purposes are slightly different; it is unlikely, however, that they would appear in the same programme. The consultancy exercise falls into two parts, the second half of which is optional.

In the first part, which is an individual task, the participants are told that they are working for a consultancy firm and that at short notice they have to take over the assignment of one of their colleagues who has met with an accident. He is due to give a 10 minute presentation to the managing director of the client firm, detailing his recommendations, on the following day. He must go through the previous consultant's notes and arrive at his recommendations, also preparing his 10 minute presentation.

As we have usually performed this exercise, it varies from the management development presentation in one crucial way; there are a number of possible recommendations any of which might be the right answer. Usually the 'client' is a small factory, fraught with the problems of the family firm, which has got into trouble while trying to introduce a new line. The notes cover production figures, sales records, labour turnover etc, as well as records of interviews with some of the key figures. The participant has to make sense of this; this means he has to come to terms with the jargon of disciplines not his own. He must plan not only a possible solution but also how to sell it, given the information available about the people to whom he will be making these recommendations; he must also have a back-up plan made in case his first is not accepted. It is a subtle situation, in that the technical matters are not all that difficult but it is not enough for the consultant to stop there: he must take note of the information he has on the people involved.

After he has sifted the information the participant has to present his proposal. One observer is delegated to act as the managing director, with strict instructions to say as little as possible; if the 'consultant' tries to ask questions etc, the 'managing director' is to say that he is here to get answers, not to give them and so on. The other observers watch the presentation, looking for points as they have been briefed.

The second, optional part of the exercise takes place after the presentations have been made, with the proviso that participants have not seen each others' presentations nor discussed the exercise amongst themselves. They are brought together in a group and asked to arrive at a common recommendation to the client's problems. Here certain characteristics may come to the fore: the ability to discuss subtle information about people and to plan using it; the ability to get one's proposals accepted; and perhaps the conflict between selling a good solution and selling an expensive one (the exercise can be adjusted to make this prospect more likely).

The reason for having the group discussion *after* the individual presentation is that participants will have a high degree of commitment to their own way of doing things, and to come to a group agreement after having defended their individual points of view is a testing task.

12 The Ajax task force

This is a group exercise designed to assess the ability to work to a departmental brief and the ability to form alliances etc, in a group problem solving task. Each participant is given a departmental brief to argue to in a situation in which the managing director of the Ajax company has got everyone together to discuss reactions to the loss of a major client. There are a variety of possible solutions and each participant is told which one he is to prefer and his reasons for rejecting the others; there are always two advocates for any one solution. The group has to discuss and agree a solution, under the chairmanship of the managing director, and the observers are briefed to monitor such aspects of group behaviour as have been shown to be related to effectiveness, with particular emphasis on skills in forming alliances, bargaining etc and maybe other behaviours such as stating one's own position openly. This is a useful exercise at first-line manager level in particular because the ability to be a departmental representative/delegate is unlikely to be shown in a man's track record.

13 The manufacturing game

This is a complex buying and selling game in which the participants have to cope with a great deal of information and work, many possible distractions and a constant requirement to read the small print. In groups, participants have to manufacture paper tubes and sell them in the market place, buying raw material and negotiating loans etc and (if they are careful) watching for trends in the prices of everything. They must be aware that buying and selling can take place only at certain times and watch their cash flows and the interest on the loans they will almost certainly have to take out and so on. The observers will probably be watching to see how they organize themselves, how delegation and handing over responsibilities is done, how team members adjust to the inevitable failures and whether they keep cool and can assess the importance of new information. The programme manager has an active part to play in this task, as he must judge when to add new information etc to the group's in-tray; a current copy of the *Financial Times* has sometimes tempted an unwary team member to read it from cover to cover while his work goes undone!

14 The appraisal exercise

Here participants are asked to take the part of the appraising manager in an appraisal interview with a well briefed stooge. This is unlikely to be a common exercise, but there are one or two characteristics common in effective managers which this exercise would test. For example, at the beginning of an interview always ask the appraisee how he thinks he has done. It is also possible to assess the handling of grievances or the proportion of adverse comment to praise and positive suggestion.

15 The industrial relations game

This is a commercially available board game in which industrial relations issues arise and have to be solved using the skill of the participants and where there is little luck involved, mostly skill.

16 Manager's day out

This exercise is designed to test rather the same characteristics as the Railway Planning exercise, but with less emphasis on numeracy and rather more on man management and customer relations. It is therefore especially suitable for testing whether or not participants are likely to be able to manage sales or customer service teams.

Each participant receives an identical set of documents in which are described his team members (sales or customer service), the major customers in his territory and a physical description of the territory. His 'patch' usually centres around a moderate sized town, with customers distributed all over. The descriptions are so arranged that his most difficult or sensitive customers are quite far away from each other and in the hands of the weaker members of his team. The town has a traffic problem. The participants receive a sketch map of the area with the customers located on it, together with a list of the equipment which each customer has and its potential problems. The participant is told that he is the manager of the territory and that, due to a cancelled customer visit, he now has a whole day available in which to help his team to the best of his ability. He is asked to plan his day to the maximum benefit of customers, team members, the company and himself.

Having spent some time working on the problem as individuals, the participants are then required to come to a consensus about the best solution. This division of activities can be made formal or left to the participants to manage as they see fit.

17 Real life exercise

A criticism that is sometimes levelled against simulations is that they are simulations. 'Of course, in the real world he would not tackle it like that at all.' In order to overcome this difficulty we have increasingly frequently made use of an obvious remedy, namely, to give the participants a real problem which is presently exercising the organization. The problem itself is best presented by a senior line manager not otherwise involved with the programme. He comes prepared to present the problem and to support it with sufficient facts and figures, but not too many as programmes can sometimes have rather a lot of exercises involving the reading of vast amounts of material before any action is possible. While this may itself be an accurate simulation of managerial reality it can take up more time than is available in a programme. After his presentation he is available for further relevant factual information, but the participants are told firmly that they should not expect him to volunteer information after his presentation, nor should they expect him to chair or take any further part in the discussion except by invitation and then minimally. The participants are finally told that, since this is a real problem, any solution which they arrive at and which looks workable will be seriously considered by whoever is actually responsible for solving it and that their solution may indeed be implemented.

It is a curious and possibly worrying phenomenon that this exercise has sometimes proved altogether too difficult for participants. Certainly it polarizes

117

groups and individuals very clearly. Either the participants get down to work quickly and produce workable ideas which are well targeted on the problem or they exhibit total lack of understanding and extreme avoidance behaviour. In one case this led to the conclusion that there was no management potential available in the group under observation. This harsh judgement was later shown by events to be accurate, if uncomfortable.

18 Relocation problem

The problem posed here is of a business about to diversify and requiring to relocate its head office and a number of subsidiary offices and plants in order to manage the diversification efficiently. The various conflicting requirements of the businesses into which the original organization is now to split are presented, as are the differing blandishments of a number of development areas. Government grants, EEC incentives, local labour market intelligence, the domestic arrangements of some senior managers and a number of other factors are listed. A framework for costing the various options is offered and the group has to agree how best to allocate the new functions to a limited number of the sites on offer. Since much of the firm's work is for export, for example, the availability of airports and docks has to be considered and taken into the calculation, together with the likelihood of labour disruption.

As a general comment on exercise construction it is perhaps worth mentioning that, as we have improved our ability to construct situations that echo closely the reality of the organizations with which we are working so we have been increasingly asked how we knew that such and such was being contemplated. While this is flattering as an indicator of the degree of precision with which our diagnosis enables us to focus the exercises, it can generate problems by being too close to the bone to be acceptable or by being changed too fast by changing reality. On balance, we would rather be close to reality, but it can lead to frequent redesign.

19 Psychological tests of personality and ability

This is a potentially explosive subject; some firms try to insist on them whether there seems to be a need or not, others regard them as unacceptable even when a suitable test is available off the peg. The reader should be warned that psychological testing is no place for the amateur and that a qualified psychologist should be consulted before embarking on testing. Even those tests which are relatively freely available need treating with caution if the results are to be fed back to participants. For further information on this subject the reader might consult Stewart and Stewart (1975), or Stewart (1974). These articles also contain warnings about the use of American validated tests on non-American participants.

Having uttered these warnings, we should perhaps indicate the tests which are most likely to be relevant, although detailed decisions cannot be taken until after the diagnostic stage. Frequently used tests of personality are the Eysenck Personality Inventory, which gives measures of extraversion-introversion and of normality-neuroticism; the 16PF inventory, which covers 16 personality factors and has been widely used as a general personality test; the Allport-Vernon-Lindzey Survey of Values, which does not address personality but the subject's interests – practical, theoretical, economic, aesthetic, religious and political. This last test has not been widely used, which is perhaps a pity as it is so obviously not a probing personality test that it might help calm people's fears about such tests. Eysenck has also devised various tests of simple dimensions such as conservatism-radicalism or toughmindedness-tendermindedness and readers might also be tempted to a perusal of the tests of Machiavellianism available in *Studies in Machiavellianism* (Christie and Geis, 1970) though no British norms exist for this test.

We would also like to mention the Myers-Briggs Type Indicator. Based rather unusually on Jungian hypotheses this instrument leads to quite clear statements about basic personality type and the likely consequences for behaviour in a variety of circumstances. We are particularly attracted by the range of behavioural examples given, many of which echo quite closely the behaviours which have emerged in our diagnoses of effective behaviour in several different organizations. Experience with Myers-Briggs is limited in the UK at the time of writing, but we look forward to working further with a questionnaire which demonstrates a number of promising features, together with a quite impressive track record in the United States.

There are tests of ability in common use, of which the most useful on an assessment programme would probably be the AH6 test of high intelligence, the Watson-Glaser Critical Thinking Appraisal, which tests logical thought, and many specific tests of technical abilities. The reader should probably beware of those tests which say 'Imagine you are a manager. Tell us how you would act if . . .' These tests run a strong risk of being unreliable, as people commonly report themselves in more favourable terms than are justified by their behaviour.

Psychological tests need to be validated before they can be regarded as giving useful information to the assessment programme; until this validation has been undertaken the results of the tests should probably be kept secret from the programme observers and maybe even from the client's own staff. We shall soon be in a position to observe the experience of the Americans, where Federal legislation is restricting the use of selection tests and other devices to those which have shown to be effective and valid in that particular firm; the American experience should teach us about quite a few pitfalls to avoid.

We would also like to draw attention to a publication issued jointly by the Runnymede Trust and the British Psychological Association, called *Discriminating Fairly: a guide to fair selection* (1980). While not going into great detail, this booklet does outline current thinking about fair discrimination and makes the valuable point that the object is not to avoid discriminating (that is, after all, the whole point of any selection or identification exercise) but to avoid discriminating on grounds that are not relevant to the proper performance of the task under review. There is also a useful short glossary of some of the more commonly encountered technical terms that occur in the technology of test construction and validation.

The bible of psychological tests is Buros's *Mental Measurements Yearbook* (1978) which lists all tests available to psychologists that are not restricted by commercial agreements, with validity data, references etc.

Though we have listed a number of exercises here, we should emphasize the need to be pragmatic (and not above plagiarism) in designing one's programme. There are many other exercises which we have in our library; and every time we have designed an assessment programme we have had to design at least one new exercise, so the above list is by no means exhaustive. When designing a new exercise, the clear requirement to have a specific set of objectives for that task should be at the back of one's mind. Which assessment factors should it address? How will the observers record these factors? What assessment factors shall be left out? It is not fruitful to design an exercise merely to 'put them through it' or because it made an impression on one earlier; the design must be approached with economy.

The reader will now have some idea of the breadth of exercises that are available to choose from when designing an assessment programme. We would suggest that the person designing his own programme should begin by drawing up his own matrix (like the one we show in table 16 on page 105) and constantly update it, using his own assessment factors and own assessment content. The choice of exercise then becomes simplified.

Before we discuss putting these exercises into a programme, we should examine the role of the observers in the exercises and the way the observer records are kept. There is a good deal of evidence to suggest that reliable observations are only made if the observers are given a schedule of things to look for; otherwise (as anyone who has attended a conventionl training course involving amateur, unbriefed observers will testify) the observers will remember the beginning, the end, any particularly boisterous spots and will find it easier to describe the faults of the participants than to describe their strengths. There is a good reason for this. A skilled performance always looks easy to the outsider and the observers must be given help in analysing the skills of the participants.

The following chapter describes in detail the way observers are trained.

However, in this chapter on programme design we must remember that we have not designed the exercises until we have also designed the observers' record sheets. Two examples will help illustrate the material we give the observers and are given on the immediately following pages and pages 135–138.

Leaderless group discussion

Instructions to participants

We are interested in finding out how well you can present your point of view on a problem under time pressure. Consequently we are asking you to present the case of a person who is being considered for promotion within X Y Z Ltd.

For this session we ask you to consider yourself as holding your present, real life position. You have been asked to nominate one person for the position of Public Relations Executive. Attached is a description of the person you have to nominate. Today you are meeting with some colleagues to decide who should be promoted from amongst the nominated candidates.

1 You will have 10 minutes in which to read the description of your candidate. You may take notes during this reading period. The description will then be removed and you will have five minutes in which to prepare your presentation. Your presentation should last up to three minutes. In it you should describe to the other participants your candidate for the post.

2 Your presentation should be so organized as to present as accurate and convincing a picture of your candidate as possible. Your associates should be made to believe that you know this person well and that they are well qualified for the job. To assist you in giving a truthful presentation, one other participant has for their information a copy of your candidate's details; and you have for your information a copy of the details given to another participant. During the presentations of each participant's candidate you may, of course, take notes.

3 After the presentations are made you will spend the remaining 45 minutes discussing the qualifications of each candidate. The purpose of this discussion is two-fold:

to do the best you can for your candidate

to help to select the best candidate for the position.

Since there will be other openings you will also rank each candidate in order of promotability, ie the number one person promoted now, the number two person next and so on.

Joyce Carroll has been with X Y Z for 10 years; she worked as a secretary and realized that her talents were being under-used. She took an Open University degree and moved to the training function.

Joyce is enthusiastic and hard-working, with an infectious cheerfulness which contributes to her popularity at all levels within XYZ. She has met most people during training courses and her services are often sought for unofficial advice and counselling. She also knows most of the lower level jobs in the company backwards and for that reason she is a fair but firm taskmaster. People cannot pull the wool over her eyes, nor say that she doesn't know what she's talking about, because the chances are that she has done their job at some point and knows all the finer details.

She is a good developer of people, taking her view that it is a manager's job to shield his or her people from above and to keep them free of silly requests so that they can be free to do their jobs and expand their responsibilities. She is a critical consumer of training courses, making a point of debriefing her people on their return from a training course and getting them to tell the rest of the group about the course at the next management meeting. She is an excellent trainer and her presentations in her own field of management development are regarded as the best in the business.

Where Joyce falls down is in administration. She seems to prefer the company as she knew it in the old days, when everybody knew each other and if you wanted to fix something then you could do it face to face with a quick meeting. She has little patience with formal reporting systems that seem to her to prolong the business of taking decisions.

Joyce is happily married to a senior police officer and they have two young children.

Leaderless group discussion

Fault sheet

A	Tommy Allan's fault:	confidential information leak
B	David Burton's fault:	slow to recognize and correct mistakes
C	Joyce Carroll's fault:	weak in administrative systems
D	Bill Drury's fault:	too many outside interests
E	Mary Eldon's fault:	prefers clear problems with definite solutions
F	Jeremy French's fault:	carelessness through emotional strain of domestic difficulties

Leaderless group discussion

Evaluation report guide

To assist you in the evaluation of participants in the Leaderless group discussion exercise, and to indicate the type of report that has been developed in the past, the following typical reports are presented.

1 Observation of Mr X

Mr X gave a good, but rountine, friendly presentation. Although direct and forceful he did not seem to make much impact on his associates, and ran out of steam at the end of his presentation. During the discussion he did not seem to have much to offer, and though he made various attempts to influence the group, he was not too effective. At one point he stood up and walked about as he talked, but again he ran out of things to say and others stepped in and took over. He simply was unable to hold the ball more than a moment when someone else would take it from him. He seemed to be under slight tension in this exercise, rubbing his lips, pulling his nose and grimacing on occasion. His presentation was marked by many short pauses, and 'ah's', etc, as he felt for ideas. In general, low average performance.

2 Observation of Mr Y

Y's three minute talk was very good, concise, well organized, well delivered. Seemed to seek leadership after hanging back for about 10 minutes, but he never held it for long. Operated from the easel occasionally in his selling efforts. Aggressiveness. His sales approach was more dogged than skilful.

Y sought allies occasionally, though no alliances formed. No loss of control – displayed frustration now and then. Seemed to retreat from the situation by complaining about its lack of realism. When challenged on his failure to disclose his man's weakness he attempted to pass it off as a qualified asset, not too successfully.

3 Observation of Mr Z

Mr Z makes a positive and forceful presentation, with good logic. He could have done a better job of defining what was needed and then showing how his man satisfied those needs. He was very honest, almost to a fault. The more he talked, the more his man's minor fault got out of perspective. Mr Z appeared to have self-confidence and confidence in his man. He was active in trying to steer the group towards a consensus and was generally listened to when he spoke.

Mr Z stayed calm during the exercise. He could have done a better job of pushing his man. He was almost too objective at times, sacrificing his own man to secure an agreement. Kept hammering at 'objective measurements' without relating them to his man. In general, even though his man finished last, Z did a reasonably good job.

Leaderless group discussion – oral presentation rating form

Observer: _____

Rating

Instructions: On the basis of your observations of the oral presentations, rate each participant on the quality of his performance. Any comments concerning the content of a particular presentation should be written on the evaluation sheet for this exercise.

This rating should be based on the effectiveness of his presentation. Was it well organized? Does he speak clearly? Is he verbally fluent? Is his vocabulary adequate? Does he speak forcefully?

	A	B	C	D	E	F	G	H
An excellent presentation of his candidate	—	—	—	—	—	—	—	—
A good presentation of his candidate	—	—	—	—	—	—	—	—
A fair presentation of his candidate	—	—	—	—	—	—	—	—
A poor presentation of his candidate	—	—	—	—	—	—	—	—
Completely failed in his attempt to present his candidate	—	—	—	—	—	—	—	—

Ranking

Write in the appropriate letters

Best	1	-----------
	2	-----------
	3	-----------
	4	-----------
	5	-----------
	6	-----------
	7	-----------
Poorest	8	-----------

Leaderless group discussion – observer evaluation form

Participant: _____   Observer: _____

Observe and rate these   Use this scale in your rating
assessment factors

_____ Organization/strategy/control   1 – Outstanding standard
                                                2 – Above standard
_____ Stable/stress resistant   3 – Adequate or satisfactory
                                                   standard
_____ Gets on with the job   4 – Slightly below standard
                                                5 – Definitely below standard
_____ Bright/penetrating

_____ Company/business conscious

_____ Oral/written skills

_____ Interactive skills/team man

_____ Social skills   OVERALL EVALUATION _____

Please write a one sentence summary of the participant's performance on each assessment factor.

Organization/strategy/control: _____

_____

Stable/stress resistant. _____

_____

Gets on with the job: _____

_____

Bright/penetrating: _____

_____

Company/business conscious: _____

_____

Oral/written skills: _____

_____

Interactive skills/team man: _____

_____

Social skills: _____

_____

Please write a comprehensive summary of this participant's performance in this exercise tying together the above points into a narrative. Be sure to elaborate on any area rated 1 – Outstanding, or 5 – Definitely below standard.

Leaderless group discussion – overall rating and ranking form

Observer: _____

Overall rating

To what extent did he contribute to the success of the group?
Mark only one space under each letter. More than one person may have the same rating.

	A	B	C	D	E	F	G	H
Very effective A definite leader	–	–	–	–	–	–	–	–
Above average performance Definite influence on others	–	–	–	–	–	–	–	–
Average effectiveness Satisfactory performance	–	–	–	–	–	–	–	–
Relatively ineffective Little influence on others	–	–	–	–	–	–	–	–
Ineffective, practically no participation	–	–	–	–	–	–	–	–

Overall ranking

In the space provided below, rank the group members on their overall contributions to the success of the group. Select the best performer first and record his letter. Then select the second best performer and record his letter. Then select the next best performer, etc. Do not assign the same rank to two or more participants. Include all members of the group.

Write in the appropriate letters

Best	1	-----------
	2	-----------
	3	-----------
	4	-----------
	5	-----------
	6	-----------
	7	-----------
Poorest	8	-----------

On the previous pages we quote part of the package given to the observers who are observing the leaderless group exercise (in this case designed for a firm giving financial advice). The participants each receive the instructions (page 122), a sheet giving the description of their supposed candidate (page 123), and a further sheet similar to page 123 containing the description of the supposed candidate supplied to one of the other participants. This tactic is designed to prevent too much evasion or inaccuracy on the part of the presenting participant. It has not been unknown for adventurous participants to embellish their candidate's descriptions or to omit to mention the weaker parts of their candidate's profile. If participants know that one other participant has a copy of the description of their candidate, then opportunities for this kind of manoeuvre are more restricted. The observers receive all candidate descriptions and a further five pages. Page 124 summarizes the faults built in to each candidate description. Page 125 gives some examples of performance summaries that other observers have produced on this type of exercise to illustrate the kind of short summary that is required. On page 126 each observer rates the performance of each participant on his oral presentation of his candidate only. Since these presentations are made in sequence it is possible for each observer to rate all participants' performance on this stage of the exercise. On page 127 the observers record their detailed observations of the behaviour of the particular participant whom they are observing during the group discussion and record their preliminary evaluation of the participant's performance. On page 128 the observers record their rating of the performance of all participants during the group discussion. These ratings form the basis of the quick reliability checks referred to in the following chapter on observer training. All these forms should be completed immediately after the end of each exercise.

Close study of the observer rating forms will give the reader an insight into how they are designed. Each set of rating forms is unique to its exercise, concentrating only on the assessment factors appropriate to that exercise. This could mean that observers are briefed to look at only one or two factors but this is quite acceptable. They are asked to make judgements in two different forms; by rating and by narrative. It is not sensible to ask for ratings on a scale greater than five points; seven points is the maximum discrimination the average adult can make, and given a seven point scale many people treat it as a five point and ignore the lower range. We prefer to use a five point scale and to persuade people to use all the scale.

Narrative summaries put flesh on the bones of a numerical rating, and a good narrative summary will not merely rephrase the rating (very good . . . poor . . . below standard . . . splendid) but will describe in detail what happened and what the person did. These rating forms are designed to get the observer to concentrate on reporting what happened and to refrain from making an overall evaluation of the candidate until the very last. Even the final page of the observers' rating sheets offers little encouragement to making general evaluative comments; the observers' job during the programme is to record in detail what goes on, and only after the participants have ceased taking part in assessment exercises are the observers asked to turn their observations into evaluations.

Book review

Instructions

Will you please take the next two hours (less any time required for other tasks) to review the accompanying book *The Hazards of Work*. You are to pay particular attention to any points which you think are of interest to the Company in general or to your own position in particular. The book is commercially available.

Please be sure to write your name on the review.

Book review – observer guide

Not all the assessment factors are relevant to the evaluation of the Book review. Some guidance is given below on the interpretation of the factors which are relevant.

Coping with stress: How does he react to the pressure of too much material to absorb? Does he do too much or too little? If he is interrupted how well and how quickly does he get over it?

Decision-making: Does he assign priorities to the material presented, or does he start at page 1 and work on through? When pointing out the relevance of the book to the company and to his own job, does he distinguish clearly between things that are within his (or the company's) control and things that are not? When reading the polemics in the book, does he distinguish or attempt to distinguish between fact and opinion?

Large scale operations: does he concentrate on the detailed information in the book at the expense of regarding the large-scale implications of its content? Does he examine the implications of such a book being published – the next likely steps, both generally and in the company?

Technical competence: Does he absorb the technical information rapidly and accurately? Can he correct any misunderstandings or distortions in the reporting and can he separate his dislikes (if any) of the political bias of the book from any valid technical points it may contain? Is his assessment of the implications for the company valid? If he puts forward any specific proposals, are they clear and concise?

Communications: Is his writing clear, grammatical, well set out and properly spelled? Does he clearly indicate when he is quoting? Does he indicate how much of the book he has covered in the review?

Company policy and PR: Is he aware of the implications for the company (from the industrial relations viewpoint and the viewpoint of the general public) if this book were to be misused or distorted? If there are any exposures, has he indicated how these could be dealt with? Has he indicated any special strengths the company has to deal with the misuse of this book? Is his general approach constructive and concerned, or defensive and rejecting?

Book review – observer evaluation form

Participant: .... Observer: ....

Please assign a rating to each of the following assessment factors:

	1 Out- standing	2 Above standard	3 Meets standards	4 Below standard	5 Very poor
Coping with stress:	....	....	....	....	....
Decision-making:	....	....	....	....	....
Large scale operations:	....	....	....	....	....
Technical competence:	....	....	....	....	....
Communications:	....	....	....	....	....
Company policy and PR:	....	....	....	....	....
OVERALL EVALUATION:	....				

Will you now please write a one paragraph summary in narrative form of the participant's performance, using the space below.

In contrast to the previous example, this second excerpt from a typical observer manual shows the guidance given to observers when the task is an individual one. While the participants are actually doing the task which is here reviewing a book, the observers will be engaged in another activity; they might be filling in their reports of the previous exercise or checking the internal consistency of their observations. They will not actually see the participants at work and supervision of the participants and attention to their queries may be left to the programme manager or his assistant. When the reviews are handed in, the observers will fill in the rating form, assigning a rating to each participant on the basis of the assessment factors which are relevant to the task. Some of these assessment factors are intrinsic to the job in hand – coping with stress, for example, and the clarity of the man's communications. (The participants experience one interruption each while they are doing this task in this particular programme.) Some of the other factors are determined by the content of the book to be reviewed – this was a book about safety and health at work, with direct implications for the jobs the participants were doing, and so it was appropriate to assess their technical competence, their attention to the company's relations with the outside world, and their ability to take the 'helicopter effect' view and see the implications on a broad scale within the company.

It is useful to give the observers each a looseleaf folder with the paperwork for the whole programme in order within. We usually staple the individual exercises together and have each exercise printed on different coloured paper. This helps when collecting the papers relating to particular exercises. In front of each exercise set it is useful to give a contents listing of the material; the observers will be working hard and anything that minimizes time spent searching will be welcome.

It is necessary to pilot each exercise if this is one's first assessment programme and it may be wise to pilot the exercises separately and then go on to pilot the programme. Should the reader design his own exercises and set about piloting them, we suggest that he also pilot the observers' contribution at the same time, paying attention to the clarity of instructions to the observers and also to the time it takes them to fill in forms etc.

The following chapter discusses in detail the training of the observers and also our experience of administrative requirements etc to get the programme running smoothly. But the design of the actual programme must be discussed first. Opposite we show a programme designed for six to eight participants, with four to six observers, taking just over two days spread over one afternoon, a full day, and a morning and part afternoon. We selected this as an example because it illustrates some of the constraints one meets when designing these events; the observers were very senior managers indeed, whom it was not possible to spare for longer than two and a half days and this programme leaves little breathing space and some work to be done back at the office.

The principle of design is that after observing each group exercise the observers must immediately be able to record their observations. Thus we start with the leaderless group discussion: this group exercise requires no preparation beforehand, so it is an ideal starter. After tea the participants work as individuals while the observers are completing their records, and then collating their observations, doing reliability checks if appropriate and generally making sure that things look as if they will run smoothly. It is important to allow the observers plenty of time here to address any potential problems (people not agreeing in their ratings, for example) and the programme manager will probably stay with the observers during this time to make sure that potential problems are nipped in the bud. So although they are supposed to stop work at 17 30 according to the programme, they could well run on. The participants must stop work at 17 30 sharp and they should be encouraged to do something other than have an early postmortem themselves. After dinner the observers are busy marking the in-trays, one or two to each observer; the participants meanwhile are busy with the individual consultancy exercise. First thing the following day the participants carry on with their preparations for the consultancy exercise and are also taken away for part of the time for an interview, with the observer who marked it,

132

Overall programme – Assessment of 6 to 8 participants

DAY ONE		**DAY TWO**		**DAY THREE**	
Participants	*Observers*	*Participants*	*Observers*	*Participants*	*Observers*
1400–1540 Leaderless discussion (promotees)	1400–1540 Observe leaderless discussion	0900–1050 Preparing consultancy reports and having interviews	0900–1030 Conducting interviews	0900–1020 Group consultancy exercise – part II	0900–1020 Observe group consultancy exercise
1230 LUNCH	1400	1030 COFFEE	1050	1020 COFFEE	1040
1540 TEA	1600	1050–1250 Negotiation exercise	1050–1250 Observing negotiation exercise	1040–1140 Listening exercise	1040–1140 Observe listening exercise
1600–1730 in-tray exercise	1600–1730 Collate and check observations	1250 LUNCH	1400	1140–1245 Individual assessments of own and others' performance	1140–1245 Collating observations
1730 DINNER	2000	1400–1530 Individual consultancy presentations and performing book review task	Observing the consultancy presentations	1245 LUNCH	1400
2000–2130 Preparation of individual consultancy exercise	2000–2130 Mark in-trays	1530 TEA	1550	1400–end Individual interviews and finishing rating and reaction sheets	1400–1730 Individual interviews and collating results etc.
		1550–1700 Ajax task force	1550–1700 Observe task force		
		1700–1810 Writing work Environment report	1700–1810 Collating the day's observations		
		1810 DINNER	2000		
		2000–2130 Just a minute	2000–2130 Observe just a minute		

about the in-tray exercise. Observers are given firm guidelines about how to conduct these interviews and how to record the participants' reactions in the interview.

The programme continues along these lines, mixing group tasks with individual assignments, until the middle of the final morning. The observers then have to work very hard collating their observations about the programme as a whole to give them sufficient information to plan to interview the participants in the afternoon. While they are thus engaged, the participants are filling in self-assessment forms and forms on which they assess each others' performance. The purpose of this activity is twofold; first, in this organization the ability to assess one's performance accurately is indicative of managerial effectiveness, so we are asking them to assess their own performance to see how well they agree with the observer ratings; secondly, there is evidence (Kraut, 1975) to suggest that the ratings of one's peers are a good predictor of future success and we wish to test this prediction. So while participants' assessment of their own performance is material for the assessment overall, their assessments of each other are being obtained for research purposes only and will not be shown to the observers.

After lunch on the third day, the observers split up and each interviews a candidate, getting the candidate's first impressions of the programme, his performance and any questions he might have. In this particular programme, the interview here must be supplemented by a longer counselling interview when the people concerned have gone back to their jobs, with the proviso that the longer interview must take place before a fortnight has elapsed. It would be preferable to give the observers more time to collate their observations and recommendations, and to give the participants a full interview at the end of the programme, but time does not permit it in this programme. However, before the observers leave, they must have agreed their final evaluations of each candidate and settled any other outstanding matters. We now give an example of a final evaluation sheet such as the observers are typically asked to fill in about each participant.

Management Assessment Programme

Final evaluation

Participant: ....

Date: ....

Final evaluation – exercises

Participant: .... Observer: ....

Please write a one sentence summary of the person's performance on each exercise.

Exercise	*Rating (1–5)*
Leaderless:..	
....	....
In-tray:...	
....	....
Negotiation exercise:	
....	....
Consultancy exercise part I:	
....	....
Consultancy exercise part II:	
....	....
Listening exercise:..	
....	....
Task force:	
....	....
Work environment report:	
....	....
Just a minute:	
....	....
Assessment of own performance:	
....	No rating
Assessment of other's performance:...............................	
....	No rating
Response to in-tray interview:.......................................	
....	No rating
Response to individual interview:..................................	
....	No rating

Final evaluation – assessment factors

Participant: .... Observer: ....

Please write a one sentence summary of the person's performance on each assessment factor.

Assessment factor	Rating (1–5)

Self-assessment: ....

....

Coping with stress: ....

....

Concern for improvement: ....

....

Decision-making: ....

....

Preference for quality: ....

....

Large scale operations: ....

....

Absence of self regard: ....

....

Technical competence: ....

....

Delegation: ....

....

Training his staff: ....

....

Personal relations: ....

....

Social skill: ....

....

Communications: ....

....

Group behaviour: ....

....

Final evaluation – overall comments

Participant: ....   Observer: ....

I believe that the highest position that this person is likely to attain in the company is:

His next position should be:

Within what period of time?

_____

You should spend the next five to 10 minutes listing the participant's:

1 *Strong points:*

2 *Weaker points:*

3 *Recommendations:*

Summarizing the principles of programme design, they consist of planning parallel activities for participants and observers so that all are busy, with careful balancing of individual and group activities. Give plenty of time in the early stages for meeting difficulties before they grow, a little light relief in the evenings if possible and with time allowed for final discussions between the observers and for interviews with the participants.

What form should the interviews take? This is partly dictated by the people concerned but there are some fairly reliable golden rules:

1 the interview should not contain any promise of a job. Circumstances may prevent this promise being fulfilled and, if the rumour is allowed to develop that the assessment programmes are directly linked to the candidates' promotion, unhealthy competition is likely to develop

2 the best strategy for any interview is to begin with 'You tell *me* how you feel about your performance' or some similar form of words. The advantages are obvious: it gets the participant talking, it ensures that the participant does not have to begin by arguing against the interviewer's stated assessment of him and in instances where people have not performed well they usually are aware of this and will spare the interviewer embarrassment by giving an honest evaluation of themselves

3 the interviewer should not be trapped into justifying the design of the programme or the assessment factors. There should be no need for him to be on the defensive: the programme is based on thorough research, the interviewer's strategy has been settled by discussion and agreement with the other observers. He should be on safe ground and should not need to defend himself, although he must be prepared to back up any evaluations with the appropriate evidence

4 the interviewer should be prepared to deal with the occasional person who, having completed the assessment programme says, in effect, 'If that's what management is about then I don't want to know, thank you.' This sometimes happens with professionals, specialists and salesmen, who might think that the only way to achieve promotion is up the management ladder and get a glimpse of the management job for the first time on the assessment programme. If a number of people show this reaction, it may be worth the organization's while to investigate the whole area of professional career paths (*see* Stewart and Stewart (1974) for a discussion on the management of specialists and professional staff). If, as happened to one of our clients, one highly-valued participant who had been tipped for very senior management decides that he does not want promotion and would rather gather seniority in a non-managerial job, an imaginative one-off solution is called for, to meet the man's unique needs

5 the interviewer should be thoroughly conversant with what will happen to the actual evaluation forms, the procedures to be followed in reporting back to the participant's manager (if at all) and so on, so that he can meet any such questions easily

6 the interview should concentrate on that participant's performance. Comparisons with other participants, or comments on them, should be discouraged

7 the interview should either involve the production of a development plan for the participant to increase his skills in areas where he is deficient, or should prepare the ground for the participant and his manager to draw up a development plan when he gets back to work. The plan should include measures of success and failure and a procedure for reviewing progress at regular intervals. Whether the plan is prepared during the feedback interview or later is a matter for the 'culture' of the firm concerned.

We set out in this chapter to share our experiences in designing an assessment programme and we should stress that this is very much a personal viewpoint; we are constantly learning and changing our approach and other people may find that different methods work for them. Our constant concern is always to tailor the programme to the specific needs of the firm concerned and, while the purpose of this book is partly to encourage plagiarism in our readers, may we suggest that you start plagiarizing at the very beginning, drawing up your own matrix of tasks x assessment factors and carrying on from there; and please do not be despondent if the design is not right first time; the very best of servomechanisms requires two corrections before it stays on target and those standards are quite high enough.

Chapter 6

Observer training, administration and accommodation

We have emphasized the need to have the observers carefully briefed and trained: we take it as an axiom that observers must be trained to certain high standards of reliability and consistency before taking part in a live assessment programme. It does not seem fair to the participants to have anything other than the highest standards of skill in the people making the observations.

The topic of observer training is one that has concerned social psychologists for decades. The protagonist of one of the first systems for analysing group behaviour, Bales (1950), derived a multi-category system and claimed that training observers to use this system might take as long as six months. Other methods have been tried but perhaps the most striking is that reported by Rackham, Honey and Colbert (1971), and Rackham and Morgan (1977), in which they describe the use of simple job related analysis schemes containing no more than a dozen or so categories which they used on training courses, giving feedback to participants based on their regular reviewing of the observations made. One of us was involved with Rackham's early work, including the training of observers to use these behaviour analysis categories, and with simple category systems it was possible to train most willing people to high standards of reliability in observing. We therefore design observer training programmes to take one or two days, with the possibility of later refresher courses, and our record shows that only one in 20 trainees fails to meet the required high standards after training.

Let us go through a typical two day training programme for novice observers (senior line managers) in a firm where assessment programmes have never been run before.

The first necessity is to familiarize the observers with the history and background of the work leading to assessment programmes in their own organizations and to acquaint them with the basic skills which they will need to exercise. They then need to become familiar with their programme so that mere administration will not distract them when they are working in a real event. Finally, they will learn how to collect and interpret all the information at the end of the programme and how to conduct the different kinds of interview in which they will become involved.

In the initial presentation they will hear something of the history and development of assessment programmes, both overseas and in the UK. The observers need to know where the programmes come from, who uses them and whether they appear to work for other people. It is important to stress, within UK companies, that industrial assessment programmes differ from the WOSB and CSSB selection procedures in a number of ways, chiefly, with the factors observed and the provision of detailed feedback on results with consequent individual action planning. In fact, such has been the emphasis on this follow up in most of the UK organizations with whom we have worked that they have offered to change the name of the programme from Assessment Programme to Individual Development Programme, which they feel more accurately describes the activity they are undertaking. We entirely support this change.

The next step is to present the method by which their particular programme was designed, showing the results of the diagnosis and how they were arrived at, the people who were interviewed, possibly the statistical basis of the analysis and the arrangements which have been made for the validation of the present programme. One must be specific about the level and type of management potential which the programme has been designed to assess and the uniqueness of the programme to this particular firm should also be emphasized.

The third step introduces a detailed discussion of the assessment factors which are being looked for *on this programme*, with reference also to any assessment factors which the programme cannot help to identify but which are being sought elsewhere. This emphasizes that the programme is only adding to current information and management practice, not substituting for it. Each of the assessment factors should be discussed in terms of the individual behaviours which go to make it up and the observers are encouraged not to opt for the shorthand single word names of the assessment factors which are bound to be less precise. If the observers are very senior it may also be advisable to seek a final interrogation of the factors to make sure that they really are representative of what the organization feels it should be looking for in the future. This may extend the early part of the observer training somewhat but our experience is that the time is well spent. It can be disastrous if managers decide that the factors are not quite right after, or worse still during, a programme. In addition, the fact that the observing managers have been actively involved in the formulation of the final

142

list of assessment factors is likely to induce a greater commitment to the whole programme.

The fourth step is to introduce the observers to the discipline of observation. They are given some general information about common pitfalls of live observation, but this is quickly followed by some simple, practical advice. We introduce the mnemonic ORCEF. This mnemonic gives observers a sequence in which to do their work and they report that, while the job is never easy, following this sequence does help a good deal. This sequence is set out below:

ORCEF

O – *Observe*   Do nothing else. Look and listen. That is all.

R – *Record*   Write down what you have seen and heard. It is not possible to look, listen *and* write. It *is* possible to switch rapidly from observing to recording and back again. The recording is done on a piece of A4 paper, divided as in the illustration on page 144. In most programmes the observer has special responsibility for observing two named individuals in any one exercise and for keeping a general eye on the remaining participants so that he has some context in to which to fit his primary observations. For this reason we have found that it is helpful if the A4 paper is turned sideways and three columns made. These columns are made up with one wide one at each side of the paper for each of the observer's primary participants and a narrower central column for brief notes about what the rest are doing. It can be especially helpful if a record is made of the fact that one of the other participants has reacted to something that one of the primary participants has said. This is indicated in the example by an arrow. It is also helpful to keep a note of the progress of time on the record. This is easily achieved by drawing a line across the page after every 10 minutes of the exercise.

C – *Classify*   Categorize your observations according to the list of assessment factors. This happens after the exercise is over. There is no time during the exercise to do more than observe and record. After the participants have moved on to their next activity the observer goes through his raw record, putting by each observation the number of the assessment factor of which he believes it to be an example. Next, he transfers and organizes this raw record on to the prepared record form (illustrated previously on page 127). At this stage he can begin the first part of the next activity.

E – *Evaluate*   The observer can now, and only now, begin to make some value judgements about what he has seen. His first task is to make as accurate and complete a record as possible of what his participants are doing. Only on the

143

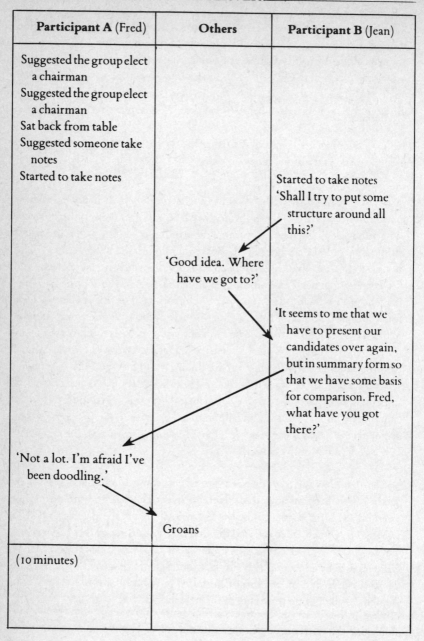

Participant A (Fred)	**Others**	**Participant B** (Jean)
Suggested the group elect a chairman Suggested the group elect a chairman Sat back from table Suggested someone take notes Started to take notes		Started to take notes 'Shall I try to put some structure around all this?' 'Good idea. Where have we got to?' 'It seems to me that we have to present our candidates over again, but in summary form so that we have some basis for comparison. Fred, what have you got there?' 'Not a lot. I'm afraid I've been doodling.' Groans
(10 minutes)		

basis of this record can he begin to evaluate their behaviour. Many of the difficulties experienced by observers spring from attempts to observe, record, classify and evaluate simultaneously. We do not believe this to be possible. Most observers react well to the discipline of doing one thing at a time once they have seen what it is that has to be done.

F – *Feedback* This is given after the programme has been completed and all the observations have been discussed and challenged during the Observer Conference.

Whenever the observer transfers a statement to the formal record form he is encouraged to ask himself one question: 'How do I know that?' If the answer is: 'Because that is what the participant did', then that is probably a good observation. If the answer is: 'Because he did such and such, from which I deduced that . . .' the observation is a poor one. It is the primary behaviour that should be recorded, and the combination of the raw A4 record and the formal record form should enable the observer to track down exactly the event from which an evaluative comment is drawn.

In addition to all the foregoing, the observers are encouraged to make simple reliability checks with each other. This is done by means of the Overall Rating and Ranking Form illustrated on page 128. The easiest way of proceeding is probably to display on a flip chart all the ratings and rankings given by all the observers and then to probe discrepancies. As a rough guide, we usually recommend that it is not necessary to worry if two observers have ratings that are the same or next to each other. If there is a larger difference, then the observers should discuss the raw evidence upon which their rankings or ratings have been based. For example, if observer A has ranked Bill Bloggs 2, and observer B has ranked him 3, then there is no need for concern. If observer A has ranked Bloggs 2, but observer B has ranked him 4 or lower, then they should probe the basis on which their respective judgements rest. The objective of this process is not necessarily to achieve uniformity among the observers. If the difference is due simply to an administrative error (the use of an incorrect form, for example) then one would expect the erring observer to change his position. If, on the other hand, observer A has seen a number of behaviours which observer B has not seen, then the positions should not change. This is something which can be argued out at the Observer Conference at the end of the programme. Similarly, if the evidence upon which the judgements rest is very nearly identical, then one is looking at a genuine difference of interpretation and this can also be left for resolution at the Observer Conference. The point of the reliability checks is to establish that the *procedures* are being followed correctly and that the reason for any differences of view is well understood and can be backed up by hard evidence.

If observers are finding real difficulty with the process outlined there is a further stage which can be introduced. They are shown a sample Behaviour Analysis form, such as the one illustrated on page 147, and encouraged to use it in recording people's behaviour in some simple group situations. Half the observers might engage in a short group discussion, with the other half recording their behaviour on the analysis form using a simple tally mark for each contribution; then the observers would change places and the discussion group be repeated. Using very short discussion groups (10 minutes maximum) the observers learn to concentrate on observing to a schedule, begin to understand how to keep records and follow what goes on, and above all learn to concentrate on recording the participants' behaviour and *not* their own feelings about the reactions to the participant.

As well as observing themselves in groups, the trainee observers are given one or two transcripts of group discussions to analyse using the behaviour analysis forms, working in groups so that they have plenty of chance to discuss the meaning of each category. When they are familiar with the analysis categories and used to working with them, they may be given one or two prefacing games to increase their skills. The prefacing game consists of a small discussion group where there is a rule that nothing shall be said without the speaker first prefacing it by stating into which behaviour analysis category it falls. This is a remarkably effective way of teaching people to analyse group behaviour and it is usually also highly enjoyable.

It should be pointed out, however, that taking the Behaviour Analysis route to observer training does, in our experience, take a good deal longer than the procedure which we outlined earlier in this chapter. With some regret, because it is a powerful and elegant technique, we recommend its use only if real difficulty is being experienced. The major problem lies in transferring the Behaviour Analysis skills on to the organization's assessment factors, which could be regarded as conglomerate behaviour categories. One attempt to solve the problem involved breaking down the assessment factors into their component discrete behaviours and listing those behaviours on a large Behaviour Analysis record form. It was very large, involving, as it did 168 different behaviours. It is, of course, unusable albeit a valiant attempt. If observers are experiencing that much difficulty it is worth asking what else might be wrong. Possibly some step in the sequence of development of the programme has been skipped, leading to confusion or lack of commitment; possibly the observers are not as able as had been thought. In either event, observer training is unlikely to solve the problem. For a very thorough exposition of various approaches to observer training we would recommend the account in Moses and Byham (1977).

The remainder of the time available (the bulk of it in fact) is spent in putting

146

OBSERVER: **EXERCISE:**

Names / Behaviour categories							Σ
Supporting							
Disagreeing							
Building							
Criticizing							
Bringing in							
Shutting out							
Innovating							
Solidifying							
Admitting difficulties							
Defending/attacking							
Giving information							
Seeking information							
Other							
Σ							

the observers through the exercises as participants. This gives them knowledge of the content of the exercises more rapidly and more thoroughly than any other method we know. It also generates behaviour of the kind they are likely to encounter so that their colleague observers can take the opportunity to practise their skills and check the results. This process also permits detailed changes and additions to exercise design to take place to increase their credibility to the participants, to avoid unnecessary errors, and to help to obtain commitment to the whole programme on the part of the observers. They find it much easier to believe in a programme which they have themselves, in part, designed.

With a group of well motivated managers it is likely that by this stage they will have escaped most of the pitfalls that await the amateur observer and the emphasis on uniformity can relax a little to allow the particular strengths and weaknesses of the observers to come through. Some people may be particularly good at reading 'body language', for instance, or others at keeping track of five arguments at a time; once they have acquired the routine behaviour analysis skills, it can be fruitful to allow for their special contributions.

The remainder of the time is spent discussing the interviews which the observers will have to give, one at the end and maybe one about the in-tray exercise. By this time they will probably be in a position to anticipate themselves what the requirements of the interviews will be and to discuss the best strategies to adopt. Guidelines to good interviewing practice are given at the end of the previous chapter on page 139.

The day concludes with a discussion of any unresolved questions and the participants depart with a manual of reading matter for further study. This will include the programme design, sample record forms, summary of the assessment factors, guidelines for observing, some behaviour analysis forms and a transcript for further practice, some examples of completed observer rating forms (good and bad examples), guidelines on interviewing, career counselling and perhaps the company appraisal system or manpower planning system.

What are the potential problems and difficulties in training observers? We can list several below, most of which are easier to prevent than cure:

1 Observers are not committed to the idea of the programme

The beginning of an observer training programme is no place to discover that one or more of the observers have yet to be convinced that assessment programmes are a good idea. If such an unconvinced manager decides to hold up the proceedings until he *is* convinced, deadlock can result, because it will in all likelihood be difficult to sell him the idea at such a late stage and in the midst of a perhaps similarly ill prepared group. We drew attention to the need to get agreement and full discussion of the results of the diagnostic stage before going on to programme design and a similar effort to get people's feelings and to ask for their commitment is necessary before asking them to become observers. The job of getting commitment is much better suited to the firm's manager responsible for the programme than to an outsider, though the outsider can help. We have once been put in the position of starting observer training with an uncommitted group; it was not possible to achieve the training objectives and we had to delay the implementation of the programme until the dust had settled.

2 Observers show consistent but inadequate reliability

Sometimes an observer will show agreement with the others at about the 60 per cent level, not completely inaccurate but not good enough for a task where people's futures may be at stake. Every time this has happened to us the 'culprit' has been someone who has already had some experience of group behaviour analysis but has not enough flexibility to put his old habits behind him and meet the different needs of the new situation. One firm of our acquaintance, having taken to the Rackham-Honey-Colbert approach of using behaviour analysis on training courses, hired at great expense a social psychologist and an ex-Coverdale trainer, neither of whom lasted more than a month. They had learned one system of looking at groups and had not the breadth of experience to see that their system was only one from a number of possibles. We admit to being a little wary whenever we are told that a group of observers boasts amongst its membership 'someone who's done a lot of work with groups' just in case he has fixed ideas. In most cases, though, it is enough to explain to the person having difficulty that the observers' schedule for the assessment programme is examining only a small segment of people's behaviour (the behaviour that has been shown to be associated with managerial effectiveness) and that this requires a change of focus in someone who has till now been looking at a much broader spectrum of behaviour. This explanation usually suffices, and the trainee must be given help in discarding some of his usual analytical categories and pursuing others in greater depth.

3 Observers say they don't need an assessment programme to help them spot potential

If the groundwork in getting their commitment has been properly done, this objection should have arisen earlier and been coped with. Sometimes it comes up again on the training programme, though. The best way to deal with this statement is probably to arrange to test it, by the method described later in detail in the chapter on validity. This requires that before the assessment programme takes place the participants' managers, and the observers if appropriate, try to make assessment of their potential using all the management information that would normally be available to them. In programmes that we have designed, we hold these predictions until after the programme; we check to see what extra information the programme generates and whether it is different in

149

quality as well as quantity; we also compare, in due course, the long term predictive validity of the managers' ratings with the predictive validity of the ratings from the assessment programme.

4 Observers making allowances

In one of our early observer training programmes all the observers except one were in agreement – one pair agreeing 100 per cent. However, one man was showing a high negative correlation with his co-observers' ratings and it was obviously necessary to pursue this difficulty. We were running a mock assessment programme at the time, to give the observers practice and the maverick observer said of one of the participants: 'I know him well. I know this is how he's acting on the programme, but in real life I'm sure he wouldn't do that, I'm sure he would do such and such instead.' We discovered that in making his ratings he was not recording what he observed but had built in a correction factor according to how he thought the people would really carry on. So we had to convince him that it was necessary to record what he actually observed and to leave 'corrections' until later if at all. This problem of the observers making allowances is an extension of the well known 'halo effect' whereby a favourable rating given to a man on one characteristic can wash over into a general attitude of favourableness to all the man does; it is necessary to warn the observers against it and to structure the programme so that opportunities for it to arise are reduced by varying the participants assigned to each observer and discouraging the observers from making inferences about or evaluations of the behaviours they observe.

5 'Nobody from personnel can tell us senior managers how to train/observe/promote/judge potential'

Some senior managers in some firms are prone to making this sort of complaint, if the personnel department (which is probably in charge of the assessment programme) is held in low esteem. This can develop into a particularly sore point if, for example, someone's ratings are awry and he will not admit difficulties or enter into discussion about the difference between his ratings and his colleagues. The best remedy for this is probably to have the observer training conducted by, or shared with, an outsider. It helps to have a psychologist handy when discussing group behaviour and training to high standards; and we have to admit that sometimes our outside status as qualified consultants has enabled us to be listened to by people who would not have asked for or taken advice from the personnel department people with whom we shared the training programme.

6 'I can use these skills back at the job!'

Most certainly he can. This is one of the great spin off benefits from the assessment programme; very senior managers, whom it would probably have been impossible to interest in a training course in group behaviour, spend some time learning practical skills in following what is going on in a group discussion, a negotiation, a sales presentation and so on. They learn these skills to high standards and realize that there is nothing mysterious about them, just a few tricks of the trade and some habits to break. This realization, which usually comes to most participants as they learn behaviour analysis, adds to their enthusiasm and commitment.

So far we have indicated how the programme is designed and how the observers are trained. There are some further administrative points to be coped with before the programme is ready to run: what are the administrative and accommodation requirements necessary for a smooth performance?

What does the programme require in administrative support?

We have mentioned the role of the programme manager and sometimes the programme manager's assistant. This job should be examined in more detail. As we have usually conducted assessment programmes, one of us has taken the job of programme manager for the first one or two programmes, handing over the job to the firm's manager who has perhaps served as assistant. The task is partly one of co-ordinating observers' thoughts and evaluations, partly keeping the participants in step with the observers and both groups in step with the clock, and partly acting as antennae to detect any concerns anyone might have and take appropriate action. It is not an easy task and requires unflappability and over preparation.

If the reader consults the sample programme given on page 133 of the previous chapter, he will be able to follow through the job of the programme manager during this time. He will have arrived at the hotel earlier, getting any last minute preparations out of the way and everything will be ready by the time the observers and participants arrive. If there are speeches of welcome, he will have to make them; one or two people will almost certainly buttonhole him over lunch to confide secret fears, or to say that it's quite safe to let him into the secret, or to ask where the microphone is or to say that he will have to leave at lunchtime tomorrow. He must act diplomatically to get everyone ready to start work after lunch.

At 14 00 hours he gives out the leaderless group discussion papers, one to each participant, and times them in reading their briefs; he takes their papers away from them, ushers them to the conference table and instructs them to begin discussion. Then he hovers round the observers, checking that no one has got hopelessly lost. If the participants ask him questions, other than administrative questions, he must not answer.

At 15 40 he calls a halt to the discussion and sends the participants off to tea, joining the observers to make sure that each is filling in his rating forms correctly. As soon as an observer has completed the set of rating forms relating to that exercise, he must hand them to the programme manager: there must be no opportunity for correction in the light of rationalization. The programme manager starts the participants off on their in-tray exercise and quickly gets photocopies made of the rating forms collected in the leaderless exercise. One copy of the ratings is stored safely away; then he works with the observers to check and collate their observations, do reliability checks if appropriate, discuss any potential problems he sees looming up and probably steering the observers away from the strong temptation to make premature judgements of the participants. If he has no assistant (unwise for a first programme) he will periodically check the in-tray workers and will call a halt to their efforts at 17 30 hours, spending some time with them easing their tensions and directing them towards some relaxing activity before, perhaps, rejoining the observers.

He will put the paperwork in order before dinner, collecting each participant's in-tray and putting it into a named file.

After dinner (where again he should be on the alert for people's concerns) he starts the participants off on the individual consultancy exercises and then gives each observer one or two in-trays to mark. He divides his time between the two groups, taking questions as they arise, and makes sure that the participants stop at 21 30 hours and do not try to work late into the night. He checks with the observers that they are confident of their marking of the in-tray exercises and discusses any concerns they might have about the interviews to take place the following morning; he makes sure that a notice is clearly displayed of who is interviewing whom and when and where, and then joins the participants and observers for a period of relaxation.

On the morning of day two, he supervises the participants who are alternately preparing their consultancy reports and having interviews about their in-tray performance. As each in-tray interview is completed, he makes sure that the records are photocopied and one copy kept under lock and key. He gets out the paperwork for the negotiation exercise (this is heavy on paperwork) ready to start straight after coffee; during the exercise he takes an active part, going from one group to the other with the messages and keeping the records of all transactions.

After lunch (for which the observers are slightly late, as they have to complete their rating forms) he starts the participants on the book review task, taking them away one at a time to make their consultancy presentations to the observers, one of whom plays the part of the managing director. He also makes sure that copies of the rating forms are made and filed and settles any queries that may arise; he will have to ensure that the managing director cuts off each presentation at the time limit, because little space is allowed for over run.

The observers work through tea, making any final ratings that may be outstanding from the afternoon's presentations and then they observe the Ajax task force which the programme manager starts off. He himself will probably use this time to make sure that the rating forms which he is collecting after each exercise are being carefully assembled, so that on the last day each observer will receive a complete package of rating forms relating to each participant, in their proper order. There will probably also be administrative points to take care of: messages from the observers back to their offices (inevitable, however much one tries to prevent it) and queries about travel.

After the Ajax task force the programme manager sets the participants writing their work environment report while he gathers the observers together to fill in their ratings of the task force and to talk together about any problems or special points they might want to raise. This is a good time to check that people are in broad agreement about the ratings they are giving, although they must be dissuaded from making inferences or evaluations at this stage.

After dinner the participants may be joined by the observers for the just a minute game, for which the programme manager might take the chair; or if one or two of the observers are having special concerns he may ask one of the other observers to take the chair while he confers with the appropriate people.

The following day, he starts participants off on the group consultancy exercise, works with the observers through coffee on their ratings for the exercise (being prepared to lose a little time here, because they will be hard pressed; alternatively, each observer could keep only two or three participants in view during this exercise). Then they do the listening exercise, which the programme manager has to administer, having previously decided the topics and the groupings; then the programme manager sets the participants to their task of self-assessment and peer rating, being careful to explain that this latter task is for research purposes only and the ratings they give to their fellows will not be revealed to the observers or anyone else.

Then he joins the observers who have the task of collating their observations of the whole two days in order to arrive at a strategy for interviewing each participant. The programme manager may take the chair for this session; they will need his experience and guidance on how long to spend on each individual and they will also need him to keep them to the task in hand: which is to get enough information to plan to interview and not necessarily to arrive at an overall evaluation. Then the programme manager draws up an interview schedule which covers the period after lunch; general farewells are said at lunchtime.

After lunch he keeps the interviews to schedule – though this is not now as strict a schedule as earlier in the programme – and when the participants have departed he may take the chair for the final Observers' Conference at which ratings of overall performance, assessments of potential and guides to further development are arrived at.

He must be careful not to give his own evaluations of the participants, so his job as chairman is a fairly rigorous interpretation of the role and, if he carries it out well, he can do the observers a service which any of them (with their own observations to talk about) might find difficult to perform.

We have described the programme manager's job in detail because he can make or break the actual programme. A key finding in our own and other people's assessment programmes is that if the administration goes wrong, participants lose faith in the observers' ability to do sensitive tasks like assessing their potential: after all, they reason, if they can't manage coffee on time and enough chairs to go round, how can they be right in their judgement of people? It is also particularly important to keep to timetables since the various activities are so closely interwoven that there is no provision for recouping more than five minutes.

In addition to these administrative tasks, the programme manager is the only 'neutral' person there and as such has a function to play as a lightning conductor, neutral chairman, smoother of ruffled feelings etc, and therefore needs to be sensitive and diplomatic. We would advise the reader who is contemplating running a programme to choose the programme manager wisely; to make sure that he runs at least one pilot programme before going live; to give him an assistant for the first two or three programmes at least; and to make sure that every action and every stage in the programme is contained in an administration manual which he can rely on for thorough support.

Mention of administration manuals brings us to the last point in this chapter about back up services: what is needed by way of paperwork, secretarial support, hotel accommodation etc? We try to follow the guidelines below:

Secretarial staff

Someone to assist the programme manager with tasks like copying, passing messages, dealing with hotels. Needs to know about travel arrangements so participants will not worry about getting home and to be sufficiently responsible to cope with small crises. Perhaps should be able to operate videotape machines (if used), though we have rarely found these as useful as the trouble they cause.

Accommodation

Bedroom for all participants, one or two roomy syndicate working rooms that can accommodate all participants and all observers in comfort, preferably air-conditioned for the comfort of nonsmokers. If the negotiating exercise is to be run, the syndicate rooms should not be too far apart as the programme manager has to walk between them. A room where the observers can meet, close to the syndicate rooms but soundproofed from them, with plenty of working surfaces (lots of paper to be manipulated) and also cupboard space. No telephone in the syndicate rooms; telephone in the observers' room used with discretion and probably answered by the programme manager's assistant.

The hotel should be briefed to provide tea and coffee on time and lunch should be light since people need to be alert in the afternoon. Some hotels can provide a private bar and dining room as part of their conference accommodation and this can be useful. They should pay attention to little things like fresh iced water, adequate lighting for the writing tasks and, in the best of all possible worlds a variety of chairs and room to walk about. Stressful working conditions have little part to play on an assessment programme.

Paper

The usual quantities of paper, flip charts, overhead projectors, blackboard, clip boards (essential for the observers), pencils and felt-tip writers, which accompany any training course; but be warned that the amount of photocopying required is much greater than the average course (at the end of each exercise, each observer's rating forms must be duplicated so that every other observer can have a copy, plus a couple over) and this photocopying needs to be done promptly. The copying paper taken should be enough to meet their needs in plenty and, if the hotel or conference centre does not have a copier to which access is readily available, it is worth hiring one.

Other equipment may need to be present in quantity for example, enough of the appropriate materials for each participant to put together a presentation (if used) in the manner he prefers, whether paper and flip chart or overhead projector and screen.

A polaroid camera might be useful if, for example, some of the participants prepare flip-charts which need to be preserved for further study.

Things to be discouraged

The following is a list of things to be discouraged because they upset the rhythm and purpose of the exercise: telephone calls to participants or observers during the day; hidden microphones; visitors who do not have a definite and worthy purpose of value to the programme (people coming to 'see what it's like' should definitely be told to stay away); late arrivals and early departures; late night drinking sessions (in one firm we worked with, the ability to use alcohol sensibly was characteristic of effectiveness); people carrying on regardless even though they are sick; participants being given the chance to see each other's work or the observers' paperwork.

Finally, we should consider the process whereby people are nominated to the assessment programme and what we have learned about mixing participants on the programme.

How are participants nominated?

There are at least three possible strategies: the programme could be compulsory for everyone, it could be available to anyone nominated by his manager or it could be open to self-nomination. There are potential problems to be weighed in the balance when selecting a strategy for nominations in any particular firm.

the 'crown prince' effect, if going on an assessment programme is thought to be a sign of special management favour and likelihood of rapid promotion

the 'wallflower' effect, if not going on an assessment programme is taken as a sign that there is no further potential

the presence of chronic coursegoers and concomitant absence of good people whom their managers cannot spare to go on a course

people feeling threatened if they feel they must go on a stressful event such as an assessment programme might prove to be

people who are performing badly because they are currently in the wrong job not having the chance to show their potential on a programme because their managers will not nominate them

people who have an unnecessarily low opinion of their own potential not putting themselves forward.

The balance of these risks has to be a matter for the individual firm to judge, depending on the existing practices and culture. It is worth noticing that, if there is any reasonably large throughput through the assessment programme, the crown prince/wallflower worries must fade away to some extent, as there will not be room to promote everyone who has been on an assessment programme. We have worked with some small firms where virtually everyone participates in an assessment programme, and these programmes have a strong element of individual development and counselling conducted in an atmosphere of overall helpfulness rather than a search to fill a particular position. On the other hand, some large firms beginning assessment programmes could not hope to offer everyone a programme within a reasonable time and some rationing must take place. Probably the best strategy here is to make the nomination dependent upon the manager's recommendation in the first instance, but with some provision for people to request a programme themselves. This is a matter for individual judgement.

The question of mixing participants will not always arise. If, for example, middle or junior managers in the production department are being assessed for their potential to achieve production director level, there is no problem about mixing. But if all employees below management level are given the chance to go on an assessment programme, there will be a question of mixing occupations. Is it all right to mix salesmen with engineers, debt collectors with actuaries?

One firm we worked with tried mixing across occupations and reports that when he mixed salesmen with actuaries the results were depressing. Under the conditions of short term pressure which an assessment programme is bound to bring about, salesmen are quite likely to shine. Faced with the task of putting together a presentation at short notice, they were on more familiar ground than the actuaries. Even though the latter group did not see the presentations, they divined that the salesmen were finding it easy and became unduly depressed about their own performances. In addition, the observers found it difficult to cope with such disparate performance, even though on an all salesmen or all actuaries programme they could probably have coped well.

This is a difficult problem, because there are two rival considerations. On the one hand, if the salesmen shine on a management assessment programme in comparison to actuaries, does this not indicate that salesmen have greater management potential and is not the purpose of the programme being served by this discovery? Another of our clients, disturbed at the low proportion of engineers on the board of directors, was forced after rigorous examination to conclude that this was less due to innate pressures to exclude engineers and much more to the lack of essential skills in the senior engineering managers. There is no point, this argument runs, in trying to impose a spurious uniformity of representation when some groups just do not have the potential of other groups.

On the other hand, it could be argued that being mixed with a group who so obviously radiated superiority (whether or not they possessed it, salesmanship being a form of lifemanship) presented the actuaries with an unfair challenge which disheartened them before they had time to grow their confidence and hence show their true potential; in a less immediately competitive situation, it could be argued, the depth of the actuaries would be pitted against the shallow brilliance of the salesmen.

The argument can be partially resolved by considering the purpose for which the programme is being run. The salesman/actuary mix occurred on a programme for very junior staff which is known within the company as the individual development programme, to which people come in order to find out their overall developmental needs. There is no specific management post in mind, and though the programme is designed to look for management potential the net is cast wider than this in practice. Given these purposes, we would think it wise to try to prevent a repetition of this unfortunate mix; the level of challenge in the programme should not be too daunting for people who are still finding out about themselves and their capabilities.

If, however, the programme is run at a much more senior level, with the intention of filling the next one or two appointments to the board, we have more sympathy with the every man for himself approach. Given that the programme has been properly designed and is looking for the right characteristics, then whosoever shines, shines; and the observers will be briefed to put that brilliance into its right context.

Just in case we have overstressed the competitive nature of the last example, we should reiterate that it is not usually fruitful to set up competition between the participants. We encountered one firm where it would not be possible ever to run assessment programmes in one division, at least until the next generation of managers had arisen; this was because there had once been an assessment course, thoughtlessly designed, where the personnel manager in charge had greeted the participants with the bald statement: 'Welcome to the assessment programme. It lasts a fortnight and the one who wins will be the next branch manager.' Though it was difficult to obtain a coherent statement of what had happened in those two weeks from anyone, one thing was clear: participants had spent an inordinate amount of time trying to spoil one another's performance, playing practical jokes of varying degrees of maliciousness, and overworking and undersleeping. Enough bad blood was generated for the episode to pass into the limbo of things unmentionable. On an assessment course, the only competition should be against oneself.

Chapter 7

What happens next?

The assessment programme is not over when the last exercise has been completed. Indeed, this stage is best thought of as the preliminary data-gathering on which counselling and planning will depend. Participants, observers and programme managers can permit themselves only the briefest of breathing space before their next series of tasks. This is to agree and systematize the information they have to counsel the participants and help them draw up development plans and to do the necessary things which make the data available for use later for participants' career decisions and for ongoing research into the assessment programme.

The following steps are possible immediately after the exercises are finished:

recording participants' reactions to the programme so far
observers agreeing on their assessment of participants, their views on
    developmental needs and their approach to interviewing the participants
counselling interviews with the participants on the results of the assessments
    and/or the participants' developmental needs and career aspirations
recording participants' reactions to the counselling interviews
systematic recording by the observers of the data in the form the company
    requires and transmission of those data to the appropriate storage facilities
transmission of assessive or developmental feedback to the participants'
    managers or to anyone else in the company who is deemed to need access
    to it.

As usual, we have encountered a wide variety of different practices in different firms on whether and how they perform each of these steps. In this chapter we shall discuss the options open to the firm beginning assessment programmes, except that the long term treatment of the data for the purposes of research will be left to the chapter on validation.

Debriefing

We separate this stage from its later counterpart – recording their reactions to the counselling interview — because the two activities serve such different purposes that if one asked for participants' reactions to the whole programme at the end of the procedure there is a danger that unexpected interview results might unfairly bias a participant's statements about the exercises. The value of having participants' reactions to the assessment tasks should be obvious, though they should be taken for what they are and should not be over generalized. The practice of evaluating training courses by asking participants to fill in 'reaction sheets' at the end of the course has been widely discredited by research (eg Stewart and Stewart, 1974b, Rackham *et al* (*op cit*), and many others), but it still continues. It is important to know whether the assessment programme *feels* fair and useful to the participant, and relevant to him and what he knows of the organization; but these feelings should be taken as feelings only, not as objective assessments.

One questionnaire we have sometimes used asks the participants to:

rate the programme on a five-point scale (very good to very poor)

state to what extent they think the programme as a whole measures qualities required in the company's managers, again on a five-point scale

state to what extent they think each of the exercises measures these required qualities

state how they felt they performed on each of the exercises, on a five-point scale from very satisfied to very dissatisfied

state how the actual programme agrees with the expectations they had formed (from pre-course publicity etc) about the programme

state to what extent they believe assessment programme information could be used to select employees for promotion to the position-level under consideration

state whether they would recommend to a good friend in the company that he should participate in an assessment programme

state whether there were any special conditions (ill-health, problems in the family etc) which may have hampered their performance in the programme.

This questionnaire takes no more than 10 minutes for the participants to do, and can be adapted from firm to firm. (Readers who wish to pursue the topic of drawing up questionnaires and surveys may like to look at *How to Conduct Your Own Employee Attitude Survey* (Stewart, 1974) which gives detailed advice on framing questions etc, or Oppenheim, 1966, *Questionnaire Design and Attitude Measurement.*)

If the questionnaire is administered at the end of the assessment exercises, the observers could be closeted together agreeing on their assessments of participants for later feedback interviews while the participants are filling in the questionnaires. Some firms take advantage of the participants' free time here by giving them one or more questionnaires about their career aspirations, or giving them other written material designed to prompt them into thinking about what they would like to achieve in future. The purpose of this is to prepare the participants for the feedback interviews, especially if these interviews are to be slanted towards the participants' developmental needs. We should warn the reader who is designing his first assessment programme that if he plans to conduct the feedback interviews immediately after the assessment exercises (only giving the observers time to agree their assessments) then some activity will probably have to be found for the participants while they are waiting. Leaving them to cool their heels, in the hope that this will relax them, is more likely to lead to stress problems as the pressure is suddenly lifted. A visit by a good speaker talking about an interesting matter not directly related to assessment programmes fills the time comfortably; but better a coach trip to the local stately home than an unstructured evening in the bar wondering what's happening behind the door of the observers' room.

Material to prompt participants into thinking about their career aspirations might contain a selection of the following items:

a listing of the 'motivating factors' present at work, with the invitation to the participant to think about which appeal to him most and least. Examples of 'motivating factors' could be security of employment, pay, promotion based on performance, good working conditions, opportunity to be 'in' on organizational plans and strategy, challenging work, good fringe benefits, congenial workmates, supportive superiors, supportive subordinates, ability to plan well ahead, acknowledged importance of the job being done, opportunity for further education, opportunity to work unsupervised, not having to work too hard, opportunity to hire and fire people at one's own discretion. The list of criterion behaviours arrived at in the diagnostic stage can often be combed to add to these 'motivating factors'

questions about how much the participant knows about the way promotions are made and the career paths that are available to him, referring both to his own division and to the rest of the company

questions about what the participant considers his strongest and weakest points, and whether he thinks his manager knows about them

questions about whether he thinks of himself as a potential manager or potential specialist and whether he wants to make a career in this firm or move from company to company

questions about what he could do himself, what his manager could do, and what the company could do, to make him more suitable for promotion in the direction he desires.

questions about what he is actually doing – apart from attending the assessment programme – to make him more suitable for promotion.

It is better to arrange this career aspiration questionnaire so that nobody but the participant sees it, and to make clear that the questions are there merely to prompt him into thinking and to suggest matters he might not have thought of unprompted. Its purpose is to bring to his attention matters that may be addressed in the counselling interview; there are no right or wrong answers and no pressure to reveal his responses to the questions.

All these activities for the participants are suggested on the assumption that they are waiting for a short while for the observers to finish agreeing their assessments, so that feedback interviews may take place. Some companies separate the feedback interviews from the actual assessment programme, making sure that they take place within a fortnight of the programme's completion. The reasons for this are usually administrative: observers (and perhaps the participants too) may not be easily spared from their offices for the extra day it may take to conduct the interviews at the end of the programme. Everybody could be recalled to the same place a few days later for the interviews, or participants may be interviewed by observers in their own job location. In either case it is probably not wise to let more than two weeks elapse before the feedback interview since the observers' memories for detail may have deteriorated and the participants need the interview to get a proper sense of closure. The programme manager must make sure that interviews take place, that plenty of time is allowed for them and that records are kept consistently. If the decision is to give feedback interviews some time after the assessment programme, then theoretically the participants can be sent home at the end of the last exercise; not so the observers, for they still have work to do that must be completed while the observations are fresh in their minds. It is usually good practice to give the participants a short interview before they leave even if the full feedback interview must wait until later. The sample programme in the previous chapter, where we discuss the role of the observers and programme manager, gives participants a short interview in the afternoon of the last day but reserves the longer ones for a meeting held a fortnight later.

The Observer Conference
The observers have a three fold task; to agree their assessments, to agree what they should recommend for the participants' developmental needs (if this is seen as part of the programme), and to agree on interviewing strategy for each participant. Depending upon numbers, each participant will be interviewed by one or two observers, and some notes on the strategy adopted for each participant should be committed to paper so that any interviewer can talk to any participant

if this becomes necessary. In fact, organizations vary a good deal in the way in which these interviews are handled. At one extreme was the company who had one senior, well-respected individual whose normal task included the conduct of career counselling interviews with those thought to have high potential on a fairly broad basis. It was therefore held to be natural for him to conduct all the counselling and development interviews resulting from the assessment programme and to accept the responsibility for seeing that the action plans were carried out. At the other extreme lay the company who felt that the advice and decisions were so critical to the future well-being of the organization that everyone with any real interest should be involved in the interview. This resulted in an interview attended by the participant, his immediate manager, the Director of the division from which the participant came, the programme manager and a staff psychologist. The company professed itself well pleased with the results of these interviews, but we must confess to some unease about the likely success of an exercise which begins to look more like a committee meeting than a personal developmental counselling and action planning interview.

The programme manager should prepare a summary form or forms on which the rating assigned to each participant on each task and each assessment factor is written. In addition each observer may now, for the first time, make an overall evaluation of each participant's performance, giving a one sentence summary of the performance on each task with a rating from 1 to 5, and a one sentence summary of the man's performance on each assessment factor, with a rating from 1 to 5. Each observer is then given a copy of all the other observers' records and the task begins of agreeing their assessments.

There is no set procedure for agreeing assessments. It is a group decision-making process; the observers should be well practised, if only at second hand, in the skills required. We can offer guidance on how to get the decisions arrived at clearly: first, to have an independent person in the chair. Perhaps the programme manager can take this job. It may not sit happily on one of the observers; it is a real chairman's job, not just a figurehead position. As psychologists, we find we are sometimes consulted at this stage and it does not seem to impair our effectiveness if we also have to chair the group; but we have to discipline ourselves not to make evaluations of the other participants. Secondly, the chairman should distinguish clearly the three jobs that have to be done and get the group to concentrate at first on agreeing assessments and not leap forward to discussing development. When it comes to discussing developmental needs they must be allowed to back track to their assessments. And thirdly, they should begin with one candidate selected at random and not stop until his assessment has been agreed. The discussion on this one candidate will probably last twice to three times as long as the discussion of every other participant, with no loss of coverage; do not despair at the time taken discussing the first man.

The assessments should be recorded as before – performance on each task and each factor – with the one sentence rule probably relaxed somewhat. The observers then move on to discussing the participants' developmental needs.

A useful tactic to follow here is to list three strengths and three weaknesses of the participant; to list ways in which the strengths could be consolidated and developed and the weaknesses overcome and to make sure that these ways are defined in operational terms wherever possible. We have seen a man who was a poor communicator recommended to improve his communications skills; that advice is insufficient! It is slightly better to advise him to go on a communications course; even better to advise a series of activities including training courses but also office activities and special projects that would help improve the skill, with assistance in standard-setting and advice on how to get him to review his performance.

Common pitfalls some observers fall into when thinking about developmental needs are:

spending all their time looking at weaknesses, none at strengths. This is partly because it is easier to talk about weaknesses; partly because remedies are more obvious usually than ways of consolidating the present position; partly perhaps unconscious jealousy can stand in the way of praising someone. (We know a university department where for 11 years no first-class honours were awarded until one of the external examiners resigned on the ground that obvious firsts were being withheld because none of the examining lecturers had more than an upper second.) The assessment record forms have been designed to help overcome this difficulty, by attempting to record strong points as well as weaknesses. The chairman or programme manager can draw the group back to strengths by pointing to written evidence

making recommendations according to what they think is available rather than being imaginative. We had a training manager as observer on an assessment programme and nearly all his recommendations were phrased 'Book him on such and such a course,' usually naming a specific course provided by his department. Obviously recommendations for development need to be tempered according to what the company can provide, but they should not stand in the way of wide-ranging thought from the observers at this stage

getting blasé about the term 'strengths and weaknesses' so that in the later counselling interview they use the terms freely, not realizing how daunting it can be for the participant to be told 'Now let's look at your weaknesses . . .' as if they were talking of the colour of his tie

getting committed to bright ideas they may have about the ways of meeting developmental needs so that they forget that the best strategy, in the later counselling interview, is to let the participant come up with the ideas himself. The chairman, or the visiting psychologist if used, should remind the observers after this phase of their task that while they have decided what they would like for the participants, the participants should ideally volunteer it themselves.

Their final task is to discuss the counselling strategy they will adopt in their interviews. They need reassuring that the amount of evidence they have, and the reliability of that evidence, is a firm foundation on which to build the interview. In our programme, we often take the observers away from their group task for a while and give them a discussion lecture on counselling strategy. In this discussion, we begin by emphasizing that there is a golden rule for nearly every interview, which is to begin by asking the man how he thinks he performed. We go on to give them a checklist by which a counselling interview could be judged; one example of such a checklist is shown below:

Counselling interview guidelines

1 Has the observer sufficiently familiarized himself with the participant's assessment file to be able to establish a definite plan or structure for the interview?
2 Did he establish an easy, non-threatening atmosphere at the start of the interview? If not, why not?
3 Did the participant talk more than the observer?
4 Did the observer use a directive or non-directive style of interview?
5 Did the observer use open ended questions?
6 Were the man's strengths and weaknesses properly identified by himself before the interview?
7 Did the observer make use of the man's self-assessment comments?
8 Did the observer make use of the observers' assessment comments?
9 Was there an attempt to allow the man to see any pattern in his performance at the programme?
10 Was the observer able to explain and justify all the ratings and rankings? If not, why not?
11 Has the man identified the major factors that affected his performance?
12 Does he see the implications of the above for action?
13 Was supportive direction given by the observer on the above?
14 Was the participant given all of the data that was to be fed back to him?
15 Was a specific plan of action for improvement arrived at in the interview?
16 Was a summary made? By whom?
17 Do you feel the participant left the interview with a positive intention to undertake a real programme for self-development? If not, why not?

18 Whose responsibility is it to see that actions agreed during the interview are actually carried out? Does he know?

This list is not intended to be exhaustive. Please add and amend in the light of your own needs and experience.

The observers then go back to the notes on individual participants and discuss the best ways of approaching each of the interviews, making clear notes so that any observer could interview any participant. Obviously the programme manager will draw up a schedule of who-interviews-whom, but this schedule is flexible according to how long the interviews take.

' Several organizations have found it worthwhile to provide observers with a structure for the counselling interview. One such structure is shown below:

Counselling interview structure

Opening – Request participant reaction to his own performance
  Readjust his reaction as necessary in broad terms (participants are often over-critical of their own performance)
Feedback – Taking each exercise, provide feedback to the participant using the observer comments. All comments must be capable of justification.
Mutual agreement – Obtain agreement, so that subsequent actions are committed to by the participant.
Development plan – Agree basis for development activities in as much detail as possible. If further work on constructing such a plan is necessary, commit to this work.
  Explain role of observer, future role and responsibility of immediate line management.
  Explain relationship to Performance Appraisal and the use of the performance appraisal system to check that actions have been carried out to the required standard and by the agreed time.
Summary – Summarize and agree responsibilities for action.

The counselling interview

We have proceeded in this chapter on the assumption that the feedback interview and development counselling will take place in the same interview and that this interview is the responsibility of one or more of the observers. Not all firms think it necessary to include developmental feedback; some organizations give no feedback at all. We cannot help thinking they are missing enormous opportunities. However, there is much more room for disagreement on who should do the counselling interview.

In some firms the programme manager is a qualified psychologist whose main activity is running assessment programmes, and the counselling is handed over to him (the reader will guess that his role in the rest of the programme is different from the one we have described earlier); some firms employ people from the personnel department to counsel, usually on the participant's home territory; some firms employ professional counsellors – the term may be unfamiliar in the United Kingdom, but in the United States degrees in counselling may be obtained in many universities. Our own feeling is that if line manager observers can be trained in counselling, they can usually do a better and more imaginative job, and in learning to counsel they increase their own skills and their own commitment to the assessment programme. They also become more adept at using assessment programme data when, later on in their career as managers, they have to make promotion decisions and are shown the assessment data from the candidates. It is slightly riskier to use observers as counsellors, because they are laymen and the occasional one may be unsuitable; but the possible benefits are unique.

Oversimplifying somewhat, there are four possible outcomes to the matching of participant's feelings with the observers' views. The participant may feel he has done well or done badly; the observers may agree or disagree with him. Each of these outcomes is illustrated in the following real life case studies.

Outcome 1: participant thinks good, observers think good

The participant was a young woman who had done outstandingly well in an assessment programme for first line managerial ability. Her grasp of administration and her verbal ability were especially good. (We have not seen enough women on assessment programmes to be able to generalize on a statistically sound basis but so far the women we have seen have been either outstandingly good or abysmally poor, very rarely in the middle range of ability.) The observers who counselled her were convinced that this one would be an easy one to counsel, so they selected her as their first interviewee; in fact they later agreed that it is much more difficult to counsel someone who has done well and who knows it. One observer said that he was actively looking for something to criticize, as he insisted she must have her 'share' of denigration. He highlighted the difficult problem of counselling for development someone who starts from a strong position; it is much easier to counsel someone who knows he or she needs improvement and is anxious for advice.

The observers went to some trouble to point out that good performance on an assessment programme did not guarantee a job, and the fact that the observers had agreed she performed well did not mean that they were promising her promotion. They pointed out that the man-manager ratio was such that statistically only one fifth or less of the participants on assessment programmes could expect promotion to management and that it was important not to become smug and believe that advancement was in the bag.

When considering her performance in detail, they adopted the tactic of letting the young woman do most of the talking, getting her to evaluate her own performance in her own words and (where possible) they confined themselves merely to agreeing with her. Paeons of praise would have made them, and her, feel uncomfortable. They tested to see if she was thinking of herself as the 'statutory woman' but she did not appear to be concerned about this. After the counselling interview, one observer said that he was glad to have had the advice to frame his questions starting 'Why . . .' and 'Tell us more about . . .' because otherwise he would have found little to say except 'You did well in this one . . .' and 'Your verbal skills are high'.

The participant did in fact receive promotion soon after the assessment programme to a responsible first line managerial post in the central administration function, where her subsequent performance was highly satisfactory. The assessment programme in which she had participated was one of the first run by that particular firm, and some years later she became informally involved in restructuring the programme and giving it greater internal publicity. Often an assessment programme's 'old boys' can be of great use to the people responsible for maintaining the programme, if they can be persuaded to look back on what the programme did for them.

When training observers in counselling skills, we usually find that they show themselves most fearful when anticipating counselling a poor performer. In fact, the good performer who knows it is a much more difficult person to counsel adequately, and the trainer needs to give this problem extra attention; perhaps the best time for this attention is after the observers have counselled one or two good performers, as they may not believe how difficult it is without the experience.

Outcome 2: participant thinks bad, observers think good

The participant was a middle-aged man, rather quiet and thoughtful, who had done solid work throughout the programme. In particular he had done a great deal to keep work groups on track, making sure people didn't stray from the task; he was a good follower though a rather pedestrian leader, an excellent listener and delegated sensitively and with an eye to passing down the interesting work. His was a splendid example of the need to give the observers detailed briefs on what to look for on the assessment programme, because his low opinion of himself was founded on the belief that 'he hadn't acted like one of those flash sales managers with three telephones and an E-type and ulcers.' The observers' tactics in counselling him were (after the standard opening of 'Tell us how you think you did') to go over with him the criteria of effectiveness derived from the survey and to indicate how few of them were in fact characteristic of the flash sales manager. They indicated how the exercises were designed to bring out the criterion behaviours and how the observers were trained to look for them, so that his ability to listen to points of view he did not like had been carefully noted by people who had been specially trained to look for this rather than for 'flashiness'.

It took some time to convince him that the observers were not just being kind, and of course his opinion of what was necessary for his development became modified when he saw the criteria of effectiveness to which he should be working. Some training in self-presentation was recommended to increase his self-confidence. He received promotion to management of a technical support function, where his people show him great loyalty.

This participant is a classic case of someone having got the wrong idea of what management is about; and we admit that some assessment programmes carry with them an air of stern purposefulness which may give the impression that the managers looked for are power crazed two ulcer men hungry for three ulcer jobs. Television and novels also give the impression that effective managers are flashy and jutting chinned, running over the world making high powered decisions. Participants often need reassurance that what one is looking for has not been dictated by a stereotype but is based on research and observer training.

Readers should be warned that this paradigm – participant thinks bad, observers think good – sometimes occurs when the participant is merely saying he thinks he did poorly in order to protect himself from a shock and to avoid giving the impression of over confidence. The degree to which this strategy is adopted varies from participant to participant, as does the deliberateness with which it is used. One way of testing whether the participant is bluffing deliberately is to agree with him, mildly, when he says he thinks he did poorly, and watch to see if he looks surprised. (We learned this tactic from a medical doctor who was almost infallible in detecting malingerers.) If this tactic is not appropriate, and it does need using with care, the observer can venture to suggest that accurate perception of one's own performance is an indication of a good manager. (It nearly always *is* in the diagnoses we have performed, so the observer is safe in making the suggestion.) The observer-counsellor's main strength in this situation is having a great deal of evidence available allowing him to point out in detail the strong points of the performance and how they relate to the requirements of the assessment programme. General comments, without the detail, are not likely to convince the participant who genuinely thinks he performed poorly.

Outcome 3: participant thinks bad, observers think bad

The participant was an outstandingly successful salesman who was nominated for a programme assessing first line manager potential. As happens with so many firms his selling abilities (discovered late in life, after a period as an actuary) had led to his consideration for rapid promotion to manager, and he had been virtually promised a job as a senior manager when someone thought that he should go on an assessment programme, a mere formality in his case, of course. He performed excruciatingly badly on nearly every task; the higher the managerial content the worse he was, so that his in-tray exercise was appalling but his sales presentation exercise was not bad. The observers, well aware of the future predicted for this man, were terrified at the prospect of the counselling interview. We reminded them of the golden rule – ask him how well he thinks he performed.

'Awful,' he responded. 'Don't you think so too?'
'Afraid we do,' said the observers, relief spreading over their countenances.
'If *that's* the manager's job, then I don't want it. Thank God I came on the programme,' he went on.

The observers were taken aback to hear this, but went on to talk about his performance and guided the conversation around to asking him why he had come on the programme since attendance was by no means compulsory. With a good deal of prodding it became apparent that his desire to be a manager was entirely due to his wish (and his wife's wish) that he be *called* a manager. His great successes in selling had led him to the possession of a fine house in an exclusive district; at coffee mornings and golf clubs, surrounded by knights and lords and directors and their ladies, the title of salesman did not go down well. The firm was sufficiently sensitive and adaptable to create for him a position with a fancy sounding title with director in it, and to leave him happily to sell as before.

This situation is perhaps a special case of the participant who is known by everyone including himself to have performed badly, but we mention it for two reasons. First, we suspect that more and more people in professions and specialisms are deciding they do not want to become managers; suspicions are often borne out by attitude surveys. If we are right, and if a firm uses assessment programmes widely, hoping that everyone will come along to discover their self-development needs, then an increasing proportion of young professionals may see the assessment programme as a way *they* can assess the manager's job to see if they feel like doing it. Secondly, we should emphasize how sensitively the firm cited handled the problem. This is not always the case. Perhaps an observing manager, confronted with someone who says he does not want the managerial job, thinks back to the time when he himself, faced with the same choice, elected reluctantly to take the managerial path because he could see no career except in management; and perhaps he resents the new freedom the participant has to reject his – the manager's – values. Before introducing assessment programmes on a large scale, it is important to check that career paths for managers and for professionals are clearly defined in case someone needs to be counselled about the latter.

Cases other than the one we have quoted – cases where the participant *wants* to be a manager, has done badly and knows it – are probably the easiest to counsel. After all, there is so much room for improvement and both parties know it. Care should be taken to see that the counsellors do not dismiss the man out of hand and that they stress that the assessment programme record is not the last word about the man; in many senses it is almost the *first* word. What matters now is the use he makes of the plans he is about to draw up with the observers' help. In many firms assessment data have a limited life, so there is no permanent record and plenty of chance to improve.

We are not, by the way, just uttering platitudes here. A surprisingly large proportion of successful businessmen have great failures in their background. Refusal to learn from failure is much more reprehensible than failure itself; looking back, all mistakes can be viewed as initial.

Outcome 4: participant thinks good, observers think bad

The participant was a young, highly-intelligent graduate who had asked for nomination to an assessment programme as soon as he was eligible. His basic problem was that he spotted the technical answers very quickly but could not see the need to sell them to other people, to delegate them rather than derive them himself etc, and his idea of effective group behaviour was to withdraw into himself until he had come up with an answer and then (irrespective of what progress they had made) to berate the others for their slowness. He had enjoyed the solo parts of the programme better than the group part. He seemed to think that the group exercises were there to slow him down, rather than for any assessment purpose they may have.

The observers' strategy in the counselling interview, once they had asked for his own opinion and got confirmation of their view that he thought he had done well, was to begin by looking at one of the areas in which he had shone. (This was the Just-a-Minute game, which he had virtually dominated.) Then they went on to talk about the developmental aspects of the programme – that promotion decisions would consider not only his performance on the programme but the progress he had made since. From this topic they led on to the performance criteria and the way they had been derived, and waited for the light to dawn. As they went through a routine exposition of the performance criteria they could see realization growing; as they explained how each of the exercises related to the performance criteria the participant became crestfallen. Finally he said that perhaps he hadn't done as well as he had thought. The observers let him go on talking, discovering for himself the areas in which his judgement had to be reversed. Then they selected one of the exercises (the leaderless group, as it happened) and went through his performance in detail. Then they talked development plans, working hard to get him out of his gloom and into a spirit of resolution. The development plans concentrated on relations with people, on delegation and on following arguments he didn't like, and he was specifically encouraged to share them with his manager and enlist his support.

He has not been promoted to management at the time of writing, though his seniority has been raised. He made some startling improvements in one or two development areas; he was fortunate in having a manager who could explain the niceties of people-management in a way that appealed to his analytical sense. Whether he will actually become a manager is still in doubt, partly because he is wondering about staying as a specialist.

Sometimes the person who thinks he has done well when the observers think the opposite would in fact be better off in a different firm. We know one firm where effectiveness is seen as keeping busy and another where effectiveness is seen as pausing before you speak. A man with one set of values putting himself up for assessment in a firm that has the other set is likely to fail by his lights or by theirs. That is why it is always advisable to discuss the criteria of effectiveness in any case where the observers' views differ from the participant's. Then if the man or the firm are sufficiently flexible the position may be changed; but he may honestly be better off somewhere else; whether the observers tell him is a matter for the firm to decide.

These four sketches of different outcomes to the counselling interview should provide guidelines for interviewing strategy. The interviewer will need to record the participant's reactions to the interview before turning his attention to the next interviewee. Then when the interviews are all over, the observers and the programme manager should meet to de-brief each other and review their thoughts about the programme.

The programme generates a great deal of data. The next chapter will treat how they are used by the people who should be constantly researching to make sure of the data's validity. (And we cannot emphasize too heavily that all the work described in the previous chapters, all the heartache and effort and excitement and good resolutions, will be good for nothing unless somebody *is* in charge of research into the validity of the assessment programme.) However, there are problems of physical storage etc which need addressing.

First, a straw in the wind. We should not be surprised to see legislation allowing individuals access, as of right, to any data the firm may have about them. This may encourage personnel managers either to store the data accessibly or to have them printed on edible paper. We have never seen any great difficulty in allowing individuals access to their assessment data – it can only come as a surprise to them if they had no feedback interview – and it has the merit of being far more objective than most of the material stored in people's personnel files.

Present practices are usually more circumspect. In some firms the assessment programme data are kept under the same circumstances as data from the performance appraisal system, under the lock and key of the personnel manager. Neither the participant nor his manager has access to the data; when a promotion decision is being made, the assessment programme material is passed to the promoting manager(s) along with all the other usual information. In other firms, the assessment programme data go into the man's personnel file for his manager to keep. Some firms distinguish assessment data from developmental data and keep them under different storage conditions. In nearly every firm we know, the man's manager is involved in the developmental process following the assessment course: either he has a copy of the development plan or the participant meets the manager to tell him about it. This latter course of action is probably better for getting the participant's manager involved.

An anonymous, summarized version of the assessment findings and the developmental needs should go to the firm's training or management development department, to give it some idea of the needs of the market and the demands which will be made on it. Sometimes the department will need to meet these demands fairly quickly; in one firm the assessment programme is followed immediately by two days' developmental activities organized by the training department.

The assessment programme lends itself well to publicity in the company newsletter, if it has one. Publicity must be carefully judged, though. On the one hand, there is the 'look who's been through the mill' type of article, giving the impression that the programme is stressful; on the other, journalists must be discouraged from approaching participants to get an 'I'm sure I'm ready for promotion now' type response which is bad for that participant and for everyone else.

Chapter 8

Validation

In this chapter we are seeking an answer to the question 'Do assessment programmes work?' There are several different ways of asking this question and one will get different answers of different value, depending upon one's initial orientation.

Validity

The types of validity most frequently encountered are face validity, content validity, construct validity, concurrent validity and predictive validity. *Face validity* has little value beyond public relations but should not be underestimated in that role. *Content* and *construct* validity take us delving into the theory behind assessment programmes and, while important, tend to be more the concern of the design people working in the background. *Concurrent* and *predictive* validity fall into the group that Dunnette (1971) calls practical validity. It is these two that should concern us most here and our efforts will be concentrated upon predictive validity. It will also be useful to spend a moment or two on consistency.

1 *Face validity*

'Does it look as if it does the job?' Or even 'Do I like it?' As Ungerson points out in his review of research findings on assessment programmes (1974), their face validity can be almost frighteningly high. Clearly, both observers and participants should find the programme acceptable and credible. If it is not, then its chances of being adopted at all must be slim. While the public relations value of face validity must not therefore be disregarded, it does not constitute satisfactory evidence that the technique actually works. Among the cynical, face validity is sometimes known as 'faith validity'.

2 *Content validity*

'Do these measures tell us something about the much larger range of behaviour that we really want to know about?' It is quite unlikely that any one assessment programme will present participants with all the possible circumstances which they may meet in some future role. Content validation is concerned with establishing that the coverage of potential tasks is both wide and deep enough for the satisfactory prediction of future performance. Initially, at any rate, content validity will nearly always be a matter of judgement rather than empirical correlation. Its importance is possibly greatest when one is attempting to define and measure the criteria against which validation will take place.

3 Construct validity

'Does what they are talking about make theoretical sense?' We are thinking about discovering the potential of individuals for growth, both in their present positions and in some future role. Is the notion of an individual's potential a defensible one? Construct validity becomes important from a practical point of view when one is trying to sort out genuine validity from 'nonsense correlation'. For example, Gulliksen and Wilks (1950) have noted a correlation of .90 between the number of stork's nests built each year in Stockholm and the annual human birth rate in that city, but we doubt that many would want to spend time investigating the nature of the relationship. Operationally, construct validity is a judgement that a technique does in fact measure a specified attribute, or construct, to a significant and appreciable degree, and that it can be used to promote the understanding and prediction of behaviour.

4 Concurrent validity

'How do present job holders perform on this measure?' An early step in the implementation of most assessment programmes is to run a programme in which the participants are those senior managers who are going to act as assessors in later programmes. The rationale is that if the performance observed during this pilot programme agrees in most respects with that already known to occur on the job, then the assessment programme is likely to make a good job of predicting people further down the line who have it in them to grow towards more senior posts. As Guion (1965) points out, this is weak reasoning as it ignores both the effects of motivation and experience. Concurrent validity is no substitute for predictive validity, although it may well indicate that it is worth persevering to the point where predictive data have had time to accumulate. A high concurrent validity implies that one may at least be within reach of the target area.

5 Predictive validity

'Does this technique tell us something now that will be shown later on to have been correct?' If performance of a particular kind on an assessment programme can be shown, over time, to be associated closely with growth towards a particular position or level in an organization – and with effectiveness at that position or level – we have achieved a technique upon the results of which we may place some reliance. Until and unless some measure of predictive validity has been achieved, no procedure concerned with the future of an individual in an organization can be relied upon, be it assessment programme, psychological tests, management development programme, promotion board, initial selection interview or straightforward performance appraisal interview.

The reality of validation in most organizations is that certain compromises are reached. Innovation has a reluctant market more often than not. It is therefore necessary that the new technique being offered should demonstrate face validity. Then, in order to be permitted to continue the experiment, results of some kind have to be produced rather quickly. It is here that a concurrent validation can pay off. For example, it may be possible to show that, for a given group of sales managers who have gone through an assessment centre, performance on the programme is closely related to performance against sales quota of the teams for which they have responsibility. Quite often, assessment programme predictions are checked against current performance ratings and this does at least provide some reassurance that the assessment programme is more or less in step with management's current view of a particular participant. This is of no help if the current management view is wrong, of course, as it may be if the man's present job is too small for him or if he is performing badly for some other reason.

Occasionally the climate is sufficiently difficult that it is not really possible to proceed beyond a concurrent validation. This is a pity, because it means that management will never know whether it is getting value for money from its new technique. Only a predictive validation study will really show if the technique is worth using and, as we shall see from the evidence reviewed below, such studies have been pursued with widely varying degrees of rigour, acceptability and value.

Consistency

If validity is concerned with the question, 'Does it work?', then consistency is concerned with the more detailed question, 'Does it always work under all the conditions that it is likely to encounter?' The kinds of consistency with which we are most often concerned are *reliability*, *homogeneity*, *transferability* and *conspect reliability*.

1 Reliability

'Does the programme give the same results on further administrations?' If the same people go through the same programme, with the same observers, a number of times and get widely differing results, then the programme is not reliable. Any variation in the results obtained should be due only to variations in the people themselves, otherwise the programme cannot be telling us anything useful. Perhaps the best way to explain the idea of reliability is to draw an

176

analogy with a ruler. Given an ordinary wooden ruler we know fairly surely that three inches today will be the same three inches tomorrow. We can rely on that ruler. This is not the same as accuracy. The ruler might in fact be incorrectly calibrated but the error is constant and a measure made with that ruler one day can properly be compared with a measure made with the same ruler on the next day. But if the ruler were made of some elastic material it would not be possible to know from occasion to occasion what distance that ruler was actually measuring when it indicated three inches. A similar analogy can be drawn with a clock. A clock that is always five minutes fast is reliable but inaccurate. If one knows that it is fast, then due allowance can be made. But if the clock varies (sometimes five minutes fast, sometimes 11 minutes slow) then the clock is inaccurate and unreliable and useless. It follows that an unreliable instrument cannot be valid. If the behaviour of the instrument itself is unpredictable, then predictions made by that instrument must be worthless. This is one of the reasons why an interview is such a hard technique with which to demonstrate predictive validity. Most interviews are so unreliable that there is no possibility that they can be valid.

2 Homogeneity

'Do different parts of the programme measure the same thing'? If we are concerned to measure management potential, then all parts of the assessment programme should be concerned to measure management potential. Reliability will be adversely affected if there are some significant components of the programme which actually measure colour blindness, or some other unrelated characteristic. This concept is easier to apply strictly to more restricted techniques, such as a psychological test which is clearly targeted on to one specific ability or aptitude. The concept of management potential is more diffuse, and therefore homogeneity is more difficult to maintain, but it is none the less important for that. The specificity of the diagnostic results upon which, we suggest, the programme should be based, will make this aspect of consistency easier to satisfy.

3 Transferability

'Does it matter who the participants are?' If the programme measures one set of characteristics when the participants are male and white, and turns out to measure something different – or not to measure anything useful at all – when the applicants are black and female, then it has failed to demonstrate transferability and needs re-design. Either the nature of the participants should make no difference to the characteristics which the programme explores, or certain categories of people should be excluded from the programme. For example, if a programme has been designed to assess the management potential of people who already occupy first line management positions, then it would not surprise us to discover that junior professional staff without any managerial experience receive inequitable treatment. They require a different programme. Similarly, it is not reasonable to expect a programme that has been designed to assess management potential to predict accurately, validly and consistently potential for senior professional positions. That also would require a new programme, designed for the new purpose. In summary, the concept of transferability is best handled by defining clearly the purpose and the groups for which the programme is intended and by being extremely cautious in extending it beyond that original definition.

4 Conspect reliability

'Does it matter who the observers are?' Does the information gained by the programme vary depending upon whether or not the observers hve a direct line relationship with the participants, or whether the observers are male or female, or over 50 or under 50 years old? This concept is also known as inter-rater reliability and is well tested. Much of the observer training outlined in chapter 6 is aimed at achieving a satisfactory level of inter-rater reliability and maintaining it. It should not matter which observer watches which participant. Any observer on a given programme should record much the same evidence as any other observer would have done. This can often be checked by overlapping the responsibilities for observation, so that observer 1 watches participants A and B; observer 2 watches B and C; and so on until the last observer, who watches participants F and A. Then, at the reliability check after each exercise, observers are comparing like with like to some extent.

In case any of the foregoing should appear too theoretical and academic to be of much interest, it may be worth pointing out that legislation already exists in the United States to require employers to be able to show that any procedure which they are using for selection purposes is valid in their organization and for the specific purpose for which they are using it. Originally drafted to safeguard the interests of racial minority groups, this legislation is now being used by women and by older employees to attempt to ensure that any discrimination that takes place is solely on the ground of their suitability for the position being offered. It was amusing to note how many assessment centres became development programmes at about the time this legislation came into effect. It would not be a great surprise if something rather similar were to occur in the United Kingdom in the near future. A thoughtful account of the American experience will be found in Willis and Becker (1976).

In order to keep the scale of the survey down to what is reasonable, given the overall purpose of this book, emphasis is placed on studies in civilian industry and those studies which are primarily military or concerned with government have been given less space than pure merit would dictate. There is by now a great deal of published material on the subject of assessment programmes. We have ourselves reviewed over 600 books and articles in the course of the preparation of this chapter. After considerable thought we have concluded that the clearest method of presentation is perhaps also the simplest – namely to present those studies which seem to us to have something of significance to say in approximately the chronological order in which they were published. In this way it becomes relatively easy to find one's way about and to observe particular lines of enquiry as they developed. Since many of the reports deal with several aspects of the problem of validation, an attempt to arrange the studies by theme seemed likely to lead to a good deal of repetition or backtracking over the same material for different purposes.

It will be recalled that assessment programmes in the form in which they are most often encountered today were evolved during the second world war in order to provide better selection of officers for the British, American and German armed forces. The account given by the Office of Strategic Services (1948) of the American experience puts the early German work in context, and points out why there had to be some changes in design before the procedures became acceptable to the Allies. In Britain the direct forerunner of present day assessment programmes was the War Office Selection Board (WOSB). An account of the development and effectiveness of the WOSBs will be found in Vernon and Parry (1949). In its review of personnel selection in the British Army, the War Office Directorate for Selection of Personnel (1947), reported a validation of the 'new' WOSBs against Officer Cadet Training Unit (OCTU) ratings, compared with the results of the old selection procedure, which was basically a combination of a recommendation from the Commanding Officer and a 20 minute interview. OCTU ratings were held to be well correlated with later success as an officer. Of those who had arrived at OCTU via the 'old' method, 22.1 per cent received 'above average' ratings as compared with 34.5 per cent of those who had arrived via WOSB. Of those who had come via the 'old' method, 12.5 per cent received OCTU ratings of 'markedly below average' compared with only 7.9 per cent of those who had arrived via WOSB. Since WOSBs passed the same proportion of total candidates as were passed by the old Boards, 'the improvement could therefore be explained only by improved selection'. In a rather more detailed account, Ungerson (in Parry, Wilson and Ungerson, 1950) states that, where the criterion was the grading obtained by cadets at the end of Officer Cadet School (OCS), the correlation between all WOSBs and all OCS ratings was low but significantly better than chance. The correlation between single WOSBs and single OCS ratings showed that there were very large differences between different WOSBs, and that their predictions were better for some Arms than for others. The correlation between individual board members and single OCS ratings was widely variable

– in one case ranging from zero to 0.6 between two personnel selection officers with identical jobs on the same board. There were differences between individual officers and between individual technicians. All this pointed out a need for work on the selection and training of board members. It is not without significance that much attention is paid today to the selection and training of observers on assessment programmes.

The direct descendants of the WOSBs are, of course, the Civil Service Selection Boards (CSSBs). Both were, and are, primarily concerned with selection and much less with providing the starting point for guided and planned development of individuals. Nearly all assessment programmes place heavy emphasis on the feedback which participants receive on their performance during the programme; to trace the history of the validation of this type of programme we have to go to the United States.

Many assessment centres have as one of their component exercises some form of leaderless group discussion (LGD), where the participants are given some kind of a problem to solve and are effectively left to get on with it. Bass (1954) reports an early study of the LGD at the interface between military and civilian applications. In 12 studies, involving 1,065 assessees, inter-rater agreement (reliability) reached a median level of 0.82. The amount of agreement between observers was noticeably increased when standardized behaviour check-lists were used. LGD performance was tested against status (rank) for 180 ROTC cadets after one year, and for 131 oil refinery supervisors where a correlation of 0.88 was achieved. An analysis of 2,361 test scores yielded 17 correlations with various personal characteristics associated with leadership, notably *capacity* and *achievement* (median correlation 0.3, range 0.17 to 0.57), and *responsibility* and *participation* (median correlation 0.3, range 0.07 to 0.60). Comparing LGD with other simulation exercises for over 2,000 candidates a median correlation of 0.60 was achieved, with a range of 0.30 to 0.78 over 16 correlations. Comparing LGD results with real life performance measures, a median correlation of .27 was achieved for seven correlations. Interestingly the range was 0.27 to 0.36 for 'holding leadership office'; 0.32 for 'initiating structure'; but 0.25 for 'welfare of subordinates and associates'. An interesting follow up study was conducted by Glaser, Schwarz and Flanagan (1958), using two groups of 40 supervisors from two US military depots. The criteria were: a supervisor's performance report, a rating of supervisor effectiveness and a performance record, all wrapped up into one composite criterion. The aim was to investigate the relative contribution of interview and situational performance procedures to the selection of supervisory personnel, the LGD being the main situational performance procedure. The two groups of supervisors were matched for age, number of years as a supervisor, present job grade or level, sex, race, and on two psychological test results – the Basic Abilities Test and the Supervisory Practices Test. The results indicated that the LGD was the best predictor; that the panel interview and the individual interview, contrary to expectations, were about equal, together with a role play situation; and that a small job management problem involving the use of personnel and materials had not added much. The authors add a note on efficiency, pointing out that the LGD deals, in their case, with four people at a time as against the one at a time of the interviews.

Bray (1964) reports an early result from the plant department of Michigan Bell Telephone, wherein he compared the performance ratings given to the first 40 men appointed to management after an assessment programme with the last 40 appointed before an assessment programme became operational in that company. Each man's performance after appointment was reviewed with himself, his supervisor and his supervisor's immediate superior. Of the assessed group, 62.5 per cent were rated as doing a better than satisfactory job as against only 35 per cent of the non-assessed group. Of the assessed group, 67.5 per cent were rated as having potential for further promotion, as against only 35 per cent of the non-assessed group.

Albrecht, Glaser and Marks (1964) report another early result from a full blown assessment programme, involving a personal history form, intensive interview, two objective intellectual ability tests, a sentence completion test and a human relations problem test. The procedure was used to predict the performance of 31 industrial managers, all having similar jobs. Predictions were judgemental rather than actuarial – a distinction we shall meet again, and one which continues to generate controversy; people appear unable to decide firmly whether a statistical combination of numbers or an overall judgement based on the impression given by the number and reports yields a more accurate prediction. Nine of the 12 validity coefficients derived from rankings were significant, and none of the four coefficients derived from ratings proved to be of any help.

Anstey (1966) reported a follow up study on the British Civil Service Administrative Class and the Diplomatic Service, in which several attempts to reduce criterion contamination are illustrated with relatively large sub-samples. Validity coefficients of as high as .617 are reported. It is worth pointing out that, although we are not looking at an industrial application in the Civil Service work, their efforts to improve methodology have been considerably aided by the opportunity to work with large numbers over a fairly long period. However, 1966 also saw the publication of the first major results from the American Telephone and Telegraph (AT&T) work and the importance of these results still overshadows more recent work. Bray (1966) and Bray and Grant (1966) describe the assessment process in the Bell System Management Progress Study and present the results of several analyses. They include studies of assessment staff evaluations, contributions to the process of selected techniques and the relationship of assessment data to subsequent progress in management. The results, based on 355 young managers, indicate that the evaluations by the assessment staff were influenced considerably by their overall judgements of the men assessed, but that many intra-individual discriminations were made. The results are also held to show that all of the techniques studied made at least some contribution to the judgements of the assessors. Situational methods (group exercises and in-basket) had considerable weight; paper and pencil ability tests had somewhat less weight; personality questionnaires were given the least. It is claimed that the relationship between assessor judgements and subsequent management progress has been shown to be good over a period of eight years. It is also claimed that a complex of personal characteristics is more predictive of progress than any single characteristic, but that some of the characteristics appear to have a higher relationship to progress than do others. The situational methods and the paper and pencil tests are more predictive than the personality questionnaire. The major distinctive feature of this study is that the results of the assessment programmes were *not* made known to management, or used to make appointments, during the whole of the eight year period. We have therefore a collection of assessments, made by independent outsiders, stored by them, not released to the company for eight years and then compared with what.had actually happened to the assessees, who had meantime been promoted through the normal machinery. This is a uniquely strong predictive validation study. Unhappily, it also has a major flaw: so far as we have been able to discover, there was no control group. Although it is extremely difficult in all this work to avoid contamination (decisions have to be made, frequently by the people involved in the initial assessments, about promotion and development), it would have been most desirable to have assessed the potential of a matched group of people at the outset of the study, using the normal methods of assessment then current in the Bell System, to have locked them up for a similar period of time and then to have compared the efficacy of the two methods in parallel. There is a further point, while we are examining methodology: Bray (*op cit*) gives the figures for those of the original samples who are still employed. While 98 per cent of the non-graduates had remained with the company only 63.5 per cent of the graduates had done so (range, 52 per cent to 72 per cent). In contrast to Anstey's painstaking work, we can find no evidence that the statistical calculations have been corrected for the restricted range that the leaving rate of the graduates produces.

While in no sense wishing to detract from the major importance and significance of the Bray and Grant study, it is unfortunately true that the shortcomings we have mentioned are common to nearly all the studies reported. It is for this reason, among others, that it is still not possible to say that the case for assessment programmes is proven – it is very strongly indicated but a watertight case has not yet been presented. Nor, however, has it been proved for any other selection or development technique.

Table 17 below shows the relationship of assessment programme staff predictions to subsequent management progress.

Table 17
Relationship between assessment staff predictions and level actually achieved by July 1965
(Bray and Grant, 1966)

Sample	Staff prediction (will make middle management)	N	Management level achieved		
			first	second	middle
			%	%	%
Graduates	yes	62	2	50	48
	no or?	63	11	78	11
Non-graduates	yes	41	7	61	32
	no or?	103	60	35	5
All samples combined	yes	103	4	54	42
	no or?	166	42	51	7

In all cases $p < .001$. In other words, there is less than one chance in a thousand that the above results could have occurred by accident

Similarly encouraging figures are given for the relationship between assessment staff prediction and salary programme (median correlation of .71, range .38 to .84). Table 17 is the one that is usually presented when it is desired to make the strongest possible case for assessment programmes. Bray and Grant were themselves rather more forthcoming, and it is clear that, although the overall result is as quoted, some of the component parts of that result are not so convincing. The result of the non-graduate sample for one year is given in table 18 on page 184 and clearly the predictions were not very helpful in this case.

On occasion, Bray and Grant find a most forceful way of communicating their findings. For example, they say, on the basis of their detailed analysis of the results, that 80 per cent of those who have advanced to middle management were judged as having such potential. Conversely, 95 per cent of those who have *not* advanced to middle management were correctly identified in advance. Even without a control group, given the other conditions under which they operated, that is a distinctly promising result.

Table 18
Relationship between assessment staff prediction and level actually achieved for one sub-group by July 1965

Sample	Staff prediction (will make middle management)	N	Management level achieved		
			first	second	middle
			%	%	%
Non-graduate	yes	8	38	38	24
	no or?	14	43	36	21

Result shows no meaningful relationship between assessment programme staff and subsequent management progress at all.
Source: Bray and Grant 1966

Bentz (1966) presents data from the Sears, Roebuck investigation, description and prediction of executive behaviour. A combination of situational tests (in-tray and group problem solving simulation), the Sears executive battery of psychological tests, a biographical data sheet, and various other tests, was used. Bentz claims that 'some of the experimental tests (notably the in-tray and the group problem solving simulation) have demonstrated excellent validities'. These validities in fact range from .29 to .51, where the number of people involved was 56. Rather curiously, Sears tried to observe more variables than there were people in the study, which led them into some statistical difficulties (51 people overall and 86 variables). The criteria used were a personnel director's rating (rank order, general effectiveness and rating of future potential); self-ratings; immediate superior's ratings (future potential, creativity, executive style); and personnel records (job mobility index, salary progress index). Bentz concludes, 'the extent of the validity underlying the data in this presentation is such that we have made reasonable inroads into the problem of discovering, gaining an understanding, comprehension and prediction of the extraordinary complexities underlying and contributing to executive behaviour'. We would add that most of the studies we have seen, and our own work, lead us to believe that it is most unlikely that there will be any simple solution to the problem of finding and developing future managers, because both the problems they face and the people themselves are extremely complicated phenomena.

Campbell and Bray (1967) continue the AT&T story with results from a number of Bell companies. They conclude that promotion of those who achieved a good rating at the assessment programme led to an improvement in the quality of management at the first level of supervision, particularly in building a pool of men who have the potential to advance to higher levels, *see* table 19 below:

Table 19

Relationship between assessment rating, performance, and potential ratings

Assessment rating	Percentage above average performers* (N = 471)	Percentage high potential men† (N = 425)
acceptable	68	50
questionable	65	40
not acceptable	46	31

* Above average performance means:
  1 The man is ranked in the top half of his working group by his supervisor.
  2 He was rated 'completely satisfactory' or 'outstanding' at his last performance appraisal by his supervisor.
  3 He was similarly rated by his supervisor's supervisor.
† High potential is derived from his supervisor's ranking and rating:
  1 The man has been promoted to second level.
  2 He was in the top half of his work group.
Source: Campbell and Bray 1967

They further conclude that the assessment programme produced a modest but significant improvement in performance at the first level. The difference in the results for performance and potential suggests that the management skills measured at the assessment programme are more important in higher levels of supervision: promotion of a small percentage of the total group of men assessed to be neither fully acceptable nor clearly unacceptable, after careful review by the line organization, resulted in generally good selection for management; promotion of a small, select percentage of the men assessed to be clearly unacceptable did not lead to a favourable outcome; promotion of men who had never been assessed led to satisfactory results in terms of performance at the first level, but only a small percentage of these men were rated as having potential to advance to higher levels of management. They conclude that the pay-off seems well worth the time and effort required to operate the assessment programme.

Grant, Katkovsky and Bray (1967) report on the contribution of projective techniques to the assessment of potential at an assessment programme. Rather surprisingly, at least to us, something of value seems to have emerged. The projective data were obtained by coding reports written by a clinical psychologist from three projective instruments (Rotter Incomplete Sentence Blank, Management Incomplete Sentence Blank, six cards from the Thematic Apperception Test). Relevant information was obtained from the projective reports concerning managerial motivation, and the variables pertaining to leadership and achievement motivation were reliably related to progress in management. Since projective tests require particular care in their administration and interpretation, and since simpler methods of achieving the same ends appear to exist (Fineman, 1975), we still doubt the justification of using this approach.

Greenwood and McNamara (1967), working in IBM, reported some work relating to the vexed question of whether or not it is essential to use professional evaluators (usually psychologists) in an assessment programme. They report both the degree of inter-rater reliability in situational tests, and the relative effectiveness of professional and non-professional (line manager) evaluators. Using the results from 288 participants they show that inter-rater reliabilities on a task force exercise ranged from .62 to .86; on a leaderless group discussion from .48 to .83; and on a manufacturing exercise from .49 to .89. While it could be seen that the variability between professional observers was rather less than that between the non-professionals, it was in one 12 man group during a leaderless group discussion that the difference between professional and non-professional ratings reached a level where it could be shown to be significant. While reassuring for the majority of organizations, who would balk at the idea of having people other than company employees – and preferably line managers at that – evaluating other employees in an assessment programme, the foregoing merely shows that there was a measurable degree of disagreement between professional and non-professional observers. It says nothing about which of them was right, if either.

Jaffee (1967) reports a reassuring result to do with the influence of exercise content on the results of a leaderless group discussion: 180 supervisory personnel from a large American company participated in groups of six in a leaderless group discussion, in which each member of the group was designated a particular position to defend in regard to the expenditure of school board funds. One member acted as chairman. The discussion positions proved equitable in that the money accumulated by each position over the 30 groups involved proved to be more or less equal. We have ourselves carried out similar checks on a task force exercise, where participants are required to fight for particular commercial decisions regarding the future of their mythical company. So far, with over 60 participants, no advantage has accrued to any one alternative although it became apparent at the end of the first run of this exercise that some re-design would be necessary as one of the alternatives presented was rendered highly unlikely by governmental legislation.

Bray and Campbell (1968) record the results of the use of an assessment programme for the selection of salesmen. Newly hired candidates for sales positions were evaluated by means of an assessment programme consisting of paper and pencil tests, an interview and individual and group simulations. Assessment staff judgements were compared with job performance some months later as evaluated by a special observational team. Assessment results were strongly related to this criterion. Supervisors' and trainers' ratings were *not* significantly related to the job performance criterion nor to the assessment programme results. The findings (see table 20 below) are held to lend support to the idea that assessment programmes have a valid role to play in personnel selection.

Table 20
Assessment staff judgements of acceptability for sales employment and field performance ratings

Assessment judgement	N	Percentage of group	N meeting review standard	Percentage
more than acceptable	9	12	9	100
acceptable	32	41	19	60
less than acceptable	16	20	7	44
unacceptable	21	27	2	10

Source: Bray and Campbell 1968

Dodd and McNamara (1968) report the results of a study carried out in the field engineering division of IBM. The overall assessment rating (OAR) was compared with subsequent management progress, as indicated by increase in position code level, and position code level achieved in January 1968. (IBM had a sophisticated and highly detailed position level coding which enabled quite fine changes to be recorded.) The results are summarized in table 21 on page 188.

Dodd and McNamara state that there is no evidence that knowledge of assessment ratings contaminates or inflates the relationship between those ratings and future management progress under conditions where knowledge of OAR ratings is most widespread. While their studies have pointed out some needed modifications, the assessment programme is considered overall to be a valid indicator of future management success. While we can see the support for the second statement, we have been unable to reassure ourselves that the first, concerning contamination, has been adequately proved.

Hardesty and Jones (1968) recorded the characteristics of judged high potential individuals, as learnt from 250 men between 25 and 40 years old in a major mid-West oil company. High potential (HP) individuals did better than low potential (LP) individuals on a range of psychometric tests, and HP individuals

OAR (1=high, 5=low)	Increase in position code level N=64					
	1 or less		2 or 3		4 +	
	N	%	N	%	N	%
1 and 2	4	21	9	47	6	32
3	8	47	8	47	1	6
4 and 5	18	64	10	36	0	0

OAR (1=high, 5=low)	Position code level in January 1968 N=66					
	57 and below		58		59 +	
	N	%	N	%	N	%
1 and 2	3	16	2	10	14	74
3	7	37	11	58	1	5
4 and 5	16	57	8	29	4	14

Correlations: $r=0.38$ for OAR compared with increase in position code level
$r=0.49$ for OAR compared with position code level in January 1968
Source: Dodd and McNamara 1968

significantly dominated the top 25 per cent of rankings on the exercises. On ratings by *peers*, the HP individual was seen as a good personal and company representative, generally more effective, a better leader and having higher potential for upward mobility in the company. The HP individual was *not* seen as more friendly, better in interpersonal relations, a good counsellor or salesman, a good adviser or technical contributor. The *observers* saw the HP individuals as significantly higher on business motivation, oral communications, assertiveness and compatibility. There were also some interesting biographical differences between the HP and LP groups. HP individuals were younger, better educated, more likely to have technical degrees, athletically successful, had held student government positions, enjoyed their maths and science courses more and were less likely to have gone in for drama. Their family background was that of being moderately mobile (two to five moves, rather than very mobile or stationary), father being in the professions or management (not self-employed or unskilled), mother working, father has a degree and has done some graduate study. He is likely to have been an officer in the armed forces. Bearing in mind that we are looking at American norms in this picture, it is instructive to see so clear a view of the culture pervading this particular organization.

While not constituting a validation study in any sense, Korman (1968) provides a useful summary of the evidence to hand at that time. It is also helpful that he takes a hard look at the results and is a harsh judge of what he sees. His chief conclusions can be summarized as follows:

1 Intelligence, as measured typically by verbal ability tests, is a fair predictor of first line supervisory performance but not of higher level managerial performance. Restriction of range is probably the explanation for this finding
2 Objective personality inventories and 'leadership ability' tests have generally not shown predictive validity, with the exception of the projective measure of managerial motivation developed by Miner (1965)
3 Personal history data as predictors are fair for first line supervisors but less so for the higher level individual
4 Judgement prediction methods, as exemplified particularly by executive assessment procedures and peer ratings, are generally better predictors than psychometric procedures, although allowances must be made for the generally small samples involved
5 Little has been learned from selection research which can contribute to a theory of leadership behaviour
6 Changes in the orientation of predictive research are needed.

Byham (1969) puts a fresh angle on some of the AT&T data. Discussing the results from 123 graduates in four telephone companies, he looks at the relationship between the assessment staff prediction at assessment – 'will make District within 10 years' and the outcome at the eight year point. It was said of 50 per cent of the sample that they would make district within 10 years; 36 per cent of this high-rated group had got as far as sub-district, and 64 per cent had already reached district or higher. Of the 50 per cent of the group who were rated as not making district in 10 years, 68 per cent had stuck at sub-district, and only 32 per cent had got as far as district. When they looked at non-graduates, 38 per cent had been predicted to reach district within 10 years (from a sample of 144 men), of whom 39 per cent had actually reached district, 61 per cent had reached second level management, and none had stuck at first level management. Of the 62 per cent of non-graduates who had been assessed as unlikely to reach district in 10 years, 9 per cent had done so, 41 per cent had reached second level management, and 50 per cent had stuck at first level management.

Occasionally we are asked if it is possible to do away with all the old, traditional techniques in favour of this brand new 'management flavour of the month', the assessment programme. Our reply is usually that the assessment programme can provide information of a kind that it is hard to get in other ways, but that it would be an uneconomic proposition, as well as unsafe, to place all one's eggs in this particular basket. Grant and Bray (1969) investigated the contribution of the interview to the assessment of management potential. Analysis of their data clearly indicates that information from the interview report contributes to assessment programme evaluations. Judgements of career motivation and, to a lesser extent, work motivation and control of feelings, appear to have been influenced by the interview information. In addition, judgements of interpersonal skills were reinforced, if not influenced, by the interview reports. The results of the study also indicate that extensive and reliable information on many personal characteristics can be obtained from the interview. In addition, several of the interview variables, especially those reflecting career motivation, dependency needs, work motivation and interpersonal skills are directly related to progress in management. The findings are held by Grant and Bray to indicate clearly that information on personal characteristics important to managerial success was obtained from interview reports. Eighteen variables were explored in total, with numbers of interviewees on each variable ranging from 111 to 198. It should be pointed out that the interview itself, the method of recording and coding, and the thoroughness with which the variables to be explored were defined, are all unusual in normal interview practice. It would be quite unjustifiable to generalize from this study to the rather casual and impressionistic interviews that are more frequently conducted.

Guyton (1969) reports something of the Sears, Roebuck experience in the identification of management potential. Since the vast bulk of the Sears results are based on psychometric tests (the Sears executive battery of psychological tests) we can deduce little from them about the validity of assessment programmes. The way in which the study was set up is so clearly stated that it seemed useful to include it. They started from four basic hypotheses:

1 There are differences in the personal characteristics of more successful and less successful executives
2 These differences can be identified
3 The chances of a candidate's success are better if his personal characteristics are like those of the more successful than if they resemble those of the less successful executive
4 These characteristics can be measured early in his career.

Prediction of potential revolves around a three step procedure:

1 Select criteria of executive success
2 Identify characteristics associated with successful executive
3 Develop instruments to measure predictors of success.

Sears used 2,500 men to obtain their executive descriptions and then went on to use psychological tests exclusively in their assessment procedures.

We now arrive at a study which is potentially of great importance but which has two major weaknesses. Hinrichs (1969) looks at the problem that we mentioned earlier, of trying to establish whether an assessment programme is doing anything that existing methods do not already do as well. He tried to compare 'real life' assessments of management potential with situational exercises, paper and pencil tests of ability and personality inventories. He reached the conclusion that ratings of management potential developed from a careful review of company personnel records were as highly correlated with the criterion as were overall ratings from the two day programme, *except* for ratings dealing with interpersonal behaviour. It should be pointed out that his sample is not very large (N = 47), that it is a concurrent study, not a predictive one, and that it has not yet been reported that it has been replicated elsewhere. Nonetheless, important questions are raised concerning the economics of designing elaborate programmes to perform tasks that might as well be performed by some easier and more traditional technique.

Two more studies from IBM now follow. Kraut (1969) investigated the relationship between intellectual ability and promotional success among high level managers. The Concept Mastery Test was administered to 235 middle managers and 130 higher level executives who attended advanced management training programmes. The Ship Destination Test was also given to about half the trainees. Both tests are held to discriminate well among superior individuals. Those managers who earned high scores were rated more favourably by their peers and the training staff, but advancement in the four to seven years after the training programme was unrelated to test performance. Here we have a clear case where some form of concurrent validity may be said to have been achieved but where predictive validity failed to be demonstrated.

Wollowick and McNamara (1969) explored the relationship of the component parts of an assessment programme to management success and examined the overall validity of the assessment programme approach. Results, based on 94 individuals, using a criterion of change in position level after three years, are held to indicate that the approach is valid and that situational tests add to the predictiveness of paper and pencil tests. It was also claimed that predictiveness was increased by the use of statistical combination of the programme variables rather than a subjectively derived overall rating. Table 22 on page 192 tabulates the correlations between change in position level after three years and the exercises; also the characteristics but not the psychological tests.

Wollowick and McNamara then ask whether the assessment procedure can be justified in the light of its additional time and cost compared with the use of paper and pencil tests alone. They show a multiple correlation with the criterion for tests alone of .45 but for tests plus characteristics plus exercises of .62 thereby nearly doubling the amount of the criterion variance accounted for. They go on to claim that this indicates that the assessment procedure makes a substantial unique contribution to the prediction of management success. They also compare the multiple correlations obtained from the impressionistic, subjective, overall assessment rating with that obtained by a statistical combination of the scores; .37 for the subjective method as against .62 for the statistical method. It has proved oddly difficult to replicate this apparently clear result. It should be further noted that Wollowick and McNamara attempted to conduct their study as had Bray and Grant in AT&T: in other words, data were collected from the programmes and not shown to management, who went ahead and promoted or not as they saw fit, thereby providing the material for an incomplete predictive validation study. The length of time taken is three years, not eight; the number of people involved is lower; and the data were stored within IBM by IBM employees, not by independent consultants off the premises.

Table 22
Correlations between exercises, characteristics and changes in position level after three years

Exercises	R	Characteristics	R
Manufacturing	0.28†	Self-confidence	0.32†
Leaderless	0.25†	Written communications	0.29†
Task force	0.15	Administrative ability	0.02
In-basket	0.32†	Interpersonal contact	0.00
Job environment	0.07	Energy level	0.26†
Stock market	−0.07	Decision making	0.29†
		Resistance to stress	0.26†
		Planning and organizing	0.23*
		Persuasiveness	0.22*
		Aggressiveness	0.24*
		Risk taking	0.11
		Oral communications	0.22*
		Overall rating	0.37†

* $p < 0.05$ † $p < 0.01$

Source: Wollowick and McNamara 1969

Carleton (1970) reports briefly the relationships between follow-up evaluations and information developed in an assessment programme run by SOHIO (Standard Oil Company of Ohio), known as the FACT programme (formal assessment of corporate talent). In August 1968, between two and a half and five years after attending FACT, follow-up ratings were obtained on the 13 standard scales from 93 key managers on 122 participants from the first 24 programmes. Each man was evaluated independently by two different managers who each knew him and his current work performance well. A correlation of

192

.65 was achieved between the overall rating from FACT and the managers' ratings.

Dodd (1970) explored the question of whether assessment programmes merely ensure that we select more of the same old types, rather than look for genuinely new talent. He appeared to show, on the results from about 250 salesmen, that there was some evidence that those low on conformity might never make it to an assessment programme past the pre-selection procedures. This suspicion was confirmed when he looked at the differences between those who had been through a programme (N=49) and those who had not been through a programme but had been predicted to have been assessed highly if they had appeared (N=47), of whom 20 were still in sales and 18 had removed themselves voluntarily from sales. The assessed and non-assessed groups were found to differ significantly on both conformity and independence, the non-assessed showing both higher independence and lower conformity. This apparently worrying result is turned to some positive good in Dodd's hands, as he points out that a combination of psychological test results and supervisor ratings to assess a man's suitability for a programme could be used to remove this conformity problem. From our own experience we would add that it may help to distinguish between conformity and compatibility. We *have* come across organizations where the route to the top was clearly to be achieved through being a yes man, but not often. More frequently we have met concern that the bright young thing, whoever he or she might be, should be able to fit in with the rest of the team, on the sound grounds that he may be extremely able and of extraordinarily high potential but that he is not much use if no one can live with him. This kind of discussion is usually held at the point in our procedure where we are defining what it is that the company should be looking for. It is a little late in the day to start worrying about it when you have already started the process of assessment. Dodd, Wollowick and McNamara (1970) then go on to explore the influence of task difficulty as a moderator of long-range prediction. Results of 396 maintenance technicians followed up over nine years and of 103 sales trainees followed up over 11 years supported the hypothesis that personality variables should predict early in time for high aptitude people and late in time for low aptitude people. The ascendancy scale of the Gordon personal profile was found to predict the progress criterion at least thee years earlier for those high compared to those low on initial training performance. In addition, the predictability for low aptitude people appeared to be more complex, suggesting that the task of 'getting ahead' contained additional personality correlated elements for the low aptitude group. There is little doubt that some tasks on assessment programmes are more difficult than others, and that the more able people yield much clearer and easier to interpret behaviours. And yet Bray and Grant achieved much clearer results in their study (1966) for non-graduates than they did for graduates, and we have hypothesized in the past that this might be because the greater spread of ability amongst non-graduates makes discrimination easier. The problem appears to be unresolved at the moment.

Jaffee, Bender and Calvert (1970) report early results from an assessment programme being run by Union Carbide's Oak Ridge Tennessee Gaseous Diffusion Plant. They use a rather compressed one day event, involving the participants in four controlled simulation exercises. They conclude that, based on their experience to date, the quality of supervisors selected by means of the assessment programme has been good; and the trend indicates that the assessment programme technique is a dependable tool for use in the total process of selecting new supervisors. It also provides a mass of information that can be incorporated into personnel development programmes for those who have been evaluated through the assessment programme technique. They used one conventional criterion, superior ratings of job performance, and one most unusual one – subordinates' ratings of the promoted individual's job performance. Very small numbers were involved in this study ($N = 13$) and the authors say, quite rightly, that the results can hardly be conclusive – but one is fascinated by the possibility of using that second criterion elsewhere.

Meyer (1970) investigated the validity of the in-tray as a measure of managerial performance. A plant manager in-tray was developed and administered to 81 unit managers in the manufacturing sections of seven departments. The in-tray was evaluated upon 50 dimensions, which were reduced to 27, and then factor analysed (centroid method) to provide a four factor measure. A performance rating was used as the criterion. The performance rating was divided into two dimensions: supervision and planning/administration. The validities of the in-tray proved to be higher for planning/administration. In a cross validation on 45 additional unit managers the predictive validity of the scores against the planning/administration factor was significant. In a second comparison, a group of 165 men with no managerial experience was tested and studied with the original manager group. Age in both groups correlated negatively with in-tray scores and education level correlated positively. The face validity of the in-tray, and its apparent validity in predicting one aspect of managerial performance, is held to demonstrate its potential value as a selection device.

Walker, Luthans and Hodgetts (1970) asked the question 'Who are the promotables?' Working with the marketing force of a major petrol company ($N = 3{,}202$) they drew up a simple matrix, *see* table 23 on page 195. From the normal company records they divided their group into those who were promotable now, within two years, within five years, and the non-promotable. They then obtained values for each individual on his performance rating, his educational level, his age, time in current job, service with the firm, job level and his annual salary. The results seem to us to have considerable relevance to both the way in which results from an assessment programme might be interpreted, and to the way in which people are selected initially for attendance at an assessment programme.

Table 23
A comparison of various characteristics with overall promotability (N=3202)

Mean personal characteristics	Promotability			
	Now N=732	2 years N=1002	5 years N=526	Not N=942
Performance rating (1 – high, 4 – low)	2.03	2.55	2.80	2.65
Educational level (1 – low, 5 – high)	2.31	2.60	2.44	1.86
Age	41.3	33.3	35.0	51.0
Time in current job (years)	2.67	1.50	1.75	3.30
Service with firm (years)	15.0	7.7	8.2	23.0
Job level (6 – low, 15 – high)	9.44	8.40	7.92	9.26
Annual salary ($5,300–$26,000)	12,347	10,179	9,726	12,670

Source: Walker, Luthans and Hodgetts 1970

To summarize: comparing the immediately promotable person with the non-promotable person, we find that the immediately promotable person has a better performance rating, he/she is better educated, younger, has less time in his current job, has less service with the company, is slightly higher in the hierarchy and earns a slightly lower salary. Comparing the potentially promotable groups with both the immediately promotable and non-promotable groups, we find that the potentially promotable person is better educated than either of the others, that he/she is younger and has less time in his present job and with the company, has a lower level in the hierarchy and a lower salary – and a *much lower performance rating* than the immediately promotable and slightly lower than the non-promotable. Where candidacy for an assessment programme – or indeed for consideration for promotion in any way – depends upon a high performance rating in the present job, may we assume therefore that the potentially promotable candidate has little chance of actually being promoted, leading to his decision to leave, or at least to become thoroughly demotivated because his job is too small for him? We have met companies where precisely this rule applies.

The Fulton Committee of Enquiry into the Civil Service (1968) commissioned a follow-up study on the efficacy of Civil Service Selection Boards and other methods. Anstey reported the results of the follow-up (1971a, 1971b) based on 1,064 entrants to the Fulton Administrative Class between 1948 and 1963, who had survived until 1 September 1966. Various methods of entry were compared, including open competition (open to all graduates with at least Class II degrees) which leads to entry as an Assistant Principal. Method I (N = 297) involved a written qualifying exam in English and general subjects, a two day CSSB and a final selection board. Limited competition entry was also possible (N = 80) which was confined to serving lower grade civil servants.

Three main kinds of information were looked at:

1 Rank attained on a four-point scale (0 = Assistant Principal, 1 = Principal, 2 = Assistant Secretary, 4 = Under Secretary and above).
2 Grading for present performance on a five point scale (5 = very good indeed, 1 = among the less able). This was further subdivided into three cognitive factors (paperwork, figurework, effectiveness at meetings); two affective factors (short-term contacts, relations with colleagues – long term); and two conative factors (drive and stability).
3 Assessment of future potential on a three-point scale (3 = expected to reach Under Secretary, 2 = expected to reach Assistant Secretary, 1 = not beyond Principal).

The main criterion was the combined criterion score (CC). CC = (3 × rank) + present performance + (2 × future). The main findings are summarized in table 24. It is noted by Anstey that validity for method I was rather low at .18 (written exam alone was 0). Validity for method II was .3 for CSSB, rising to .42 for the final selection board (which had the CSSB results available to it of course). These figures are then corrected for various statistical reasons to do with the nature of the sample to .36 for CSSB and .48 for FSB. Vernon has previously achieved .5 and .56 respectively, but he was working with reconstruction candidates who were older and about whom more was known. He had in addition a small team of regular assessors. Not much difference was noted between men and women in their performance on CSSB, men tending to be slightly higher on dominance, influence, emotional stability and numerical ability; women tended to be slightly higher on tact, sensitivity, written expression and on overall intelligence ('g').

Anstey (1971b) calculated the cost per successful candidate as £542, which is broken down into £15 each for the 1,200 candidates sitting the qualifying examination; £100 each for the 450 candidates going through CSSB; and £49 each for the 350 candidates attending a final selection board. Clearly costs will have increased since 1971, and this becomes a very expensive proposition. The work that Anstey reports is thorough and painstaking. The statistical analysis contains many lessons for anyone undertaking this kind of work, particularly in its attention to corrections for diminishing samples and unsafe criteria. Our present understanding is, however, that CSSBs remain selection devices, and that feedback on performance which can form the basis of planned development for the individual does not occur. This is both a strength and a weakness. From the research point of view it removes one possible source of contamination, since the candidates' performance on the CSSB will not have any detailed effect on their performance back at work. From the practical point of view it seems to us that a singular opportunity to help civil servants to develop themselves in directions helpful to both themselves and the Service is being lost.

Table 24
Main findings from the follow-up study commissioned by the Fulton Committee
of Enquiry into the Civil Service

Method of entry	N	Mean CC score (adjusted)
For 596 entrants at Assistant Principal		
Method II	219	12.39
Limited competition	80	11.75
Method I	297	10.99
For 883 officers compared at Principal		
Method II	132	13.78
Limited competition	71	12.35
Method I	217	12.17
Direct entry principals	76	10.64
Department promotees	387	10.51

Source: Anstey 1971a

Byham (1971) provides us with another 'pre-digested' review of results. He has a happy knack of presenting material in a fresh fashion, and, while his contribution is not always original, he is usually highly informative. He quotes the Supreme Court Case (Griggs et al vs Duke Power, 1971) which affirmed the guidelines laid down by the Equal Employment Opportunities Commission in the United States, that organizations must be prepared to prove that their standards for selection and appraisal are job related. This includes assessment programmes. At the time of writing he states that there were 22 published research studies attempting to evaluate the overall validity of assessment programmes, on which 15 were positive, six were too small to be of any value, and one very small one was negative. AT&T had by this time assessed more than 70,000 candidates. He quotes the Bray and Grant work on 123 new graduate hires and 144 non-graduate first level managers, pointing out that after eight years (during which the results of the programmes were not known to the company) 82 per cent of the graduates and 75 per cent of the non-graduates who had reached middle management had been correctly identified; 88 per cent of graduates and 95 per cent of non-graduates who were never promoted out of first line management had also been correctly assessed. He adds that professional psychologists were used as assessors, and that some clinical techniques were employed in addition to the more usual industrial ones – neither of which points holds true for many other studies, placing some small doubt on the possibility of generalizing from these strong results. A second AT&T study is reported, involving 78 newly hired salesmen who were assessed immediately after hiring. Again, the results of the assessment were kept hidden from management. A review team went out and observed the assessees during live sales calls and then rated their performance. Nearly half the assessees were predicted to be 'not acceptable' in review, and of these only 24 per cent actually gave acceptable sales calls. Of those predicted to be acceptable, 68 per cent were so rated. Of those predicted to be more than acceptable, 100 per cent were so rated. The correlation between the assessment ratings and the field panel review was .51, and the correlation between four paper and pencil tests and the field panel review was .33. Supervisor and trainer ratings were found to be unrelated to job performance as seen by the field review team. Finally, he quotes an operation study (where the data *were* used for promotional purposes) of 5,943 assessees in AT&T. The criterion was 'advancement above first line manager'. Those who had been rated 'more than acceptable' were more than twice as likely as those who had been rated 'acceptable' to be promoted two or more times. Those who had been rated 'more than acceptable' were 10 times as likely as those who had been rated 'not acceptable' to be promoted two or more times. The correlation between assessment programme prediction and the actual event was .46

A study of first line sales managers in IBM yields the result that of the 46 assessed as having potential and who were then promoted, 4 per cent were demoted for job failure, whereas of the 71 assessed as having *low* potential but promoted nonetheless, 20 per cent were demoted for job failure. And Byham concludes by quoting a study in Caterpillar Tractor which showed that both the traditional methods and assessment programme approach could be highly accurate, with a slight edge for the programme – but this result is based on 37 men through the programme and 27 through the traditional route so the sample is relatively small. Byham calculates the costs of an assessment programme as between $5 and $500 per person depending on the assumptions that are made.

Turney, Rosen and Conklyn (1971) take a brief look at the problem of early identification of managerial potential in a technical/professional organization. Both paper and pencil tests and group interaction indices were used as possible predictors of managerial emergence in a fairly unstructured organization. The criterion was the number of promotions during a three year period. The data indicate two different patterns characteristic of managerial emergence depending on whether an employee is young or older. Successful young employees are characterized as aggressive or forceful; successful older employees as agreeable or passive. Successful young employees are rated as more technically competent by their superiors than successful older employees. These results, important as they are for the interpretation of performance on assessment programmes by employees of different ages, may achieve further significance if legislation is introduced in the United Kingdom which affords the same protection against discrimination in employment on the ground of age as presently exists on the grounds of race or sex. We have ourselves met one case in which an employer was most anxious to be seen to give all employees a fair chance to seek advancement through an assessment programme, regardless of age, sex or race. One participant was already receiving pre-retirement counselling and was therefore vociferous in his condemnation of the selection procedure for the programme. Had he been excluded, however, might he not have been just as vociferous and with just as good cause? This is a problem regardless of what form of assessment is undertaken. It is perhaps more obvious where an assessment programme is used because the programme itself makes the whole process more open and apparent.

Ginsberg and Silberman (1972) report a study conducted in the New York Hospital Administration. While this is not quite an industrial application, the technique appears to have been used in a manner indistinguishable from that most frequently encountered in industry. They used a one day programme, which included an interview, tests, a leaderless group discussion and an intray. On 54 administrators, the assessment programme ratings correlated between .30 and .36 with supervisors' ratings and they hold that their centre is predictive of management ability. While the study itself is of interest insofar as it adds yet another brick to the validation edifice, perhaps most interesting are the parameters which they set themselves for their programme:

1 It must validly measure management potential. Decisions made on the poten-

tial and development of the individual must be related to the actual job performance factors.

2 It must have high face validity or acceptability to both the organization and the persons being assessed.

3 It must be administered as an integral part of the organization manpower development programme.

4 It must be flexible enough to permit assessment of management potential at various levels and functional areas of specialization and provide for future alterations as the need arises.

5 It must be comprehensive enough to tap a wide variety of management potential characteristics.

6 It must have a high pay-off value in relation to investment and cost of administration.

7 It must be flexible in terms of the realities of the company's particular organizational structure and climate, and be practical as well as theoretically sound.

We would find it difficult to dissent from any of those points.

Returning to IBM, Kraut and Scott (1972) review the validity of an operational assessment programme in the office products division of that company. The career progress of 1,086 employees in sales, service and administrative functions was reviewed after they had been assessed. Although participants were nominated for the programme on the basis of being thought promotable, raters found that more than 25 per cent of them were unqualified for further advancement and the remainder were widely differentiated, see table 25 on page 201. Ratings were used to move men into first line management, but the relationship of ratings to first promotions is held to be moderate enough to reduce fears of 'crown prince' or 'kiss of death' effects, see table 26 on page 201. Nor is participation held to demotivate these employees. Assessment ratings are claimed to be substantially correlated with two major criteria – second level promotions (for which the results were not used) and demotions from first line management (based on performance after promotion, see table 27 on page 202). We agree with Ungerson's view (1974) that, while it may be true that the assessment programme results were not used to make promotion decisions beyond first level, it is hard to accept that all memory of the candidates' performance on the programme is expunged at the moment of first promotion – some form of contamination, the extent of which is uncertain, seems likely to have taken place.

Kraut (1972) takes a hard look at management assessment programmes and their future, covering such topics as validity, acceptability, morality, value added, impact on the organization, characteristics measured, impact on careers,

Table 25
Ratings of non-management candidates assessed from 1965 to 1970

	Function		N = 1,086
Assessed potential	Sales %	Service %	Admin %
Executive management	3	6	3
Higher management	13	16	22
Second line management	26	23	23
First line management	28	29	25
Remain non-management	30	26	22
	N = 437	N = 433	N = 216

Source: Kraut and Scott 1972

stress, developmental aspects, development of observers and future needs. While much of his time is spent reviewing ground previously covered in this chapter, he has some very useful data from participants' reactions to an assessment programme. This information was updated in a later publication (Kraut, 1973), and some extracts are highlighted below.

On the question of morality Kraut is quite clear. He maintains that one should concentrate less on the process and more on the consequences of potential assessment. People's potential for development is going to be assessed anyway, Kraut

Table 26
Percentage of assessment candidates promoted to first line management

	Function					
	Sales		Service		Administration	
Assessed potential	Assessed	Pro-moted	Assessed	Pro-moted	Assessed	Pro-moted
		%		%		%
Executive management	14	86	26	85	7	100
Higher management	57	60	71	37	48	52
Second line management	114	44	99	35	50	50
First line management	123	33	127	23	54	35
Remain non-management	129	24	110	26	57	19
Overall	437	35	433	33	216	40

Source: Kraut and Scott 1972

Table 27

Assessment candidates promoted to higher levels after becoming first line managers, and assessment candidates demoted after becoming first line managers (sales only)

| | Function | | | | | | |
| | Sales | | Service | | Admin | | Sales |
Assessed potential	*Mgrs*	*Pro-moted*	*Mgrs*	*Pro-moted*	*Mgrs*	*Pro-moted*	*De-moted*
		%		%		%	%
Executive management	12	42	22	30	7	28	
							4
Higher management	34	50	26	27	25	12	
Second line management	50	30	35	34	25	12	14
First line management	40	15	29	17	19	0	
							20
Remain non-management	31	13	29	3	11	0	
Overall	167	28	141	23	87	9	14

Source: Kraut and Scott 1972

points out, so one might as well go about it in as methodical a fashion as possible. He claims that assessment programmes encourage decisions to be open, objective, based on agreed standards, based on relevant and systematically gathered data, and explicit. He adds to these advantages the fact that multiple raters are involved, making more objective, trained judgements of management skills through attentive observation of standardized tasks, with all candidates being compared on a common yardstick. He fails to see what is immoral about any of that – a view to which we would subscribe without reservation if we thought that it always happened that way. We are not certain that all programmes meet the high standards that Kraut proposes, and there is occasionally real difficulty in achieving some of the aims. The establishment of a common yardstick has caused us to be involved in long discussions, for example, at the end of which we have agreed a procedure which has sometimes fallen short of a truly common yardstick.

McConnell and Parker (1972) present the answers to a range of important questions about the value of an assessment programme. While the questions they ask are critical, the answers they give, while encouraging, cannot be taken to give very strong support to the concept because of the small samples involved. One would like to see further work on all the questions raised but with answers provided on the scale of Kraut and Scott (1972) or Huck (1973). First McConnell and Parker tested the internal consistency within assessment categories and found reliability coefficients ranging from .64 to .90, with eight out of the 14 at .80 or higher. (12 participants, five observers.) Next they tested the internal consistency of estimates of overall management ability within groups of five assessors in six different programmes, achieving a reliability coefficient of .9 across 129 participants. Test-retest reliability coefficients of .79 and .74 were achieved for two programmes (one of nine participants, one of 12, both using five assessors). Concurrent validity coefficients were obtained for 70 participants across four programmes ranging from .28 to .64 (average .57). The low .28 coefficient is attributed to the use of a two point scale in making evaluations on this programme – 75 per cent of the participants had been correctly evaluated when compared with the criterion. They also present data to support the claim that the assessment programme is accurate at identifying people with particular job performance ratings; that the dispersion of assessors' judgements is greatly reduced by training and that there is no evidence that black or female participants suffer particularly in the rating process compared with white males. We would question their interpretation of the data on this last point as some 22.2 per cent of females were misjudged by two scale points on a nine point scale, while none of the white males or the blacks was misjudged by this amount at all. However, since the total group size was only 24 (eight black, nine females, nine white males), we do not lean too heavily on this result.

Moses has produced a large scale report on the AT&T work (1972). He studied the validity of assessment programme performance measures as predictors of managerial success using data collected from 8,885 participants in a personal assessment programme from 1961–1970. The predictor variables were: behaviourally based ratings on various management abilities, mental ability scores on the School and College Abilities Test, and a global rating of managerial potential based on all assessment programme information. The criterion of managerial success was two or more promotions since evaluation. Results are held to indicate a highly significant relationship between the global rating of managerial potential and managerial success. Assessment variables showed the same rank order of contribution both to the rating of potential and the managerial success measure. Ratings based on behavioural observation correlated more highly with the global assessment rating and with managerial success than did mental ability scores. A previous study by Moses (1971) had recorded a correlation of .46 between assessment programme ratings and management progress over 10 years, using the results from 5,943 participants. Sleven (1972) uses this and several other reports to support his view that 'at this point it seems relatively safe to say that the assessment centre technique as a method of managerial selection is as valid and probably more valid than any other currently used techniques' (Sleven was at the time Professor in the Pittsburgh University Graduate School of Business).

Reporting a study in the field engineering division of IBM (1972), Palmer derives his results from over 400 individuals already in first and second level positions who had been assessed between 1964 and 1970. He presents a striking picture of the success of the programmes for 142 managers assessed between 1963 and 1966, see table 28 below. Of those managers who were predicted in the programme to be rated among the top third of the group back at work, in terms of position level achieved, 67 per cent actually appeared in the top third and none appeared in the bottom third. Of those managers who were predicted to be in the bottom third of the group in terms of position level subsequently achieved, 89 per cent actually were in the bottom third and none was in the top third. Although this result looks superficially exciting (given the usual caveats about control groups, contamination and so on) it is unfortunate that Palmer chose to use percentages rather than give us the raw numbers as well. We can only assume that the participants were split into three groups of 44, meaning that some rather arbitrary decisions may have had to be made at the boundaries.

Table 28

Actual versus predicted position level progress for 142 managers assessed between 1964 and 1966

	Actual		
Predicted	Bottom	Middle	Top
	%	%	%
Top	0	33	67
Middle	18	68	14
Bottom	89	11	0

Source: Palmer 1972

Gardner and Williams (1973) present data from a 25 year follow-up of an extended interview selection procedure in the Royal Navy. The first 269 naval officers selected by the extended interview procedure between 1947–1949 were followed through. Various criteria were used to enable validities to be assessed at all stages of training and in the later career up to the rank of Commander.

Wherever possible the criteria used were the actual measures employed within the Service for assessment of progress. It was found that the interview scores correlated well with an assessment of 'officer-like qualities' at the end of initial training; that written examination results made an important contribution to the validity of selection scores at all stages of training; and that certain biographical and psychometric variables were potentially useful selectors. Initial training results were found to be particularly well correlated with long-term success. As with Anstey's work, close attention is paid to the problem of finding adequate criteria and to the use of the appropriate statistics. Unfortunately, as the authors themselves state, after all this detailed and careful effort the research does not provide indications of the relative contributions of the situational tests (individual command and group tasks, group discussions, short talks) to board mark and subsequent performance. So we have a result which gives us some encouragement that the assessment programme technique may have worked in another form and in another situation, but it is not possible to disentangle the specific information that we would like to have.

Huck (1973), basing much of his comments on earlier work by Moses, returns to AT&T, who had by this stage put more than 100,000 people through their assessment programmes. He concentrates on 5,943 individuals assessed by the Bell System companies. Table 29 tabulates the relationship between assessment programme rating and progress in management, and demonstrates a correlation of .44 between final assessment rating and management progress.

Table 29
Relationship between assessment rating and progress in management

Assessment rating	N	Number receiving two or more promotions	Percentage
More than acceptable	410	166	40.5
Acceptable	1,466	321	21.9
Questionable	1,910	220	11.5
Not acceptable	2,157	91	4.2
Total	5,943	798	13.4

Source: Huck 1973

Huck's conclusions are worth quoting in full:

1 Multiple assessment procedures have consistently been related to a number of performance effectiveness measures. Future studies must investigate different

aspects of behaviourally relevant multiple criteria to determine which can best be predicted by the assessment process.

2 Procedures unique to the assessment programme approach, essentially the situational exercises, contribute a substantial element to the prediction of managerial performance, beyond that which is found in paper and pencil tests alone. However, multiple assessment procedures provide a number of sources of data and the contribution of each to the assessment dimensions, to the final assessment rating and to the multiple criterion measures must be further clarified.

3 The assessment process focuses on the behavioural demands of a manager's job. A wide range of supervisory skills can be observed at an assessment centre. Other relevant dimensions of job performance must be identified and defined, and assessment techniques designed to measure them. Likewise, those variables and exercises which can be eliminated from the assessment process without an adverse effect must be identified.

4 The assessment process is not limited by low reliability. This results from the intensive training provided to the assessment staffs in evaluating performance and from the standardization incorporated into multiple assessment procedures.

5 Essentially no difference exists between psychologists and *trained* managers in the role of assessors. The psychologist can be most efficiently used in the training of assessment staffs and in research associated with the process.

6 No differential validity data have been reported on sub-groups of assessees or assessors in regard to sex, race and job differences.

7 Future research must be designed systematically to investigate the effects of the assessment process on:
   (a) the assessee: attitude, self-esteem, motivation, career planning
   (b) the staff observer: training value of serving on the assessment staff
   (c) the organization: identification of training needs, morale, manpower planning, organizational change and development.

Partly in answer to Huck's conclusion 3 above perhaps, Moses (1973) compared the results of the early identification assessment programme (EIA), a one day programme for assessing and evaluating management potential in short-service employees, with those of the personal assessment programme (PAP), which was currently used more widely but is more time-consuming. Eighty-five employees, black and white, men and women, who were evaluated by EIA staff as having high, moderate or low management potential also took part in PAP. Overall management potential ratings correlated .73 for EIA and PAP, with similar correlations for all sub-groups. Significant correlations were found for all variables common to both groups. The advantage of EIA over PAP for rapid assessment is then discussed. Clearly there is no point in measuring something several ways if one can be sufficiently certain that just one measure will do – but the advantages of multiple measures and multiple criteria are so clear that we would hesitate before recommending that a company should automatically opt for the trimmest programme possible. There remains a significant possibility that one could be quick, cheap and wrong.

Kraut (1973) updates the information given in an earlier paper on participant reactions to assessment programmes in a variety of countries, including Austria, Brazil, Germany, Japan, The Netherlands, the United Kingdom and the United States. Sample sizes vary from 11 in the United Kingdom to 70 in Germany. Responses are uniformly favourable. The questions asked were:

1 To what extent do you believe the assessment programme measures important qualities required of your company's managers?
2 To what extent do you believe assessment information could be used to help in the selection of employees for promotion to first line management?
3 How do you rate the programme's . . . value in giving you additional information . . . for your self development?
4 Would you recommend to a good friend at about your level in the company that he volunteer to participate in an assessment programme?

Scoring on a five point scale, the vast bulk of the responses fell into the first two points, the third being still mildly positive. The highest negative response came from Austria to question 3, and totalled some 10 per cent of the responses out of a sample of 59.

Wilson and Tatge (1973) working with the Pacific Telephone Company, introduce a healthily sceptical note into the proceedings. They state: 'Assessment centres have been established as a valid selection method, but considerable research is needed to justify claims for superiority over the traditional methods.' Working with three years' throughput of female supervisors ($N = 401$) the authors claim that scores from the California Psychological Inventory, the School and College Abilities Test (verbal) and overall ratings from the assessment programmes correlated significantly in all cases, with the exception of two scales from the CPI in year three. Interpretations based upon the test results alone yielded the following description of the successful supervisor, and the authors ask whether the assessment programme will improve upon it sufficiently to justify the extra time and cost.

She is aggressive, self-confident, forceful and enthusiastic. She is sensitive and insightful in interpersonal situations. She is quick to take charge of the situation in a group of peers. She tends to be self-centred, dominant and outspoken, but as she is sensitive, articulate and versatile, her dominant behaviour is acceptable to others whom she influences.

They then go on to report the results of a test in which they used psychological test results to predict the performance of supervisors on the assessment programmes. They were correct in 82 per cent of the cases (N = 120).

The authors hold that the critical question is not whether assessment programmes are too expensive but whether they contribute significantly more to the validity of the selection decision than other measures. This is indeed a critical question, which numerous studies have failed adequately to answer, but Wilson and Tatge have not considered the information which is yielded by an assessment centre for *development* purposes. If one were only concerned to select people for promotion, it is arguable that the assessment programme approach might be thought unduly expensive. One is usually concerned, however, to help the individual participant to develop his abilities so that he can perform more effectively in his present job as well as beginning a planned growth towards a range of possible future jobs. Under those circumstances we would hesitate before jettisoning so rich a source of information as assessment programmes have shown themselves to be.

Having established that assessment programmes appear to be measuring dominance, capacity for status, social presence and self-acceptance, Wilson and Tatge then go on to ask whether those characteristics are significantly different from those measured by more traditional methods. They conclude that, while it may be true that the programmes do measure characteristics not measurable by other methods, it has not been established that they do. They remain unimpressed by the difference between paper and pencil tests and overall assessment programme ratings for predicting management performance. While recognizing that assessors must gain something from their work in the centres, they are not certain that these skills could not be more economically provided in some other way – although they do not go on to show that some other way has in fact been shown to be more cost-effective. Finally, they express the belief that people would rather be judged on real life performance than by being processed through the quite threatening assessment. This belief has not been borne out by our experiment, although it is true that some anxiety is sometimes expressed by participants before the programme starts. Provided that entirely open discussion is encouraged, we have not found that people find the situation particularly threatening. We believe, since it is beliefs that are being matched here, that it is better to face the possibility that people may be initially uneasy about an open and clearly stated method of assessment than it is to live with the thought that no one really knows how development decisions are made.

Barnett (1975) working in Edgars Stores in South Africa, reports that they have put 270 individuals through their assessment programme. More than half have subsequently been promoted, and 'we have to date not had one single obvious disappointment'. Three individuals who did rather poorly have been promoted and performed 'reasonably well'. None has been promoted to grade four level at the time of writing, and that is the level for which potential is being sought. It will be interesting to read of further progress in this study.

Farnsworth (1975) reports that 3M in the United Kingdom were sufficiently pleased with the results of their newly installed assessment programme to extend the procedures to a further 200 salesmen operating in three of its largest product groups. Mitchel (1975), working with SOHIO, presents data on 254 managers attending an assessment programme. These data were examined for changes in validity over time. Twenty four predictors were correlated with a criterion of salary growth measured one, three, and five years after the managers were assessed. Before conducting the analyses the managers were grouped into three generations based on the year in which they were assessed. Peer and assessor ratings, along with linear combinations, were found significantly correlated with the criterion. The multiple correlations generalized across time and generations. A general increasing trend in the validity coefficients was noted over time. Comparison of overall assessor rating with multiple correlation did not indicate any marked superiority for actuarial prediction.

Moses and Boehm (1975) have examined the relationship of assessment programme performance to the managerial progress of women. Data concerning their current management level at the end of 1973 were obtained for 4,846 women assessed between 1963 and 1971. Performance at the assessment programme was strongly related to subsequent promotions into management and advancement within management, see table 30 on page 210.

The distribution of the women's assessment ratings was very similar to a corresponding distribution for men assessed using the same techniques, *see* table 31 on page 210. The assessed dimensions relating most strongly to subsequent management level (organizing and planning, decision making and leadership) were the same for men and women. They conclude that assessment programme methods appear valid for the selection of women managers and do not result in the promotion of proportionately fewer women assessees.

Huck and Bray (1976) studied management assessment programme evaluations and subsequent job performance of white and black female employees. The sample consisted of two groups of (a) non-management women (91 white, 35 black) who attended an assessment programme during 1966–71 and who were later promoted to a supervisory position, and (b) women (238 black, 241 white) who attended the same assessment programmes but had not been promoted. The purpose of the programme was to help in the selection of non-management employees for promotion to the first supervisory level. Each

Table 30
Distributions of final assessment ratings and corresponding subsequent promotions

| Performance criteria | Assessment performances | | | | Subsequent promotions women only | | | |
| | Women | | Men (Moses, 1972) | | 1 promotions | | 2 + promotions | |
	N	%	N	%	N	%	N	%
More than acceptable	294	6.1	638	7.2	208	71.4	20	6.9
Acceptable	1,364	28.1	2,279	25.6	954	70.4	82	6.1
Questionable	1,403	29.0	2,902	32.7	736	52.6	39	2.8
Not acceptable	1,785	36.8	3,066	34.5	552	30.9	11	0.6

Source: Moses and Boehm 1975

Table 31
Correlations between each assessment measure and management level of men and women

| Assessment measure | Management level (Moses, 1972) | |
	Women (N=4,846)	Men (N=8,885)
Overall assessment rating	0.37	0.44
Organizing and planning	0.30	0.34
Decision making	0.28	0.34
Leadership	0.26	0.38
School and College Ability Test (total score)	0.25	0.31
Oral communication	0.24	0.27
SCAT verbal score	0.23	0.20
Perception	0.20	0.31
SCAT quantitative score	0.20	0.18
Written communication	0.20	0.25
Rank order correlation between men and women is 0.75 ($p < 0.01$)		

Source: Moses and Boehm 1975

participant was given a rating on each of 18 dimensions as well as an overall assessment rating. These results were then compared with supervisory ratings of performance and future potential. The findings confirm earlier research (a) that assessment programme results are good predictors of later performance, (b) that the overall assessment rating is the single best predictor, and (c) that assessment programme results are more predictive of potential for advancement than of performance on the current job. No difference was found in the validity of predictions for blacks and for whites. Finding (b) might especially be noted by those managers who are reluctant to make overall assessments. We have some evidence that UK managers quite like to avoid making that overall judgement, perhaps because it is more unequivocal than they are used to handling.

Klimoski and Strickland (1977) offer a valuable review of assessment programme studies with special regard to the criteria used, staff composition and number of organizations involved. They note impressive, consistent results, but they also identify a disturbing trend. Acceptance of the method, they suggest, is often based on relatively few studies, conducted by fewer organizations, using a limited range of criteria. It is argued that possibly the assessment programme evaluates candidates based on familiarity with the preferences of the decision makers who will actually promote, thus merely duplicating existing decision studies incorporating alternative predictors and criteria. The reality in most UK companies is that the numbers do not exist to support that kind of study. This is regrettable, but may not be so disturbing as Klimoski and Strickland fear. At the Observer Conferences with which we have been involved there has sometimes been very vigorous discussion between the senior line manager observers about whether they were in danger of perpetuating what already existed. In the absence of absolute criteria of effectiveness for organizations (and their existence seems unlikely), we are forced back on to the judgement of existing senior managers in the light of the information gained during the programme. This would be more worrying were it not that the programmes do generate a great deal of new information and lead to a most thorough and informed review of the direction that management is taking. It seems to be a rule that organizations whose managers are flexible enough to countenance assessment programmes are also flexible enough to be able to change direction if the evidence warrants it. Those managers who are not flexible enough to do this do not opt for assessment programmes in the first place. This does not help the survival of their organizations but it says nothing about the contribution of assessment programmes either.

Schmitt (1977) provides encouraging evidence about inter-rater reliability (conspect reliability). His study indicated that a very high level of inter-rater reliability is regularly achieved on the major determinants of overall ratings. Since we have already seen that overall ratings are among the strongest predictors of potential, this adds strength to the argument for the acceptance of the assessment programme approach. Anstey (1977) reports further on the results of a 30 year follow up of the Civil Service Selection Boards (CSSB). While confirming his earlier results he goes on to make some recommendations which our own experience would reinforce. He indicates that more attention needs to be paid to managerial qualities (we would prefer 'behaviour'). He also feels that it is to improvements in career planning and development rather than selection that the greatest contributions can be made in the future. Possibly this is why so many of the companies with whom we have worked have chosen to call their assessment programmes 'Individual Development Programmes' instead. There is a general view that the most useful focus is indeed on development, both in the present position and in the future, rather than simply on selection.

Schmitt and Hill (1977) report a slightly worrying result concerning possible unconscious discrimination on a sex and colour basis. Using 306 non-management candidates for promotion to supervisory positions, divided into 54 groups of five or six employees in each group, they observed that there was a tendency for some assessment ratings of black women to be negatively correlated with the number of white males in the group. Further, the ratings of white males tended to be higher when the number of white males in the assessment group increased. While the results are not dramatic, they highlight the need for continual vigilance in the area of discrimination on bases other than performance relevant to the job to be done.

Hinrichs (1978) reports an eight year follow up of one management assessment centre in which the validity of the method is once again demonstrated. He makes a number of useful points about the study, however. First, the criterion is, once again, level attained after the time period selected. Hinrichs asks that future predictive studies try to escape from this procedure and concentrate instead on criteria concerned with effective performance in the management job. While admitting the difficulty of achieving this criterion, he implies that no really satisfactory study of the validity of the assessment programme will have been achieved until such a criterion has been used. This, of course, is the force behind our insistence on a thorough diagnosis and interrogation of the characteristics of effective behaviour as a manager before any programme is designed. Second, he points out that the clarity of the assessment programme procedure is a great help in determining the fairness or otherwise of the selection and development of future managers in line with equal opportunity legislation. It is much easier to spot inequity and to deal with it when the process is well understood. Less systematic approaches may be overturned simply on the basis of obscurity. This is not an area where benefit of the doubt is easily given. Third, he asks that comparative studies be carried out of the value added by assessment programmes against other, apparently simpler techniques. Our own concern for this point is shown in chapter 9, which is concerned with costs and benefits. To anticipate that chapter, the cost consequences of a wrong decision are so considerable that it is not difficult to justify expenditure on a quite elaborate process of identification and development. The question remains whether an assessment programme is necessarily the most cost effective alternative. Only further research will determine this and that, in turn, depends on other techniques being as well defined and leading to results as precisely formulated as those of an assessment programme.

It is perhaps encouraging that Huck (1977), in an entirely independent review of the research evidence concerning assessment programmes, comes to very much the same conclusions as those presented here, including the plea for more performance related measures of managerial effectiveness to be used as validation criteria.

Our own work has confirmed the view that an assessment programme designed for a specific situation can have predictive validity. So far, over 600 people, at widely varying levels and in many different organizations, have gone through different assessment programmes designed for those organizations as a result of a thorough diagnosis. The satisfaction reported with those programmes appears to be directly related to the thoroughness of that diagnosis. Where, for reasons of (false) economy, a less than searching investigation of management effectiveness has been undertaken, the resulting programme has been discovered to be less well focussed on the needs of the organization. While research continues in the various organizations concerned we are able to say that:

1 More is known about participants after an assessment programme than had been found out by any other method so far used
2 Some of the information discovered about participants is greatly different from what had been expected
3 Better development and placement decisions are being made as a result of the information obtained
4 Participants are reacting well to the assessment programme approach.

Evidence in support of 3 above varies between organizations, as they tend to use different measures which, while satisfactory to them, makes for untidy science. However, if the evaluation of the participants by senior management, once they have moved into new posts, is any guide, then very few mistakes are now being made in areas where before there was considerable lack of confidence and evidence of poor choices. Given the research evidence offered earlier in this chapter, one might be surprised if this were not the case.

Evidence for 4 above may be found in table 32 on page 214, where it will be seen that participants are confident that the programmes measure the right qualities and that the data generated by the programmes should be used to help in the identification and development of future managers.

Table 32
Participants' opinions about assessment programmes

To what extent do you believe the programme measures important qualities required of your company's managers? (N = 663)

To a very great extent	To a great extent	To a moderate extent	Not very much	Not at all
28%	50%	16%	5%	—
(186)	(333)	(108)	(36)	—

To what extent do you believe the programme information should be used to help in the identification and development of future managers? (N = 694)

To a very great extent	To a great extent	To a moderate extent	Not very much	Not at all
20%	60%	16%	4%	—
(140)	(414)	(110)	(28)	(2)

It should be noted that these opinions are not collected immediately at the end of the programmes, when there might well be some euphoria (or despondency, depending on the outcome), but some weeks after the feedback interview has taken place. In this way participants are responding when they have as much information as possible about the outcome of the programme for them, including action plans, and will have been back behind their desks long enough for any novelty effect or post-event delirium to have worn off. It is by now a commonplace that reactions to training or management development events taken as people leave are hardly worth serious attention.

Favourable reactions from both managers and managed are useful but not sufficient. To clinch the argument information is needed about the follow up to the programmes. If we are serious in our contention that the emphasis is now on development, and much less upon selection, we need to be satisfied that such development is actually taking place. This is extremely difficult to establish with any precision, which does not excuse us from making the effort. At the time of writing the most encouraging evidence we have to offer is that virtually all of the organizations which have implemented some form of assessment programme three or more years ago are now under pressure from within to answer the question, 'What next?'. The managers and ex-participants appear to feel that the assessment made was valid and that the action plans agreed afterwards were relevant to the real needs of the individual and the organization. They have now completed those action plans. Some individuals have been promoted as well although most have not because the vacancies were not there. Since the focus of the programme was elsewhere than on promotion this does not seem to cause difficulties. But there is now pressure to move on to the next stage of development, whatever that may be. We would like to think that organizations finding themselves in this position are better placed to manage the changing nature of work in the future than those who have not taken so thorough a look at themselves. We shall continue to encourage those organizations to monitor their own progress to see whether such a claim may be justified.

Attention has been drawn by Anstey and many others to the problem of achieving a satisfactory criterion against which to evaluate the results of the assessment programmes. We must confess to unease when the programmes are judged against such criteria as supervisors' ranking and rating, salary growth achieved or job level achieved after so many years. These seem to us to be derivative or second order measures and we would welcome the possibility of discovering on the job measures against which to validate assessment programmes. Some work reported by Fogli, Hulin and Blood (1971) and Campbell, Dunnette, Arvey and Hellervik (1973) seems to us to be pointing the way. These two groups have been concerned with the development and evaluation of behaviourally based rating scales. They make a clear distinction, as we do, between criterion measures that assess individual performance in terms of concrete job function and those that reflect organizational outcomes several steps removed from actual behaviour (salary level, for example). It is argued that we should be more concerned with the former and they present an example of nine criterion dimensions for department managers in a nationwide retail store. The resulting behaviourally based ratings were compared with those achieved in the more usual way on a sample of 537 department managers. The behavioural scales yielded less method variance, less halo error and less leniency error. The nine dimensions used were: supervising sales personnel; handling customer complaints and making adjustments; meeting day to day deadlines, merchandise ordering; developing and planning special promotions, assessing sales trends and acting to maintain merchandising position, using company systems and following through on administrative operations; communicating relevant information to associates and to higher management; diagnosing and alleviating special department problems. This kind of scale seems to us no more than an extension of good objective setting practice. The use of these principles for evolving clearly job related criteria against which to assess assessment programmes (or any other personnel and management techniques equally difficult to evaluate) is exercising us currently.

Referring back to the discussion at the beginning of this chapter concerning different types of validation and reliability, we believe that the evidence justifies the following conclusions:

1 Face validity is extremely high. There is ample evidence that participants react favourably to assessment programmes once the initial suspicion has faded.

2 Content validity appears to have been achieved insofar as satisfactory predictions are possible, but there is still some lack of clarity about how many measures are necessary in any one programme to achieve satisfactory coverage.

3 Construct validity appears to be satisfied insofar as no one has ever queried what we mean by potential, and we have not seen it raised as a problem in the literature.

4 Concurrent validity appears to be well satisfied in that assessment programmes have been checked quite frequently against other measures (either psychometric or supervisors' rankings and ratings) and found to be in good agreement.

5 Predictive validity remains strongly indicated but not proven. Many reports exist which purport to demonstrative predictive validity for assessment programmes, some of them using such large numbers that the case begins to look very strong. But there remains doubt because it seems difficult to produce a really watertight experimental design which will permit uncontaminated data to be compared over a suitable length of time with job related measures of performance. Until we find another management which feels able to wait for us as long as the management of AT&T, and a research group which manages to draw together the right measures and good criteria, it seems likely that the answer will remain extremely positive but short of conclusive.

Validation checklists

As will have been apparent from the studies quoted above, the business of validation is a difficult one: even the experts have not yet found a satisfactory way of answering all the questions that need to be dealt with before we can be really confident that assessment programmes are uniquely valuable as accurate predictors of future performance. However, there is a need for some form of simple procedure so that at least the basics of validation can be attended to by the reader. We outline below two procedures: one for a concurrent validation and one for a predictive validation. Neither is a complete answer, but they will both

216

provide useful data to help determine whether or not a particular assessment programme may be doing a useful job.

In both cases we assume that a diagnosis has been caried out in order to determine the characteristics of effective performance at a given level or levels, and that decisions have been taken, based largely on that diagnosis, about which characteristics can best be sought out in some existing way and which might necessitate the introduction of an assessment programme. In this way we ensure that the programme has been designed to look for only those things which it is felt cannot usefully be sought some other way. If the diagnosis has been successful it will have led to the formulation of a number of job related criteria against which any assessment technique can be validated, quite apart from the more usual, second order criteria mentioned in many of the studies. We have also assumed that inter observer reliabilities will be regularly checked, since there is little point in seeking validity if reliability has not been achieved.

Validation — concurrent

Purpose: To compare the results of a new measure with the results of existing measures in the same group.

1 Collect current performance ratings, supervisors' reports, data on performance against job related criteria for each prospective participant on the programme. Ensure that the observers have not had access to this information.
2 Run the assessment programme.
3 Compare the assessment programme results with the previously obtained measures.
4 Determine how much new or different information the programme has produced. If none, or very little, consider whether it is worth running further programmes of that design. If the new information is judged sufficient, run further programmes of the same design but continue to check concurrent validities.

Alternatively

1 Ask the observers to complete the final evaluation forms for the programme, as far as possible, some three months before the programme is due to run. They may use whatever sources of information about the participants as would normally be made available to them when gathering information for the purpose of identifying and developing potential. Seal this information away.
2 Run the programme.
3 Compare the actual performance on the programme with that predicted by the observers. Check it for amount, detail, differences and accuracy.
4 As (4) above.

Predictive validity

Purpose: To discover if a given measure taken now is an accurate predictor of future performance against some agreed criteria.

1 Determine the future performance that it is desired to predict and ensure that it is stated in measurable terms. This may be a salary growth rate or position after a period; a promotion rate or position achieved after a stated period; or preferably, some job related performance criteria derived from the initial diagnosis.
2 Run the assessment programme.
3 Divide the participants randomly into two groups. For one group, release the assessment data for operational use; for the second group, retain the data unused.
4 Check the progress of the two groups at intervals, retaining the unused data for as long as possible (three to five years would be good; 10 years would be excellent).
5 At the point when further retention of unused data becomes impracticable, determine whether the assessment programme predictions have held good
   (a) for the operational group
   (b) for the retained group
   and check whether there are any systematic differences between the groups. (A luxury touch would be to have a third group which had no experience of assessment programmes at all, but had been identified and developed through existing conventional routes. In order to match these three groups for age, length of service, sex, race etc it may be only the larger organizations that could attempt the more elaborate forms of validation.)

If pre-programme predictions have been made by the observers, a substitute for the third group outlined above can partially be achieved by checking progress of the participants as predicted by the observers without assessment programme data.

It seems possible that a truly 'clean' validation study is simply not possible since, whatever measures are taken to hold data in confidence, the participants themselves have memories and will retain knowledge of what happened and what they learnt. Even in the absence of feedback, participants come away from a programme with a shrewd idea of how they have performed and this knowledge may remain with them a long time.

Despite the difficulties, it is not merely worthwhile to conduct some form of predictive validation, it is essential if an organization is ever to know the value of the procedures it is using, be they assessment programmes or something more conventional.

Chapter 9

Costs and benefits

The discussion about the validity of assessment programmes seems likely to be with us for some time yet, despite the amount of support for the view that the programmes do work. The problem is that there is less evidence to support the view that they work better than anything else currently being used. Small wonder, perhaps, that would be users are met on occasion with reserve, if not downright hostility. Not infrequently this reserve is voiced in money terms. It is suggested, not unreasonably, that a programme costing as much as this one appears to, and demanding so much valuable management time, has got to have a better case made for it than appears to be possible at the moment before it is a serious competitor for resources. This argument tends to be put forcefully and early in the conversation.

In this chapter we attempt to show how an assessment programme may be costed, which is not particularly difficult, and how some estimate can be put upon the value side of the equation, which is more of a problem.

The costing exercise is reasonably straightforward once certain assumptions have been agreed and made. The main reason why every company comes up with a different figure for the cost of its programmes from the cost of everyone else's is that there is no consensus about what should be included in the costing part of the operation, quite apart from the fact that each company's programme tends to be more or less different from all the others. This is as it should be, since each company's needs will be different and a different programme will be required to service those needs best, but it reduces the likelihood of finding an agreed cost per head assessed. Perhaps it is not a sensible thing to try to do. We present here one basis for costing, without at all suggesting that it is necessarily the best, nor that it should be adopted as a standard: this is simply an account of one way of doing it, based fairly closely upon the way in which one company actually went about it. The factors that are considered include the scale of the programme (frequency, number of assessees and observers), the cost of professional and clerical manning, time cost of management observers and candidate attendance, equipment and materials, hotel or company accommodation and administrative costs. When there has been any doubt, the figure has been estimated high rather than low. In general, an attempt has been made to find the highest cost that can reasonably be incurred, in order to make the task of justifying the programme as difficult as possible. It will be clear from the foregoing that we are not talking about marginal costs and our approach was rejected out of hand by a major company in Sweden which held the view that the only reasonable costs to estimate were marginal costs. This may be a good point from which to begin disagreeing with our thesis!

Estimates of the value of assessment programmes – or indeed any form of identifying and developing potential – are rarer, probably because the assumptions that one can make are even more varied. There has, however, been a growing awareness that personnel need not just be a debit entry in the books. Among personnel people, the attitude that personnel should not be a debit entry has been common enough for quite a while but the numbers to prove otherwise have been a little slow in coming. Recently, however, there has been some movement to make good this deficiency. Giles and Robinson (1972) promoted the concept of human asset accounting. Smallwood (1973) approached the problem through 'added value per £1 payroll'. Logan Cheek (1973) provided an account of how cost effectiveness had come to the personnel function in the Xerox Corporation, in which he defined the key procedural steps as:

1 Define and describe each personnel programme (whether proposed or ongoing) in a discrete package
2 Separate for special treatment those programmes that are legally required
3 Evaluate all programmes on the basis of these factors: (a) 'state of the art', (b) ease of implementation, (c) net economic benefits, (d) economic risks of *not* acting
4 Rank all programmes and allocate staff and deploy resources accordingly.

While not claiming that he has a universal cure, Cheek does point out that his approach has worked in helping Xerox to plan its long term manpower strategy and has been used to develop operating budgets for selected personnel units throughout the organization. His approach seems to us more likely to provide a planned context in which assessment programmes can be evaluated than does the human asset accounting approach, about which reservations have been expressed by Cannon (1974 and 1979) among others.

The gain to be made by introducing an assessment programme depends on how good the organization has been at developing and choosing its managers so far without such a programme. This defines the level of performance that has been acceptable historically and hence the expected level of success among present candidates if nothing further is done. Let us assume that the organization is presently working on a 50/50 success ratio. In other words, the way it is presently doing the job it can expect 50 per cent of those it selects for management to be doing a fully satisfactory job. The 'fully satisfactory job' will have been defined in behavioural terms at the outset of the investigation, otherwise it will be difficult to say anything helpful about comparisons between existing techniques and new ones. Working on the 50/50 hypothesis, if nothing further were done at all, and selection were made by chance, for every 100 management vacancies 50 of those selected to do the job would be entirely satisfactory. If on the other hand all candidates in the population from which one is selecting are suitable, no further effort need be put into management selection because any of the 100, whoever was picked, would perform satisfactorily. A pool of under employed talent of this kind would pose problems of its own, quite apart from its apparent rarity. In general, an organization stands to gain most from a new selection method when only a small proportion of the available candidates is of satisfactory standard.

Next, the organization will need to investigate the absolute number of candidates relative to the number of vacancies. If there is a larger number of candidates than hitherto, in a given proportion of suitable to unsuitable, then for the same number of vacancies the efficiency of the selection should increase through the increased discrimination available, but only in the sense of having a higher proportion of the chosen proving successful. It will be achieved at the expense of also having an increased number of people *not* chosen who would otherwise have been successful. Where selection is being made from outside this is relatively less important from the organization's point of view since these individuals remain outside the organization. That is why, in selection strategy, they are known as 'selectee error', as distinct from 'selector error' which occurs when the people selected subsequently fail in the job. All selections potentially contain these two types of error. In their discussion of the foregoing considerations, Finkle and Jones (1970), present the view that selection becomes increasingly inefficient as populations are excluded on irrelevant grounds: 'Fewer Presidents in today's expanding organizations can afford the luxury of limiting their identification of talent to those men they personally can discover and develop.' They go on to review the uncomfortable fact that selectee error in internal selection becomes a problem for the selector because it is an error that stays with him:

More important, relying on cream to rise to the top – the 'Good Man Theory' – is literally using the business itself as a competitive testing ground for talent. Those who attain high positions of responsibility may be said to have passed the test. But what of those who have not? Have they failed? The serious disadvantage of using the work situation as a testing ground of ability is the great likelihood of over promoting and then doing nothing about it. The cream

221

may rise to the top, but the ranks of middle management may be saturated with those who have exposed their weaknesses.

The two types of error are illustrated in table 33 below.

Table 33
Selectee and selector error

		Rejected	Selected
Success ratio axis	Success	Rejected but would have succeeded **SELECTEE ERROR**	Selected and succeeded
Job proficiency criteria	Failure	Rejected and would have failed	Selected and failed **SELECTOR ERROR**

Rejected   Selected
Selection ratio axis
Selection decision criteria

Now let us examine the effect of different success ratios by means of two numerical examples. By chance selection, for ratios 0.5 and 0.1, the outcomes would be:

Table 34
Outcomes, by chance selection, for ratios 0.5 and 0.1, over 100 people

for 0.5			for 0.1		
Succeed	25	25	Succeed	9	1
Fail	25	25	Fail	81	9
	Reject	Select		Reject	Select

Now let us suppose that the assessment programme works perfectly: in other words, the predictions made during the programme correlate $+1.0$ with an acceptable criterion of effective management performance. In the 0.5 and 0.1 cases, selection would then be as shown in table 35.

Suppose that the assessment programme only improves performance on management selection from chance to a correlation of 0.5 with the criterion, which may be a more realistic assumption. Then selection would be as in table 36.

222

Table 35

Outcomes when the assessment programme correlates perfectly positively with an acceptable
criterion of management performance

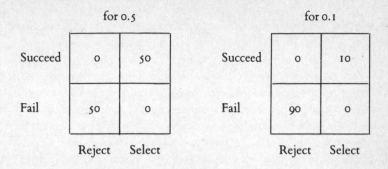

for 0.5

	Reject	Select
Succeed	0	50
Fail	50	0

for 0.1

	Reject	Select
Succeed	0	10
Fail	90	0

Table 36
Outcomes when the assessment programme correlates 0.5 with an acceptable criterion of
management performance with 10 vacancies

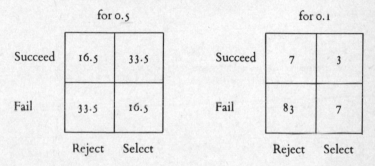

for 0.5

	Reject	Select
Succeed	16.5	33.5
Fail	33.5	16.5

for 0.1

	Reject	Select
Succeed	7	3
Fail	83	7

For the 0.5 case there has been an improvement over the chance situation (25 out
of 50 selected being successful; 50 per cent) to 33.5 out of 50 selected being
successful; 67 per cent. In other words, a 67 per cent correct choice is now being
made instead of the original 50 per cent.

For the 0.1 case there has been an improvement over the chance situation (one
out of 10 selected being successful; 10 per cent) to three out of 10 selected being
successful; 30 per cent). This is, of course, a much higher relative gain.

This demonstrates the fact that the poorer the standards of present management performance, or the worse the present success ratio, the bigger the pay off
from any method which increases the validity of what is being done.

The values are precisely calculable from the model and a set of tables (the
Taylor-Russel tables) is available. So that if the research evidence were that data
from an assessment programme gave a correlation of, say, 0.5 with accepted

criteria of effective management performance, and if the evidence were that by present standards, without an assessment programme, there would be, say, 20 selection mistakes in 100 management appointments, then the tables would enable one to say precisely what the expected gain from the programme should be, whether there would be an improvement to only 16 poor decisions out of 100, or 15 or 14 as the tables might show for this particular case.

However, this relatively simple picture is complicated by the second factor referred to previously, namely the selection ratio. The selection ratio can here be thought of as the stringency of selection dependent upon the proportion of vacancies to applicants. Let us take again the case where 10 people out of 100 are picked when the success ratio is .1 (in other words, only 10 per cent of the 100 are good enough). By chance alone we should expect to achieve only one correct choice in the 10 selected, and therefore nine incorrect (*see* table 34). An assessment programme with a validity of .5 would yield three correct choices and seven incorrect (*see* table 35).

Suppose now that there are 20 vacancies instead of 10. Then, for the .5 validity programme, the picture changes from that shown in table 36 to that in table 37 below.

Table 37

Outcomes when the assessment programme correlates 0.5 with an acceptable criterion of management performance with 10 and 20 vacancies

	The 10 vacancy case for 0.5			The 20 vacancy case for 0.5	
Succeed	7	3	Succeed	5	5
Fail	83	7	Fail	75	15
	Reject Bottom 90	Select Top 10		Reject Bottom 80	Select Top 20

In this situation, although more promotions are available, 20 instead of 10, and although more correct choices are made *absolutely*, five as against three, the *relative* performance is less good and the total error (selector error plus selectee error) has increased. There has been a move from seven wrong selections plus seven wrong rejections (14 mistakes) to 15 wrong selections plus five wrong rejections (20 mistakes).

In the case of initial selection, as was remarked earlier, selectee error is less important because those competent people who are rejected remain outside the organization. Assuming that there are sufficient vacancies it would of course be preferable to have recruited them, but the problem is less important than that of incorrectly recruiting people who are going to fail. There is no consideration here of the effect on the applicant of being incorrectly excluded from a job for which he is in fact suited. In the case of internal selection it has already been pointed out that the selectee error is important. If there are fewer promotion vacancies than competent candidates, some of the competent must remain unselected to become a potential wastage or low morale cost. But it has been demonstrated that selection methods short of perfection must always increase this number more than management might expect whenever there are more candidates than jobs.

The approach to validation discussed in chapter 8 takes some account of the interaction of success ratio, selection ratio and the validity of the selection method. The percentage success to be obtained from all possible combinations of all three can be read off from the Taylor-Russel tables.

To attempt to determine utility, let us now put some possible values into the model for a large but fictitious company. This company employs about 12,000 people in Britain and about another 6,000 overseas. It pursues a policy of promotion from within wherever possible and avoids some of the difficulties of retaining men who have reached the limit of their usefulness to the company by a scheme of voluntary premature retirement (VPR). Precise details of the scheme as it applies to any one individual vary depending upon length of service and grade attained but, generally speaking, the individual who opts for VPR will receive a tax free lump sum of between two and three times his present salary without in any way affecting his pension rights when he becomes of pensionable age. Various assumptions about the salary structure will become apparent as the example is worked through. Job grades are defined separately for labour, technical, clerical and secretarial jobs on the one hand, and professional and managerial posts on the other (roughly corresponding to 'exempt' and 'non-exempt' in the United States). The first group's grades range from level 12 to level 28; the grades of the second group from level 50 to level 62 in Britain, with some special higher grades for some overseas managers. VPR is divided into five categories, A to E, calculated according to a formula that takes into account age, length of service, salary currently paid and position held, together with rate of progress to present position. Category A VPRs are the highest grade and Category E VPRs are therefore the lowest.

The company's manpower planning model shows that for 1983, with zero growth, they should expect a total of 36 promotion moves of grades 57, 58 and 59 staffs into grades 58, 59 and 60 level jobs. This is the sum of all promotions, regardless of the number of grades moved, 1, 2 or 3. The promotable population is 415. The selection ratio is therefore .09.

Characteristic validation coefficients so far obtained for assessment programmes seem to vary in the range of 0.4 to 0.6. Let us assume that the correlation coefficient r = 0.5 for this company's programme.

We now have to make a guess at the percentage of management selection failures that the company presently has at the grade levels 57 to 60. Let us make what has been called a 'charitable' estimate of not more than two out of 10. This would make the success ratio .8. With, let us say, an average of 40 replacement promotions per annum into grades 58 to 60, it would only require an annual VPR rate of 5 per cent from the population of over 260 in these grades to support this ratio. The VPR rate among Categories C to E is thought to be one of the 'hardest' (most quantified) criteria that the company presently has of failure in management performance.

With a success ratio of .8, a selection of .1, and a validation coefficient for the assessment programme of r = .5, the Taylor-Russel tables show that 97 per cent of the promotees will perform satisfactorily. We can compare this with the Taylor-Russel table values for an assessment programme of zero correlation coefficient, which show that 80 per cent would perform satisfactorily. One way of expressing this is to say that the assessment programme identifies a further 17 per cent satisfactory performers. A more realistic way of expressing this improvement is to show this additional 17 per cent as a proportion of the 80 per cent who would have been promoted by chance, giving us a calculation of (97 − 80)/80, which when expressed as a percentage of the number of people who have been promoted by chance equals a 21.25 per cent improvement over previous practice, due to the assessment programme.

In numbers, the values of selector/selectee error are presented in table 38 below.

Table 38
Values for selector/selectee error for chance and for an assessment programme with a validation coefficient of 0.5

	for r = 0				for r = 0.5		
Succeed	303	29	332	Succeed	297	35	332
Fail	76	7	83	Fail	82	1	83
	379	36	415 in grades 57–59		379	36	415 in grades 57–59
	Reject	Select			Reject	Select	

Selection ratio   36 : 415 = 0.1
Success ratio   332 : 83 = 0.8

It is now clear that, by using an assessment programme which correlates .5 with an accepted criterion, the company has achieved two complementary things. First, it has avoided promoting six people who would have proved unsatisfactory at their promoted level. Secondly, the company has avoided leaving unpromoted six people who should have been selected. It is important to note, however, that the company still has 297 promotable people on its hands who do not get promoted. This problem is referred to again later in this chapter.

The first group of people, those who should not have been promoted and, as a result of the programme, were not, can be costed on the assumption that they would have become category B, C or D VPR cases. Length of service considerations would normally put them beyond category E at this grade level. Assume an average salary at VPR of £12,000 (the midpoint of grade 57). The minimum cost of a category C case would be £36,000 on the assumption that the calculation of present value of future *ex gratia* payments does not need to be discounted because of the effects of inflation. The minimum cost of a category D case would be £24,000. The calculated cost of six cases on a mean of C + D costs comes to £180,000. It should perhaps be noted in passing that these costs are not finally avoided if VPR cases move into a category where the pension fund takes over. Increased early retirement on to the fund would eventually mean revaluation of the pension fund loading by the actuaries. Even a small increase in loading – say by 1 per cent of the salary bill – would cost the company £½ million per year at least.

Next, the company should add the positive value of six additional correct selections. At an average salary of £12,000 plus 100 per cent oncost, this represents £24,000 per man. Assuming for the sake of simplicity that they are twice as effective as the six incorrectly selected, and therefore showing half the cost as net gain, this amounts to £12,000 per individual, or £72,000 for all six. On the not unrealistic assumption that the half life of the unsuitable candidates from selection to VPR is six years, then the total gain is £432,000.

For the six wrongly unpromoted people, the cost calculation depends in part upon whether resignation is assumed or not. If resignation is assumed, then there must be a replacement cost calculation. If resignation is not assumed, then some estimate will have to be made of the effect of being overlooked on subsequent work behaviour. Let us assume that resignation does not take place. Then, costing the survivor at a basic salary of £12,000 plus oncost at 100 per cent, he is costing the company £24,000 per annum. Making the further modest assumption of a 10 per cent decrease in efficiency as a result of the demotivating effect of being passed over for promotion, this adds a further £2,400 per man, or £14,400 for all six. Assuming, as before, a half life of six years for this group, this adds a total of £86,000 to the value.

The three sums add to £698,000. The cost-benefit equation therefore now reads:

Value of programme = £698,000 − cost of programme

Before calculating the programme's cost, the company can, if it so chooses, add an intangible to the benefit. It is stated by most programme participants, both assessees and observers, that the programme has considerable training value for them. In many cases the programmes are run consecutively with a management training course. Companies running assessment programmes rate the training value of the programmes very highly. No attempt is made here to put a money value on the training benefit but the equation may now read:

Value of programme = £698,000 − cost of programme + value of training

The assessment programme is costed on assumptions derived chiefly from American company practice. It will be seen that there is a fairly lavish use of resources, and that the assumptions about salaries and manning tend to be generous. This is done deliberately in order to load the cost element of the calculation as heavily as seems reasonable. Most programmes run in Britain will cost substantially less than this.

The assessment programme costing assumptions are as follows:

1 Six programmes per annum
2 Twelve assessees per programme, for three days, at an average salary cost of £18,000 (£9,000 + 100 per cent oncost) = roughly one man year = £18,000 opportunity cost
3 Three line manager assessors per programme, for five days, at an average salary cost of £34,000 (£17,000 + 100 per cent oncost) = $\frac{1}{3}$ man year = £11,400 opportunity cost
4 One administrator, at a salary of £12,000 per annum for $\frac{1}{3}$ year, plus two clerk/typist/test assistants, also for $\frac{1}{3}$ year at £3,000 per annum each = £6,000 + 100 per cent oncost = £12,000
5 Two professional staff (psychologists) for assessment and for research follow-up, at $\frac{1}{3}$ year for one and $\frac{2}{3}$ year for the other, at a rate of £12,000 per annum + 100 per cent oncost = £24,000
6 Materials − say £1,200 per annum.
7 One test room, 200 sq ft for three days; two interview rooms, 200 sq ft for three days; one observation room, 400 sq ft for five days and all at £20 per annum per sq ft rental, for six programmes = £1,250. Alternatively, accommodation for candidates and administrator only, plus conference rooms as above, at a fair hotel = £10,440.

The totals come to £67,850 in company premises, or £77,040 in a hotel. This works out at £942 or £1,070 respectively per candidate. To take an example from real life, one company has produced a figure of £350 per candidate, exclusive of assessors' and administrators' salaries. This figure is in line with the above calculations where these salaries are at an oncost of 200 per cent on the factors in that company's calculation. Other companies have produced figures as low as £120 per head.

The full cost-benefit equation now reads as follows:

Value of programme = £698,000 − £77,040 + value of training
(These calculations assume the higher, hotel cost.)

Finally, the question of the very low selection ratio should be discussed. This point was mentioned briefly above and it should be borne in mind that the effects of more skilful selection in the fictitious company have been only to remove six people from the pool of 297 promotables who remain unpromoted. The pool is unacceptably large and the problem will not be cured entirely by assessment programmes. In addition, it is necessary to monitor the initial quality mix and its flow through the grade structure. This should lead to better supply and demand ratios at each level and should therefore produce considerable economies, even though it might reduce the gain from an assessment programme procedure at any given level. It would reduce the level of frustration and also reduce the amount of 'voluntary' premature retirement which, for most people, still has echoes of 'being pushed on the scrap heap'.

It can be argued that assessment programmes have a role to play at all stages of this process, particularly in the context of trying to ensure that as wide a population as possible is considered for promotion, without the intervention of irrelevant variables such as the fact that a given individual may not be known to any of the selectors in his normal work situation. For many companies in the 1980s, present selection ratios will stem from the reduced promotion rates resulting from the change from growth to zero growth, or even decline. The problem for a number of organizations may not be so much one of whom to promote but of determining who will be the least damaging loss. The implications of this state of affairs for the labour market will be clear.

Cascio and Silbey (1979) present a similar analysis to that offered here, but become rather more technical than we have chosen to be. They begin by stating that the psychometric requirements of the classical validity approach to selection have been more than amply met by the assessment programme. Inter-rater reliabilities of .6 to .9; test-retest reliabilities of .68 to .77; predictive validities of .39 to .68 are quoted in support of this view. They then go on to suggest that the systemic effects of the selection process are largely ignored in classical validity studies. Utility theory is held to go some way towards overcoming this lack by placing primary emphasis on the outcomes of prediction rather than on measurement and prediction *per se*. They used the Brogden-Cronbach-Gleser continuous variable utility model to evaluate the utility of an assessment programme. After specifying several cost assumptions, they varied six parameters systematically: the validity and cost of the assessment programme; the validity of the ordinary selection procedure; the selection ratio; the standard deviation of the criterion; and the number of assessment programmes. The largest impact on assessment programme payoff was exerted by the size of the criterion standard deviation, followed by the selection ratio and the differences in validity between the assessment programme and the ordinary selection procedure. Cost, perhaps surprisingly, was a negligible element in the calculations, although this does support our long held view that the cost of one assessment programme is a very small proportion of the cost of one selection error in management. At the end of their argument they can show that assessment programmes with as low a predictive validity as .1 can show a satisfactory return on investment. Perhaps more importantly they offer a model for comparing the utility, in money terms of various different approaches to identifying and selecting future managers. Their final point is one which we enthusiastically endorse. It is most desirable that interdisciplinary teams look at this problem. We would be highly delighted to see a combination of, say, a psychologist, a manpower planner and a cost accountant, all trying to pin down the elusive concept of the £ payoff from an employee. In this way we might be able to achieve some concrete comparisons, in money terms, between many of the manpower management techniques that are regarded solely as debit entries at the moment for lack of any hard information to the contrary.

For illustrative clarity, this chapter has concentrated on methods of assessing, in money terms, the benefits to be obtained from the use of assessment programmes to improve the way in which companies make promotion decisions. It has shown that a surprisingly small increase in the efficiency with which these decisions are carried out can yield a considerable return. It should not be forgotten that any *system* which will improve the selection and success ratios can be evaluated in much the same way and it may be that there are other techniques which will pay off more handsomely. We have merely attempted to show that the payoff is, perhaps, calculable.

Chapter 10

Some common questions and answers

When we give seminars on assessment programmes and the identification of potential, there are usually many questions at the end of the day. We have therefore assembled here some of the most common questions that people ask, with the answers we have usually given. You may find the answers repeat information given elsewhere in the text; but this chapter will give short answers to questions you may have or which may come from other people should you decide to do a diagnostic exercise in your own firm.

The questions:

1 How can I get top management interested in the problem?
2 Must I use assessment programmes — won't something else do?
3 Are assessment programmes demonstrably better than anything else?
4 How do you know what qualities to look for?
5 How do they relate to existing performance appraisal systems?
6 How far up and down the organization can they be used?
7 Can they be used for non-managerial appointments?
8 Can assessment programmes be used as selection devices?
9 How are candidates selected?
10 How are observers selected?
11 Are they better held in-house or off premises?
12 Aren't they very time consuming?
13 Aren't they very expensive?
14 Is it possible to mix different occupations on a programme?
15 How do specialists and technical people react?
16 Is it possible to mix different levels on a programme?
17 Is it possible to mix different nationalities on a programme?
18 Is there any problem with women on the programme?
19 Are psychological tests any help?

20 Can I really design my own programme?
21 How are the assessment data stored?
22 How long are the data good for?
23 What happens when you stop using assessment programmes?
24 How can I tell whether it's doing any good?

How can I get top management interested in the problem?

In chapter 1 we give a list of frequently aired management complaints which might be answered by a more systematic approach to the identification of potential. Studying these questions and listening to top management's grumbles may help to get them interested.

Some manpower statistics, carefully presented, may help to catch the attention. Draw a graph of number of leavers × length of service and look at the bumps. It is likely that one bump will occur when people get dissatisfied with information on their promotion opportunities. Calculate how much it costs to lose a salesman after 18 months because nobody has told him about career paths. We practically guarantee that this cost will catch top management's attention. Or you can calculate the talent drain index if you have a performance appraisal system: look at the people leaving and see if top performers are over represented in any particular group of leavers. That information can be presented graphically, in eye catching fashion.

Top managers are sometimes cynical about the work of personnel departments. It helps if one can indicate that here is a proposal with hard numbers attached to it: real cost savings, real performance improvements, with built in measures. We also find that top managers are attracted by the notion of getting the problem diagnosed in *their* terms, not in some jargon thought up by people in management development. Stressing the uniqueness of the assessment programme to the firm involved also helps. Once the diagnostic exercise is started, and managers are interviewed in depth about their jobs and perhaps involved in the design of the assessment programme and also used as observers, the amount of education and insight this provides usually keeps their interest bubbling.

Must I use assessment programmes – wouldn't something else do?

We are not committed to the idea of assessment programmes above all else. It depends on the criteria of effectiveness which you find out with your diagnosis. This is why we stress that diagnosis should precede any commitment to assessment programmes or any other form of solution. If your diagnosis reveals that the criteria of effectiveness could be found from a man's track record, say by altering the existing performance appraisal system, then that is the obvious step to take. You should use similar validation procedures for this method of assessing potential as for the assessment programme method.

Having said that, we should add that in most cases, but not all, we have found ourselves working with firms on assessment programmes simply because track record was not sufficient. It has been necessary to simulate the actual job before deciding whether the assessees meet its criteria. In particular there are two levels in the organization where track record is unlikely to be helpful. The transition from non-managerial jobs to first line management is one example; the other is the transition from divisional to general responsibilities, where the man goes on the board or a company-wide management committee. The change in job content in these two transitions is so great that past performance is not usually a good predictor; the only way to find out is to do one's diagnosis and then make the decisions.

Adopting an assessment programme without the diagnosis is like buying a solution without knowing what the problem is.

Are assessment programmes demonstrably better than anything else?
Again, the answer to this question depends upon the criteria you discover in your diagnosis. Only after these criteria have been discovered is one in a position to decide whether assessment programmes would be a better method than anything else.

There are two functions which, as far as we know, assessment programmes perform uniquely well. One is in picking up those who are currently performing badly because their present jobs are wrong or too small. In many firms a person in this position is badly placed; he may not realize himself that he is in the wrong job, and it requires an exceptional degree of honesty and open mindedness for the managers responsible for putting him in that job to detect it. If in addition the firm imposes a rule that poor performers may not be promoted, the sufferer's only way out is probably into another firm. This is very wasteful.

Another function lies in showing non-managerial employees what management is actually like in time for them to decide that they do not like it. In the nature of things this does not happen often, unless everyone goes through an assessment programme automatically, but we have all experienced the chaos and misery caused by a salesman who finds himself promoted to manager and then decides he does not like it. Assessment programmes provide a safe chance of discovering what management is about, especially if the accompanying counselling is carefully done.

As a final answer to the question, perhaps we should be a little partisan and say that assessment programmes *can* demonstrate a higher degree of accuracy and acceptability than other procedures and that, if they are designed properly, data about their accuracy and acceptability are probably more easily available than with other methods. This is important to managers forced by legislation to give detailed reasons for their promotion decisions.

How do you know what qualities to look for?

We would suggest that these can only be found by going through some form of diagnostic exercise such as we recommend in chapter 4. General prescriptions of what makes for effectiveness are to be distrusted just because they are general; each firm is unique. We have found that some characteristics of effectiveness are constant over all the firms we have worked with so far, but others vary greatly. It's worth taking a little trouble to get things right.

We had an interesting demonstration of our philosophy that each firm requires its unique diagnosis. We had completed the diagnostic exercise for a client and were reporting back and agreeing a final list of characteristics. One manager with whom we were talking had got hold of a list of characteristics from another firm: we had used it as an example in the early stages of discussion and he had received it in error. His annotations to this list betrayed puzzlement, surprise and disbelief. The rogue list was for managers of similar seniority but in a different firm. We had our belief in the importance of individual diagnosis confirmed.

How do they relate to existing performance appraisal systems?

Ideally, very closely. The diagnostic phase which we describe in chapter 4 can, by identifying criteria of effective performance in jobs, help in checking or restructuring the appraisal system. As we make clear, the diagnostic procedure *can* reveal that there is no need for an assessment programme at the levels considered, if all the criteria can be revealed by an appropriate appraisal system. Even where it is apparent that some of the criterion behaviours are best sought by an assessment programme or some other planned experience, some of the behaviours – technical competence, financial competence, safety and security records, for example – can best be discovered in the performance appraisal system.

Most performance appraisal systems now include both a statement of objectives and a measure of career counselling. If our recommendation has been accepted, that an assessment programme should always lead to an action plan for each participant, then the appraisal system becomes the obvious place to incorporate these action plans and to make sure that they are carried out. It follows that those plans should appear not only in the assessment programme participants' appraisals, but also in their managers', since it will now be part of the participants' immediate line managers' responsibility to see that those action plans happen and to monitor their progress.

It is wise to indicate, in the attendant publicity, that the assessment programme is not the same as the appraisal programme. In many companies, appraisal systems were introduced in a rush of enthusiasm for management by objectives and have since failed to thrive. The assessment programme gathers new data; it will enhance, but should not replace, the existing appraisal system.

How far up and down the organization can they be used?

In principle, anywhere from the very bottom to the very top. It is worth doing separate diagnostic exercises for the different levels of management involved if you intend to set up assessment programmes companywide. If this seems a tall order, at least get a diagnosis of the characteristics of effectiveness at first-line level, at director or general manager level and at middle-manager level. The first two of those represent such large changes in responsibility that it is difficult to generalize from them to the middle level of management.

All other things being equal, the best place to start is at the top. The reason is a practical one. If you run a programme with senior managers being assessed for director-level posts, with directors as observers, those same senior managers will be easier to train to act as observers themselves when the programme moves down a level or two; and later when promotion decisions are being made by senior managers they will make more sensible use of the assessment programme data if they themselves have participated in one. To begin at the bottom involves one in much more training, education and 'selling' the programme as one takes it further up the firm.

Can they be used for non-managerial appointments?

Yes. Certain non-managerial appointments suffer the same difficulty as many managerial appointments: that track record is a poor predictor of success. In our experience, two such types of appointment are that of the salesman and that of the internal consultant or trouble-shooter. Moving an inexperienced person into either of these jobs could well be helped by some form of purpose-built assessment programme.

Can assessment programmes be used as selection devices?

Yes, often with great success. We used assessment programmes to select salesmen in a large firm and cut the wastage rate by half.

There is more concern with public relations when assessment programmes are used for selection. A stressful programme, with no feedback on results, could get you an unwelcome reputation. Obviously there is a change of emphasis in the matter of what is done with the results; long developmental feedback interviews are not likely to be suitable but we would advise you to give some thought to counselling all the candidates, even the failures.

One development we are pursuing with interest is the use of assessment programmes as *placement* devices – where participants go through a variety of exercises designed to examine many different criteria in order that they may be counselled as to their suitability for one of a number of different jobs under consideration. Employment services, vocational guidance experts and firms with a large intake of mixed employees might find this application useful; they also have a place in training and re-orienting redundant managers and specialists.

How are candidates selected?

There are at least four strategies for nominating candidates: they can nominate themselves; be put forward by their managers; be nominated by either themselves or their managers; or the programme can be designated for everyone of a given grade. Which is appropriate depends partly on the culture of the firm and partly on the purposes of the programme; for example, how the nominations for other training courses or assignments are handled. Clearly a programme with strong developmental content is more suitable to an 'all comers' nomination strategy than a programme with strong assessive content.

Clearly if programmes are to be rationed, they are best confined to people who are thought to have potential or to be ambitious. Existing data on performance appraisal and career counselling will help here; and candidates' immediate managers, being more likely to have formed a view about potential, must be involved in making nominations. It is vital they be briefed on the purposes of the firm's assessment programme so that they recommend people for the right reasons. But nomination cannot be left solely in the hands of candidates' managers and there must be one or two other ways of getting people nominated. A manager might refuse to nominate, for his own selfish purposes, or might not nominate someone whose potential is invisible because he is in the wrong job. Candidates should be able to put themselves forward, or be put forward by the personnel department; acceptance should not be automatic and candidates should be counselled about the programme's purpose, otherwise there is a risk of getting the chronic course attender or the man who attends because he feels left out.

There should not be a long gap between nomination and participation. Two to three months is about right and it is better if assessment programmes are regarded as slightly difficult to get on to; not secret but also not *automatic* unless they are strongly developmentally oriented.

How are observers selected?

Observers can be line managers, people from the personnel department, or outsiders such as psychologists or management consultants. We feel strongly that outsiders should not have to make judgements about who can and cannot be promoted in an organization where they will not have to live with their decisions. We have helped with a number of assessment programmes – the diagnosis, design and the training of observers – but we feel that for us to make the assessments is *ultra vires*.

Whether the observers come from line management or personnel is partly a matter of the firm's history and preferences. The benefits of using line managers for at least part of the observation team are overwhelming. They understand the job to be done, both on the assessment programme itself and the job for which potential is being assessed. They will know what use to make of assessment programme data when they have to use them later. The training benefits to the line managers which amounts to three to five days learning to analyse behaviour, to record it and discuss it objectively in the context of what is required to do a job well, are enormous; one could probably not persuade senior managers to receive this kind of training in any other way. Line managers in general seem easier to train in observation skills; perhaps they have fewer preconceptions than the average group trainer.

If the observation team is from personnel exclusively, its findings can be rejected by line managers. An exclusive 'assessment team' could come to be seen by themselves and others as king makers, with all the attendant political and morale problems. Our strong preference is therefore for the observers to come from line management, with the *management* of the programme in the continuous care of the personnel department or management services.

Are they better held in-house or off premises?
They should not be held in the normal work place of either the candidates or the observers. Telephone calls, local visitors and requests to 'pop into the office for a minute before lunch' are death to the smooth running of the programme and the concentration of the participants.

The choice of hotel or company's own accommodation depends on what is available. It is more difficult to discourage casual visitors at the company's own training centre; it is more difficult to be sure of good service and prompt attention – and office facilities – at some hotels. It is not worth skimping or cutting corners; pressures of time are great, there is much material to be handled and the place chosen must allow for this. People need to be gently discouraged from over eating and staying up late; this may be easier in the firm's own accommodation if it exists.

One word of warning: if you go to a strange hotel in an out of the way area, as many people do for this sort of event, be sure to check train times for arrival and departure before completing arrangements for the programme.

Aren't they very time consuming?

We can best answer this by giving a typical example of time taken to set up an assessment programme for middle managers. Getting agreement to some form of programme to identify potential took three meetings when we were present and two when we were not (including here the seminar which first gave the client the idea). This is perhaps less time than it takes to agree most personnel department proposals, perhaps because the criteria of success are usually quite plain. We took four days of familiarization interviews, after which we did 20 grid interviews. One of us shared the load with three of the clients' staff, teaching the techniques as we went; this took three days. Design of the questionnaire took a further three days from the four of us (again, including teaching). Fifty questionnnaires went to line managers taking about an hour for each manager. Analysis of the questionnaires took about 10 days to the stage of written reports (this was done solo by one of us). The results of the analysis were presented to the client at a meeting of all managers concerned, and agreement reached to design the programme. Programme design took 10 days, including design of observer training.

Training the observers was a two day programme. The actual assessment programme involved the participants for two days and the observers for three, plus a two hour counselling interview later, plus the time from the programme manager and his assistants. Further assessment programmes can be run from the original design, with perhaps refresher courses for observers; in addition statistical work is needed on the programme data to make sure it is doing its job. There is also the time spent in public relations work: visiting managers' meetings to tell them about the programme, briefing the company newsletter etc.

This is not very time consuming in return for the amount of data generated. The research programme outlined above is as lean as we can make it. It needs certain *blocks* of time dedicated to it, which may make it appear time consuming, but once the diagnosis is complete the programme needs little more effort than would be given by a conscientious training manager to any important training programme. Maintenance is important, perhaps more important on this programme than anywhere else, to check the validity of the programme.

Designing the programme oneself is not as quick as buying a package though the difference is not great if you count the number of people who must listen to the package salesman. Doing the initial research in-house, to design a programme to meet your unique needs, will not mean hiring new staff; two to four man months of existing competent staff (depending on whether you use outside guidance) is probably all that is necessary, plus time for managers to be interviewed and do questionnaires. How often do personnel departments get the

238

chance of such exciting and genuine research with such visible, real life outcomes?

Aren't they very expensive?

Accountants can prove anything! In chapter 9 we discuss some of the ways the costs and benefits can be calculated and give the calculations put together by a sceptic. Broadly speaking being as conservative as possible in our estimation of costs, you only have to save yourself one mistake (of the kind that would have led to redundancy and a possible action for constructive dismissal) for the setting up costs of an assessment programme to be covered with some to spare. Since our sceptic did his calculations, employment legislation has made the costs of a mistake even greater.

Assessment programmes are a new cost, of course, and attract attention in the way that existing procedures probably do not. Once established they are not much more expensive to maintain than a high quality training course.

Is it possible to mix different occupations on a programme?

Only with care. Where occupations typically attract extreme personality types those occupations are unlikely to mix well on a programme. One firm in the insurance world tells us that in the course of running an assessment/development programme for all comers, a single actuary found himself on a programme with seven salesmen, with sad results for the actuary. We thought that this was the superficial brilliance of the salesmen blotting out the actuary's more subfusc style; however, on a later programme a solitary salesman found himself surrounded by actuaries and this time the salesman suffered.

From anecdotal data of this kind we offer the opinion that salesmen, internal consultants, and other 'extravert loners' should not be mixed with other occupations if at all possible; neither should accountants, actuaries and other people in quiet staff functions. Within those broad limits, mixing of other occupations does not seem to cause problems except when there are local rivalries or other difficulties.

Mixed occupation programmes can cause design problems; we like to make the content of each exercise as close as possible to real life jobs and this could mean giving some people an advantage over others if they have more knowledge of the jobs used in exercises. Sometimes this can be overcome by a judicious distribution of tasks; at other times exercises of equal unfamiliarity to everyone have to be designed. Here may we offer a hint: we have seen a number of firms who, faced with the situation of designing (say) an in-tray that will be fair to all comers, design an in-tray for the personnel director; or designing an exercise of sorting and presenting material, take their material from the management development files. If you can possibly avoid it, do not take your material from the personnel department; a line manager wondering about the new package he is being offered will give you much more credit if you can draw your examples from the rest of the business rather than your own department.

How do specialists and technical people react?

One of the functions of an assessment programme can be to give a taste of the management job to those who have not so far experienced it. Specialist and professional employees fall into this category. Often an assessment programme acts as the start of a career discussion in which it becomes obvious to all parties that the specialist concerned has doubts about being a manager, or would need particular types of training before accepting the manager's job.

We predict that in the next decade one of the more difficult problems that personnel departments will be faced with is the increasing number of professionals who do not want to become managers. But, if your problem lies in persuading professionals to become managers (and many will have to face this) then may we advise that we have had some success with management training for professionals by altering some of the training techniques which became popular in the late sixties and early seventies. Briefly, we find that professionals do not take to 'discovery learning'; their training has taught them how to learn, and they will absorb management techniques far more readily if they are taught in a form analogous to the way they learned their professional skills. 'Book-learning followed by practical exercise' goes down better than 'group discussion followed by trainer's review'.

Technical people and managers of technical departments sometimes grumble that the performance questionnaire technique yields many behavioural and few technical items. The reason is simply that the technique is designed to get objective statements of behaviour; objective statements of technical capacity are usually well supplied. In addition, technical incompetence is often associated with ineffectiveness but technical brilliance is less well related to effectiveness.

Is it possible to mix different levels on a programme?

If the purposes of the programme allow it, there is no methodological reason why this should not happen though it is difficult to envisage a large disparity of levels being appropriate. The difficulties are more likely to be political. People in direct reporting relationships to each other should not take part in the same programme as participants.

If levels are being mixed, extra stress needs to be placed on telling candidates that they are not competing with each other but only with themselves, and general efforts should be made to ensure that rank back at work does not interfere with the running of the assessment exercises (for instance, in one firm the effective manager is one who does not insist that the chair be taken by the most senior man there if someone with more appropriate skills is present; if this firm were to run a mixed level course, observers would be briefed to pay attention to the way leadership evolves in, say, a leaderless group).

Our own work has usually involved only one level at a time, because this appears less fraught with possible hazards. We can see no absolute objection to mixing levels if it is done with great care and an eye to the programme's purposes.

Is it possible to mix different nationalities on a programme?

Yes, if you realize that different nationalities have different ways of doing business and have designed your programme to recognize these differences. This is a tall order.

The wrong way is to do what a large American multinational company did; decide criteria on the basis of American experience, design a programme to be run in Europe to select future European managers, pay no attention to differences *between* European countries, and run courses where mixed European nationals were assessed for their ability to meet American standards which were, had they known it, contra-indicated in some of the European countries where they would work after promotion.

In a multi-national company, the criteria of effective management at middle levels and above will almost certainly include some sensitivity to, and ability to use, national differences. With care, a programme can be designed to accommodate this requirement. Such a multi-national company would probably be well advised to record participants' potential in a more complex form than would a single nationality company, recording perhaps the particular strengths and weaknesses that participants would exhibit in different countries. This of course presupposes diagnostic exercises conducted in the different countries; the grid plus questionnaire paradigm suggested in chapter 4 is ideal for this purpose, as its observer bias free approach is even more important when comparing across nationalities.

Is there any problem with women on the programme?

No. On programmes that we have seen where women have been included, the women have usually been brighter than their male colleagues, simply because in order to survive in a male dominated environment a certain intellectual edge is necessary. In addition, women usually excel in exercises where verbal fluency is required. This is in line with general findings about sex differences in performance; broadly speaking, analysis of women's behaviour in work groups shows that they occupy the extremes of most distributions, for instance more conformist or more non-conformist, more talkative or more quiet.

We have never seen social problems when women participate in assessment programmes nor any male solidarity movements. It is now illegal to discriminate between men and women in matters such as career counselling and guidance and people conducting the feedback and developmental interviews should be careful not to recommend some jobs as more suitable for women.

Some studies have reported that women do exactly as well or badly as men and that there is no real difference between them — similarly for ethnic minority groups. But other studies seem to indicate that problems can arise. Weighting the studies for numbers involved, the evidence that there is no problem holds the field for the moment but the issue is not yet completely resolved.

Are psychological tests any help?

Sometimes, but like everything else on an assessment programme they need validating for your own organization. Tests that have no validation figures should probably be avoided completely; tests that have national validation data need standardizing in your firm.

The research findings on personality tests as predictors of potential make depressing reading. This is no reason to stop trying, but at the time of writing we do not know of many firms where psychological tests of personality make a rigorously tested contribution to the assessment of potential.

Tests of intelligence and capacity for logical thinking are a little more useful, often as a cut off for establishing minimum standards which are necessary before potential is present. Above this minimum standard, correlations between (say) IQ and managerial potential usually become thin.

We are experimenting with one or two other tests, including a manager's version of the Schroder Sentence Completion Test, designed to assess cognitive complexity and with Fineman's job environment questionnaire and work preference questionnaire; we shall report the results when we have enough data.

The message on psychological tests is that you can't buy one off the shelf to select your managers for you. If you use one it should be validated *before* you use the results to contribute to the assessments. If you use an unvalidated test for research purposes on the assessment programme you should make it quite clear to all concerned that this is what you are doing. You should get specific advice from a psychologist (not a test-salesman) before committing yourself to a test or tests.

Can I really design my own programme?

Yes. You need a list of the criteria of effectiveness and a 'task library'. Draw up a matrix of which tasks test which criteria and then start designing! When you have designed the tasks, *pilot* them and be prepared to change them; nobody gets it right first time. Remember you are assessing, not training; and remember that the tasks need designing with the observers in mind.

Early mistakes in programme design are more likely to be administrative than concerned with exercise content: not leaving time to mark in-tray exercises or not having a photocopier available.

A 'task library' takes time to build up, but pays dividends. Most tasks can be adapted for different assessment purposes and for training purposes too. It is a good idea to note down ideas for exercises as they come, when browsing through journals or doing general reading or discussion.

How are the assessment data stored?

This question falls into two parts: who keeps them and who has access to them? Usually they are kept either by the personnel department or by the line manager directly responsible for the candidate. Purely assessive data should probably be kept confidential until a promotion decision is being made because if assessments are common knowledge, it will not be long before they are treated casually and inaccurately. Developmental data and the recommendations from counselling interviews need be subject to no such restrictions.

We may become outdated in our recommendations here; we would not be surprised to find legislation soon giving all employees access to all data kept about them. If the assessment programme is properly planned we see only one problem – the self-fulfilling prophecy effect of knowing one's own potential rating. Even this can be coped with, by making sure that the rating does not come as a surprise; that high ratings are not seen as carrying promises; that low ratings do not mark a man for life and there will be further opportunities; by giving ratings where possible on a number of dimensions rather than just one, thus making over simple deductions impossible.

How long are the data good for?

The honest answer is, we don't know. There have been so few long term studies following up assessment programme results that we cannot generalize. Such studies as have been performed indicate that the data from an assessment programme can be used to predict performance and progress throughout the organization up to at least 10 years ahead. Obviously if the firm goes through drastic changes during the period, this must be taken into account. If data are being used from a programme run some years ago, one should also look at how the participant used the feedback and counselling in improving his later performance.

What happens when you stop using assessment programmes?

We only know one firm where assessment programmes have been stopped after running for some while and that was many years ago.

More exactly, we do know one or two firms where assessment activities have had to stop because they were ineptly put into practice. The firm who designed its own fortnight long course and began on Sunday evening by announcing, 'This is an assessment course and the one who wins will be the next branch manager,' will have trouble running assessment programmes again. Apart from such wayward examples, the programmes seem so popular with all concerned that there would be great disappointment if they stopped.

Often the programme changes and develops as the client sees fit. We designed an assessment programme for one firm who has altered it to a mixed assessment and development programme with greater emphasis on development than assessment. But we have never yet seen one come to an end, although we are beginning to encounter the question 'What comes next?'.

How can I tell whether it's doing any good?

In his excellent book *The Naked Manager*, Robert Heller points out that nobody ever devotes effort to proving himself wrong. Bernard Ungerson has made the point strongly that the face validity of assessment programmes is frighteningly high. So, unfortunately, if you buy a ready-packaged assessment programme with expensive licence fees you are likely to *believe* that it is doing you good, whether it is or not; you probably will not ask whether it could be made better.

The validation programme needs thinking about as soon as the diagnostic exercise begins. The diagnosis is, in a sense, telling you what you need to validate. It is possible to cobble together some validation measures *post hoc*, but it is much cheaper and more informative to think about validation at the very beginning. There is a do it yourself guide to validation in chapter 8; only by following some such procedures can you be sure you are getting evidence, uncontaminated by wishful thinking, on the effectiveness of the programme.

It is important to collect 'consumer reaction', too; you need to know how the participants felt, how their managers felt and how the observers felt. This is not validation evidence, and should not be confused with it, but it is important.

An assessment programme *cannot* come to you already validated. It may have been validated in some other company. It may not have been validated at all (some advocates of ready packaged assessment programmes have been reticent when subjected to penetrating questions on their validity). Whatever way you use to select future managers, it is your responsibility also to set up validation procedures to see what value you get for your money and to prevent the expensive heartache of people in the wrong jobs.

Chapter 11

The next steps

If the reader wishes to pursue further the ideas on assessing potential which we have described here, he may care to follow the checklist of stages given below. It is a rough guide to what has to be done and the order of doing it. We are assuming that the reader is a manager or specialist in a personnel department, who will not have to work hard persuading his colleagues but will have to sell his notions to line management.

1 *Recognizing the problem*
The checklist given in chapter 1 may help here. In addition – or as an alternative reason – the reader may think that he has no problem at the present, but wishes to check that the current system is operating as well as it could. It is a good idea to collect written data at this stage if possible since it helps when deciding one's purposes later. It will also help to review the current state of legislation about selection and dismissal, to see if there is any added impetus to constructing a validated system.

2 *Collecting current data*
Make sure you know in detail what methods are presently used for assessing potential in your organization. There may be informal methods that do not appear in the personnel management handbook. In addition, collect what data you can, without raising expectations unduly, about how managers and employees view the assessment of potential at the moment. Employee attitude surveys, exit interviews, management appraisal forms, etc, will provide good sources of data. If your performance appraisal system is a good one, you can look to see whether good performers are over represented in the people leaving after a given length of service. Of course, both these stages are somewhat pre-empted if a request comes from a line manager to give him help in assessing potential, but it is still worth reviewing the problem as a whole.

3 *Selecting an area to begin*
We suggest that you conduct a pilot study first, especially if you are new to the

research techniques we suggest here. You need to select a portion of the company and a given level of employee, if the company is large enough to permit this. If the company is a small one, try to limit yourself to one or two levels of employee at the most for the first pilot study. It is important that the manager responsible for the area should be committed to your plans. Select a time of relative calm for the exercise and preferably not at the same time as a job evaluation exercise, or a renegotiation of the salary scheme. You will be interviewing managers about their definitions of effectiveness and you want them relaxed and not worrying that their words will be used in evidence. Make it clear to the manager that you are doing a diagnosis first to find out how effectiveness is presently viewed in his organization, and that only when this diagnosis is complete will you be able to think about ways of solving the problem. It is inadvisable to become tied to the notion of an assessment programme, or any other device, at this early stage.

4 Familiarization interviews with some of the managers

If you know your managers intimately, you may skip this stage. But if you have had wide responsibilities and you suddenly find you are concentrating on one division only, or are working at a different location, then you need to familiarize yourself with the general nature of the slice of the organization where you will work. Visit the key managers there to discover the content of their jobs, the areas they are responsible for, the successes and failures they have experienced. The critical incident format is a good one to use: 'Tell me about the incident that has caused you the most difficulty and problems in the last month . . .' At this stage, you are only peripherally concerned with the assessment of managerial potential; you want to get the flavour of the division.

5 Repertory grid interviews – planning

Experiment in the safety of the personnel department, with one or two different formats for grid interviews – using different elements. Work colleagues or job activities could serve as elements; decide which one seems best. We usually use job activities, because some people find it objectionable to make judgements about their colleagues even when anonymous. Get someone to give the interviewer(s) a grid themselves, so they know what it feels like. The main points to watch when conducting the interview are (i) the necessity not to suggest either the elements or the constructs, beyond asking if there are any more constructs that occur and (ii) conducting the 'laddering' process with people who have produced few constructs the first time and need further examination.

6 Interview scheduling

You need to talk to people who actually occupy the job level for which potential is going to be assessed. If the appointments are made by telephone, a letter should follow explaining the purpose – a letter designed to remove any anxieties the interviewees may have about their own competence being assessed in the interview. Their managers should also be informed. Allow an hour and a half for each interview, with a little recovery time. If a team of interviewers is operating in one location, then some time set aside at the end of the day for comparing notes and experiences is very useful. We ourselves find grid interviewing less exhausting than the typically semi-structured interview – four or five a day seem to present no problem. Interviewers need clipboards and fast writing pencils.

7 Interviewing

Follow the guide given in chapter 4. If you are doing a lot of interviews, try to get them over in the shortest possible chronological time; four people working for a week is better than one working for a month, as the procedure raises interviewees' expectations. If you have so few people that a performance questionnaire will not be possible (it needs about 50 as a maximum number of people answering) then your grid interviews will be in much more depth with each interviewee – everyone will be subjected to laddering. If your pool of interviewers is very large, or spread across many different functions, or if you are under severe time pressure (either to work fast or not to take up too much of busy managers' time) then you may want to consider a group administration grid.

8 Collating the constructs

Each interview record form should be transcribed into a neat version, as far as possible giving the constructs and the evaluations and any further comments. A master version is then prepared, collecting together all the constructs from all the interviews. This is hard labour! We have three ways of doing it: (i) one person, with a good memory, writes the master list starting with one interview record and adding the second putting tally marks where duplications occur and so on. This is good when one person has done most of the interviews and knows what constructs will come up; (ii) writing each construct on 3 × 5 inch cards, preferably at the end of each interview, and physically sorting the cards into bundles that go together; this is perhaps the best way and is in fact the only way if a group grid has been conducted; (iii) conducting a group meeting with everyone having a small number of interview records and the group leader shouting the constructs for the rest to add to. We regret that this stage is a little arduous, but soon over.

9 For small firms

If it is not possible, for reasons of numbers, to go on to a performance questionnaire, then the constructs themselves provide the material on which a report must be written. They should be listed in order of frequency, with the positively valued poles all to one side. Here you have a picture of the distinctions and comparisons made by managers viewing their jobs, with the frequency with which they are mentioned. You do not have any notion of priority of those items, other than their frequency. It is a good idea also to prepare a list of the elements used, if they were taken from the man's job content rather than his colleagues.

10 For larger firms

If it is possible to go on to a performance questionnaire, it should be designed now; the closer in time this is to the actual collating of the constructs the better, as memories are fresh. If it is your first attempt at a performance questionnaire, we suggest you begin by taking the very first construct and devising as many possible bipolar statements of behaviour that can be derived from it – rather like a brainstorming session, carrying on beyond the point of fatigue. You will probably get 15 to 20 statements from this one construct. Do this for the next four or five, until you feel exhausted. Then go back over the constructs you have devised, and try to amalgamate them, throw out the most frivolous, and generally reduce the numbers to a manageable size. After this procedure you will probably be ready to go through the rest of the constructs designing the questionnaire in a more straightforward way – one or two questions per construct, followed by an amalgamation as some constructs will generate only one bipolar statement between them. The number of bipolar statements to aim for is somewhere between 100 and 200, and most construct listings we have worked with produce this number of statements fairly easily. If you have to reduce, cut out those statements where the behaviour is either not described objectively, or where it would be difficult to take action on the results of the statement should it prove to discriminate. Don't throw out constructs because they don't fit the current theory, or because they don't balance. We have no preferences between designing the questionnaire solo or as part of a team, but if you design a number of these questionnaires solo then it is worth asking someone to work with you now and again to stop you getting stale.

11 Issuing the questionnaire

Send the effective manager version out first, asking for return within the week – thus allowing yourself two weeks for chasing. The ineffective manager questionnaire goes out three weeks after the first one. Then the tabulations and calculations, as described in chapter 5, commence. Keep photocopies of working documents since they get lost easily. And do be careful about the security of the completed forms – nobody should be able to discover them.

The results from the performance questionnaire, or from the grid interviews, should be examined in detail at this stage. You have here a picture of what managers presently view as effective managerial behaviour at the level you looked at. All you have done is to collate their own observations. There is no evaluation from you yet. *Someone* needs to take the decision on whether they wish this picture to be perpetuated, or in any way altered. Who makes this decision is a matter for the individual firm, but it should be taken, only after thought, questioning and cross-questioning. If you can get access to other firms' pictures to compare with your own, this is a good inducer of thought. Only after you have had the decision to change or perpetuate this pattern of management are you in a position to decide what are the best ways of discovering these criterion behaviours in up and coming staff. You need to assemble data on how potential is presently assessed, and to consider whether any of these ways could be adapted to gather the new information, or whether new ways of discovering these criterion behaviours may be found. Some assessment of the costs of these various procedures, and the types and significance of the errors they will carry, is also important.

13 *Deciding the next step(s)*

You have a picture of the criterion behaviours associated with effectiveness. Beware of falling into the trap of viewing this picture as 'the effective manager'. More likely, it's a shopping list of characteristics, and any one manager will not have to show *all* of them to be effective. You now have to decide the best way of discovering the people who show these characteristics and developing them further in the people who do not yet show them. Most people we have worked with choose one or more of the following courses of action:

improving the performance appraisal system
improving the management selection committee
improving the initial selection procedure
improving the training offered
using psychological tests
instituting middle manager counselling programmes
doing nothing
designing and running an assessment programme.

14 *Improving the performance appraisal system*

Most performance appraisal systems have lists of criteria against which people are appraised. With the list from the diagnostic exercise, you can improve the relevance of the criteria, give tighter definitions on the forms and in the appraisal training courses and give some indication of priority to be put on those criteria. You may also want to institute a self-appraisal system, if your diagnostic procedure reveals that the ability to monitor one's own performance correctly is a sign of effectiveness. (Some form of preparation for counselling, whether or not the appraisee shows it to his manager, is nearly always useful in an appraisal programme.) If the diagnostic procedure has spread across a large part of your company, or if you have other useful information, you may want to write a guide to career counselling for appraising managers. We would advise that the criteria be communicated to employees as part of the performance appraisal system, and that they be told how well they match up to each criterion; however, there are some firms where this degree of openness would be contrary to the existing culture. Care is required in communicating the manager's appraisal of the employee's potential, because it is not wise to be seen to be promising a promotion or a particular job. Everybody involved in the process must be very clear about the difference between performance appraisal and potential appraisal. It might be wise to separate physically the forms on which the judgements are recorded, or to make the judgements at different times.

The appraising manager's judgements of potential should be subject to the same review and appeals procedure as is already supplied with the performance appraisal system. In this context we mention the Civil Service practice of having the senior manager who signs off the appraisal form answer the question: 'Would you take this employee (if high potential) into your own department and if not, why not?' This is a good safeguard against casual predictions of high potential.

There are many books and articles on designing an appraisal system and training managers to use it: we recommend Williams (*op cit*), Koontz (*op cit*), and Stewart (1976, 1977); and as an insight into self-counselling the guide by Korving (1975) is an unusual and valuable contribution.

15 *Improving the management selection committee*

We confess that we are not sanguine about committees in general as ways of assessing potential; too often we have seen political problems interfere with the training of their members and the decisions they take. However, one or two firms have management committees that work well, and these may be improved by the additional information from the diagnostic procedures. Specific improvements are: giving the committee the results of the diagnosis and encouraging them to use these criteria in making their assessments; setting them an example of the kind of objectivity which can be achieved and the kind of detail that can be used; getting them to work matching these criteria with the actual work assignments presently the responsibility of the candidates, so that performance measures can be arrived at using the criteria from the diagnosis: devising a performance appraisal form for the managers on the committee to fill out individually, before they meet, on which candidates are to be assessed on the criteria.

One problem with revitalizing management appointment committees is that they tend to get set in their ways, using shorthand forms of words and not questioning each others' reasoning. A Machiavellian way of giving them fresh perspectives is to get them somehow to compare their own diagnosis with that of another firm – by a spot the firm competition or a deliberate mistake, or a formal presentation by an experienced researcher.

16 Improving the initial selection procedure

In this book we have written as if we were assessing the potential of people presently employed in the firm; however, the material can provide the basis for refurbishing the initial selection procedure. One firm we worked with took the list of criteria and divided them into: those they could discover on the personal history form; those they could discover at interview if the interview were correctly structured; those they could discover by some form of assignment (in this case a group task) given to candidates to perform; those they couldn't do anything about or couldn't discover. They might also have added criteria to be discovered by aptitude testing or personality testing, or by assiduous taking up of references, but they did not need to. The people responsible for selection were given training in how to use the new procedures (they were also involved in designing them) and over several years the firm reports greatly reduced wastage and improved performance. Even where the diagnostic procedure has been carried out with promotion to managerial appointments in mind, there is usually some information which can be fed back with profit to the people responsible for initial selection – or indeed to the advertising agents who design the recruiting advertisements. The induction training programme may also benefit from a redesign using the diagnostic information.

17 Improving the training offered

There are at least two stages at which the training department should be consulted. They should know about the results of the initial diagnosis, because this can be the starting point for the diagnosis of training needs, the design of training courses and their subsequent evaluation. And they should know about the developmental needs which are identified on the assessment programme or as a result of the revised appraisal procedure, etc. A tightly controlled training course, with constant monitoring of participants' performance and feedback to them (along the lines described by Rackham, *op cit*), can be almost indistinguishable from some types of assessment course, but it is important to remember at all times that the two purposes are different; training is not the same as assessment, and one's design and feedback strategies will differ.

18 Using psychological tests

Useful additional information can often be gained economically by the use of psychological tests, in combination with other techniques. We would not advocate the use of tests alone to make decisions about people for the same reasons that we would not advocate the use of any other technique by itself. No technique is yet strong enough to be able to stand without support from others. The single most important factor in the productive use of psychological tests is the fullest possible knowledge of what is being sought, together with a tight specification of how the information gained will be used. These are preconditions for the efficient use of any of the techniques we have mentioned, of course, but failure to meet them becomes apparent more quickly and more obviously when psychological tests are being used than is the case with almost any other technique. A full initial diagnosis will therefore permit more accurate selection of those tests that are most likely to be helpful. It is also the case that the most useful tests are often also those under the tightest control, since their misuse would be most damaging. If tests are to be used, therefore, it will be necessary to use outside qualified assistance or, preferably, to have one of your own staff trained in the use of those tests. It is also necessary to be cautious in how the test results are communicated and to whom. Clearly, there is no point in using a test if no one can know the outcome. On the other hand the apparent precision and certainty of test results can lead the uninitiated (especially those who express hostility to tests, oddly enough) to accept what they are told uncritically and at face value. This is usually undesirable. Part of the point of training someone in the use of tests is to equip him or her to be able to communicate results clearly without over extending their applicability.

19 Instituting a counselling programme

Sometimes a diagnosis at middle manager level reveals an unsatisfactory state of affairs; perhaps 'effectiveness' is defined in terms which seem unhealthy, or maybe the picture of the less effective manager is rather too clear a picture and fits too many managers in the firm. Given the economic difficulties with which many middle managers have had to cope in the past few years, added to special restrictions on their salaries, and popular anti-business feeling, it is not surprising if some managers seem worn out before their time. The diagnosis may enable one to make this inference. A recent innovation to cope with this problem is the middle manager counselling service, where individual managers meet with one or two experts to discuss their career aspirations, their financial prospects, their physical health, their personal adjustment to their likely career prospects over the remaining years in work, and so on. The objectives are twofold; to clear the ground of financial and health problems as far as possible, and to rediscover their abilities and ambitions so as to fit them afresh into the career which the firm can provide.

20 *Doing nothing*

This is a perfectly feasible alternative, if you are satisfied with the results of the diagnosis and are also satisfied that people who meet these criteria are correctly identified and given the right chance to progress. Your effort will not have been wasted because you will have spent a relatively small quantity of resources in an interesting exercise to discover, with greater certainty than was otherwise possible, that this aspect of your personnel policies is satisfactory. You will also have learned some research techniques than can be easily employed elsewhere, see, for example, Stewart (1975, 1976, 1978), Smith and Ashton (1975), for ideas about other places where the techniques can be used.

21 *Designing and running an assessment programme*

If the examination of the criterion behaviours indicates that a substantial proportion cannot be gauged from present performance, or if you have other reasons for making assessment a more formal and objective an activity, you may decide to design and run an assessment programme. Here are the steps we recommend:

(i) arrange the diagnostic criteria roughly into 'clusters' that can be used as trait names (but never forget that the names are arbitrary and you must work from their content)

(ii) review the exercises you have available in your own task library or can plagiarize from elsewhere. Books of case studies can be useful; so can the critical incident or other interviews you conducted at the familiarization stage

(iii) draw up a rough matrix of exercises × assessment factors

(iv) find out the maximum and minimum lengths of time you would be allowed to run a programme for and decide who would make the best assessors. We would always try to use line managers as observers for reasons given earlier. You need to know these constraints at this stage because it is disappointing to design a good programme that is half a day too long. And be aware, when telling the assessors how long the programme will last, that they will probably be there for longer than the participants, discussing their final recommendations. The programme does not end at the last exercise

(v) design the programme, using the guidelines we gave in chapter 6. Remember that it is only a pilot programme and don't expect to get it right first time or let other people form that expectation. Also design the validation methods you will be using and prepare for the recordkeeping this involves

(vi) design the observer training, again using the guidelines we gave. When the observers meet for training, the programme manuals should be ready for them to study, and they should probably go through all the exercises

(vii) get nominations for participants and observers. Select the programme manager and his assistant and/or secretary. Select the accommodation. Design the introductory letters to participants, and to their managers. You may need to hold a briefing meeting for participants' managers, if they require it. Give the participants about a month's notice but no more

(viii) conduct the observer training, making it clear you are equipping them with general skills in assessing behaviour rather than training them for this particular group of participants

(ix) run the first programme, allowing plenty of spare capacity in time and resources. Take lots of notes on administration and on the exercises and the participants' reactions. If you have counselling interviews some time after the programme, set up these meetings

(x) study all the documents resulting from the programme, including participants' reaction sheets. Interview the observers and any other line managers who may have been closely involved in conducting the exercise so far. Question the administrators who helped on the programme and the managers of the participants themselves. You are then in a position to re-design the programme properly remembering your first one was only a pilot

(xi) take action on the validation measures

(xii) other courses of action include notifying the company publicity department. Here mentions in the company newsletter are useful. Then initiate action to spread the programme into different parts of the company if this is felt to be appropriate. We often find that other parts of the company hear of the assessment procedure and ask to have it implemented in their division, so you may not have to sell too hard.

We wish you success.

Bibliography

ALBRECHT P A, GLASER E M and MARKS J. Validation of a multiple assessment procedure for managerial personnel. *Journal of Applied Psychology*. Vol 48, No 16, 1964, pp 351–360

ANSTEY E. The Civil Service Administrative Class and the Diplomatic Service: a follow-up. *Occupational Psychology*. Vol 40, 1966, pp 139–151

ANSTEY E. The Civil Service Administrative Class: a follow-up of post-war entrants. *Occupational Psychology*. Vol 45, 1971(a), pp 27–43

ANSTEY E. The Civil Service Administrative Class: extended interview selection procedure. *Occupational Psychology*. Vol 45, 1971(b), pp 199–208

ANSTEY E. A 30 year follow-up of the CSSB procedure, with lessons for the future. *Journal of Occupational Psychology*. Vol 50, 1977, pp 149–159

BALES R F. *Interaction Process Analysis: a method for the study of small groups.* Addison-Wesley. 1950

BANNISTER D and FRANSELLA F. *Inquiring man: the theory of personal constructs.* Penguin. 1971

BARNETT G G. Identifying managerial potential for manpower planning. *Long Range Planning.* October 1975, pp 66–75

BARTHOLOMEW D and FORBES A F. *Statistical techniques for manpower planning.* Wiley. 1978

BASS B M. The leaderless group discussion. *Psychology Bulletin.* Vol 51, 1954, pp 465–492

BEER S. *Platform for Change.* Wiley. 1975

BENDER J M. What is 'typical' of assessment centres? *Personnel.* July–August, 1973, pp 50–57

BENTZ V J. The Sears experience in the investigation, description and prediction of executive behaviour. *Foundation for Research on Human Behaviour.* 1966, pp 59–152

BLAKE R R and MOUTON J S. *Building a dynamic corporation through grid organization development.* Addison-Wesley. 1969

BOWERS D G and SEASHORE S E. Predicting organisational effectiveness with a four factor theory of leadership. *Administrative Science Quarterly.* Vol 11, 1966, pp 238–263

BRAY D W. The assessment centre method of appraising management potential. In BLOOD J W. The personnel job in a changing world. *American Management Association Management Report No. 80*, 1964

BRAY D W . Choosing good managers. *Foundation for Research on Human Behaviour.* 1966, pp 153–165

BRAY D W and CAMPBELL R J. Selection of salesmen by means of an assessment centre. *Journal of Applied Psychology.* Vol 52, 1968, pp 36–41

BRAY D W and GRANT D L. The assessment centre in the measurement of potential for business management. *Psychological Monographs.* Vol 80 (17, whole no 625), 1966

BUROS O K. *Eighth Mental Measurements Yearbook.* The Gryphon Press, 1978

BYHAM W C. The uses of assessment centres. Mimeo report. New York. J C Penney Company, 1969

BYHAM W C. The Assessment Centre as an Aid in Management Development. *Training and Development Journal.* Vol 25, No 12, 1971, pp 10–23

CAMPBELL C. *The Times* Newspaper. 10 June 1980, p 3

CAMPBELL R J and BRAY D W. Assessment Centres: an Aid in Management Selection. *Personnel Administration.* Vol 30, No 2, 1967, pp 6–13

CAMPBELL J P, DUNNETTE M D, LAWLER E E and WEICK K E. *Managerial Behaviour, Performance and Effectiveness.* McGraw-Hill, 1970

CAMPBELL J P, DUNNETTE M D, ARVEY R D and HELLERVIK L V. The Development and Evaluation of Behaviourally Based Rating Scales. *Journal of Applied Psychology.* Vol 57, No 1, 1973, pp 15–22

CANNON J A. Human Resource Accounting – a critical comment. *Personnel Review.* Vol 3, No 3, 1974, pp 14–20

CANNON J A. *Cost Effective Personnel Decisions.* Institute of Personnel Management, 1979, pp 182–183

CARLETON F O. Relationships between follow-up evaluations and information developed in a management assessment centre. *American Psychological Association Convention.* Miami Beach, Florida, 1970

CASCIO W F and SILBEY V. Utility of the assessment center as a selection device. *Journal of Applied Psychology.* Vol 64, 1979, pp 107–118

CHEEK L M. Cost Effectiveness comes to the Personnel Function. *Harvard Business Review.* May–June 1973, pp 96–105

CHRISTIES R and GEIS F L. *Studies in Machiavellianism.* Academic Press, 1970

DODD W E. Will Management Assessment Centres ensure selection of the same old types? *Proceedings of the American Psychological Association 78th Annual Convention.* 1970, pp 569–570

DODD W E and McNAMARA W J. The early identification of management talent in field engineering, *IBM Personnel Research Studies*, 1968

DODD W E, WOLLOWICK H B and McNAMARA W J. Task difficulty as a moderator of long-range predictions. *Journal of Applied Psychology*. Vol 54, 1970, pp 265–270

DUNNETTE M D. Multiple assessment procedures in identifying and developing managerial talent. In McREYNOLDS P. *Advances in psychological assessment*. Vol II. Science & Behaviour Books. 1971

FARNSWORTH T. *Developing Executive Talent*. McGraw-Hill, 1975

FINEMAN S. The influence of perceived job climate on the relationship between managerial achievement, motivation and performance. *Journal of Occupational Psychology*. Vol 48, No 2, 1975, pp 113–124

FINKLE R D and JONES W S. *Assessing Corporate Talent*. Wiley, 1970

FOGLI L, HULIN C L and BLOOD M R. Development of first level behavioural job criteria. *Journal of Applied Psychology*. Vol 55, 1971, pp 3–8

FULTON Lord. *The Civil Service*. Vol 3, No 2. Surveys and investigation. HMSO, Cmnd 3638, 1968

GARDNER K E and WILLIAMS A P O. A 25 year follow-up of an extended interview selection procedure in the Royal Navy I. Introduction and preliminary analyses. *Occupational Psychology*. Vol 47, 1973, pp 1–13

GARDNER K E and WILLIAMS A P O. A 25 year follow-up of an extended interview selection procedure in the Royal Navy II. Multivariate analyses and conclusions. *Occupational Psychology*. Vol 47, 1973, pp 149–161

GILES W J and ROBINSON D F. *Human Asset Accounting*. Institute of Personnel Management/Institute of Cost and Management Accountants, 1972

GINSBURG L R and SILVERMAN A. The leaders of tomorrow: their identification and development. *Personnel Psychology*. September 1972, pp 662–666

GLASER R, SCHWARZ P A and FLANAGAN J C. The contribution of interview and situational procedures to the selection of supervisory personnel. *Journal of Applied Psychology*. Vol 42, 1958, pp 69–73

GRANT D L and BRAY D W. Contributions of the interview to assessment of management potential. *Journal of Applied Psychology*. Vol 53, 1969, pp 24–34

GRANT D L, KATKOWSKI W and BRAY D W. Contributions of projective techniques to assessment of management potential. *Journal of Applied Psychology*. Vol 51, 1967, pp 226–232

GREENWOOD J M and McNAMARA W J. Interrater reliability in situational tests. *Journal of Applied Psychology*. Vol 51, 1967, pp 101–106

GUION R M. *Personnel Testing*. McGraw-Hill, 1965

GULLIKSEN H and WILKS S S. Regression tests for several samples. *Psychometrika*. Vol 15, 1950, pp 91–114

GUYTON T. The identification of executive potential. *Personnel Journal*. Vol 48, November 1969, pp 866–872

HAGUE H. *Executive self-development*. Macmillan, 1974

HALPIN A W and WINER B J. A factorial study of the leader behaviour description questionnaire. In STOGDILL R M and COONS A E. *Leader Behaviour: its description and management.* Ohio State University, 1957

HARDESTY D L and JONES W S. Characteristics of judged high potential management personnel — the operations of an assessment centre. *Personnel Psychology.* Vol 21, 1968, pp 85–98

HELLER R. *The naked manager.* Barrie and Jenkins, 1972

HINRICKS J R. Comparison of real life assessments of management potential with situational exercises, paper and pencil ability tests, and personality inventories. *Journal of Applied Psychology.* Vol 53, 1969, pp 425–433

HINRICHS J R. An 8 year follow-up of a management assessment centre. *Journal of Applied Psychology.* Vol 63, 1978, pp 596–601

HIRD C. *Your Employer's Profits.* Pluto Press, 1975

HUCK J R. Assessment centres: a review of the external and internal validities. *Personnel Psychology.* Vol 26, 1973, pp 191–212

HUCK J R. The research base. In MOSES J L and BYHAM W C. *Applying the assessment center method.* Pergamon, 1977, pp 261–291

HUCK J R and BRAY D W. Management assessment center evaluations and subsequent job performance of white and black females. *Personnel Psychology.* Vol 29, 1976, pp 13–30.

JAFFEE C L. The partial validation of a leaderless group discussion for the selection of supervisory personnel. *Occupational Psychology.* Vol 41, 1967, pp 245–248

JAFFEE C L, BENDER J and CALVERT D. The assessment centre technique: a validation study. *Management of Personnel Quarterly.* Autumn 1970, pp 9–14

JURGENSON C E. Report to participants on adjective word sort. Minneapolis Gas Company. Unpublished report 1966. In CAMPBELL J P, DUNNETTE M D, LAWLER E E and WEICK K E. *Managerial behaviour, performance and effectiveness.* McGraw-Hill, 1970

KAHN R L. Human relations on the shop floor. In HUGH-JONES E M. *Human relations and modern management.* North-Holland Publishing Company, 1958

KATZ D and KAHN R L. Human organization and worker motivation. In TRIPP L R. *Industrial productivity.* Industrial Relations Research Association, 1951

KELLNER P and CROWTHER-HUNT Lord. *The civil servants: an inquiry into Britain's ruling class.* Macdonald and Jane, 1980, pp 119–124

KELLY G A. *The psychology of personal constructs.* Norton, 1955

KINNERSLY P. *The Hazards of Work and How to Avoid them.* Pluto Press, 1973

KLIMOSKI R J and STRICKLAND W J. Assessment centers — valid or merely prescient? *Personnel Psychology.* Vol 30, 1977, pp 353–361

KLINKE G. *Test: have you got what it takes to reach the top?* Neville Spearman, 1972

KOONTZ H. *Appraising managers as managers.* McGraw-Hill, 1971

KORMAN A K. The prediction of managerial performance: a review. *Personnel Psychology.* Vol 21, 1968, pp 295–322

KORVING J, KORVING M and KEELEY M. *Out of the rut.* BBC Publications, 1975.

KRAUT A I. Intellectual ability and promotional success among high level managers. *Personnel Psychology.* Vol 22, 1969, pp 281–290

KRAUT A I. A hard look at management assessment centres and their future. *Personnel Journal.* Vol 51, 1972, pp 317–326

KRAUT A I. Management assessment in international organizations. *Industrial Relations.* Vol 12, No 2, 1973, pp 172–182

KRAUT A I. Prediction of managerial success by peer and training staff ratings. *Journal of Applied Psychology.* Vol 60, No 1, 1975, pp 14–19

KRAUT A I and SCOTT G J. Validity of an operational management assessment program. *Journal of Applied Psychology.* Vol 56, 1972, pp 124–129

LAMB W and WATSON E. *Body code.* Routledge and Kegan Paul, 1979

LEWIS R and STEWART R. *The Boss: the life and times of the British businessman.* Dent, Revised edition, 1961

MANN R D. A review of the relationships between personality and performance in small groups. *Psychological Bulletin.* Vol 56, 1959, pp 241–270

McCONNELL J H and PARKER T C. An assessment centre program for multi-organisational use. *Training and Development Journal.* Vol 26, No 3, 1972, pp 6–14

MEYER H H. The validity of the in-basket as a measure of managerial performance. *Personnel Psychology.* Vol 23, 1976, pp 297–301

MINER J B. *Studies in management education.* Springer, 1965

MINTZBERG H. *The nature of managerial work.* Harper and Row, 1973

MITCHEL J O. Assessment centre validity: a longitudinal study. *Journal of Applied Psychology.* Vol 60, No 5, 1975, pp 573–579

MOSES J L. Assessment centre performance and management progress. Paper presented at 79th annual meeting. *American Psychological Association.* Washington DC, 1971

MOSES J L. Assessment centre performance and management progress. *Studies in Personnel Psychology.* Vol 4, No 1, 1972, pp 7–12

MOSES J L. The development of an assessment centre for the early identification of supervisory potential. *Personnel Psychology.* Vol 26, 1973, pp 569–580

MOSES J L and BOEHM V R. Relationship of assessment centre performance to management progress of women. *Journal of Applied Psychology.* Vol 60, No 4, 1975, pp 527–529

MOSES J L and BYHAM W C. *Applying the assessment centre method.* Pergamon, 1977, pp 89–126

OLLARD R. *Pepys: a biography*. Hodder and Stoughton, 1974

OPPENHEIM A N. *Questionnaire design and attitude measurement*. Heinemann, 1966

OSS ASSESSMENT STAFF. *Assessment of men*. Rinehart, 1948

PALMER W J. An integrated program for career development. *Personnel Journal*. June 1972, pp 398–406, 451

PARRY J B, WILSON N A B and UNGERSON B. Discussion on psychological selection of commissioned officers and other ranks. Proceedings of the Royal Society of Medicine. Vol 43, 1950, pp 857–866

PETER L J and HULL R. *The Peter Principle*. Souvenir Press, 1969

RACKHAM N. Controlled paced negotiation as a technique for developing negotiating skills. *Industrial and Commercial Training*. Vol 4, No 6, 1972, pp 266–275

RACKHAM N, HONEY P and COLBERT M. *Developing Interactive Skills*. Wellens Publishing, 1971

RACKHAM N and MORGAN T. *Behaviour analysis in training*. McGraw-Hill, 1977

RAMSDEN P. *Top team planning*. Associated Business Programmes, 1973

REEVE E G. *Validation of Selection Boards*. Academic Press, 1971

RUNNYMEDE TRUST/BRITISH PSYCHOLOGICAL SOCIETY. *Discriminating fairly – a guide to fair selection*. Runnymede Trust/British Psychological Society, 1980

SADLER P J. Executive leadership. In PYM D. *Industrial Society*. Penguin Books, 1968

SCHMITT N. Interrater agreement in dimensionality and combination of assessment center judgements. *Journal of Applied Psychology*, Vol 62, 1977, pp 171–176

SCHMITT N and HILL T E. Sex and race composition of assessment center groups as a determinant of peer and assessor ratings. *Journal of Applied Psychology*. Vol 62, 1977, pp 261–264

SLEVIN D P. The assessment centre: breakthrough in management appraisal and development. *Personnel Journal*. April 1972, pp 255–261

SMALLWOOD R E R. Added value per £1 payroll. *Industrial and Commercial Training*. Vol 5, No 8, 1973, pp 366–368

SMITH M and ASHTON D. Using repertory grid technique to evaluate management training. *Personnel Review*. Vol 4, No 4, 1975, pp 15–21

STEWART A and STEWART V. *The Management of Professionals*. Institute of Management Studies, 1974(a)

STEWART A and STEWART V. Reviewing appraisal training. *Industrial Training International*. Vol 9, No 4, 1974(b), pp 114–115, 118

STEWART A and STEWART V. *The Use of Psychological Tests in Industry*.

Conference paper. Brunel University. Institute of Organization and Social Studies, 1975

STEWART R. *Managers and their jobs*. Macmillan, 1967

STEWART V. *How to Conduct Your Own Employee Attitude Survey*. Institute of Management Studies, 1974(a)

STEWART V. First steps in plagiarism: the value of other people's experience. *Industrial Training International*. Vol 9, No 10, 1974(b), pp 313–315

STEWART V. A new technique for selection interviewing. *Industrial Training International*. Vol 10, No 6, 1975, pp 179–181

STEWART V. Appraisal: sorting the sheep from the goats. *Industrial Training International*. Vol 11, No 2, 1976, pp 49–50

STEWART V and STEWART A. *Practical performance appraisal*. Gower, 1977, pp 148–151

STEWART V and STEWART A. *Managing the manager's growth*. Gower, 1978

STEWART V and STEWART A. *Business applications of repertory grid*. McGraw-Hill, 1981

STOGDILL R M. Personal factors associated with leadership: a survey of the literature. *Journal of Psychology*. Vol 25, 1948, pp 31–75

TOWNSEND R. *Up the organisation*. Michael Joseph, 1970

TURNEY J R, ROSEN N A and CONKLYN E D. Early identification of managerial potential in a technical/professional organisation. *Proceeding of the Annual Conference American Psychological Association*. Vol 6, No 2, 1971, pp. 481–482

UNGERSON B. Assessment centres: a review of research findings. *Personnel Review*. Vol 3, No 3, 1974, pp 4–13

VERNON P E and PARRY J B. *Personnel selection in the British Forces*. University of London Press, 1949

WALKER J W, LUTHANS F and HODGETTS R M. Who really are the promotables? *Personnel Journal*. February 1970, pp. 123–127

WHYTE W H. *The organisation man*. Simon and Schuster, 1956

WILLIAMS M R. *Performance appraisal in management*. Heinemann, 1972

WILLIS D J and BECKER J H. The assessment centre in the post-Griggs era. *Personnel and Guidance Journal*. Vol 55, 1976, pp 201–205

WILSON J E and TATGE W A. Assessment centres – further assessment needed? *Personnel Journal*. Vol 52, No 3, 1973, pp 172–179

WOLLOWICK H B and McNAMARA W J. Relationship of the components of an assessment centre to management success. *Journal of Applied Psychology*. Vol 53, 1969, pp 348–352

Author Index

Index